LAST STOP
ON THE
RED LINE

LAST STOP ON THE RED LINE

Story . . . . PAUL MAYBURY
Art. . . . . SAM LOTFI
Color (Issues #1 - #3). . . . . JOHN RAUCH
Color (Issue #4) . . . . PAUL MAYBURY
Letters . . . . ADAM PRUETT
Covers . . . . SAM LOTFI AND JOHN RAUCH

DARK HORSE BOOKS

Dark Horse PRESENTS

LAST STOP ON THE RED LINE

President and Publisher . . . . . MIKE RICHARDSON
Editor. . . . . PATRICK THORPE
Assistant Editor. . . . . JOSHUA ENGLEDOW
Collection Designer . . . . PAUL MAYBURY
Digital Art Technician. . . . . . . ADAM PRUETT

LAST STOP ON THE RED LINE, March 2020. Published by Dark Horse Comics LLC, 10956 SE Main Street, Milwaukie, Oregon 97222. Text and illustrations of The Last Stop on the Red Line™ © 2020, including all text and illustrations, Paul Maybury and Sam Lotfi. Dark Horse Books® and the Dark Horse logo are trademarks of Dark Horse Comics LLC, registered in various categories and countries. All rights reserved. No portion of this publication may be reproduced or transmitted, in any form or by any means, without the express written permission of Dark Horse Comics LLC. Names, characters, places, and incidents featured in this publication either are the product of the author's imagination or are used fictitiously. Any resemblance to actual persons (living or dead), events, institutions, or locales, without satiric intent, is coincidental.

DarkHorse.com
ComicShopLocator.com

Advertising Sales: (503) 905-2315

First Edition: March 2020
ISBN: 978-1-50671-339-7
10 9 8 7 6 5 4 3 2 1
Printed in China

Library of Congress Cataloging-in-Publication Data

Names: Maybury, Paul, 1982- author. | Lotfi, Sam, artist. | Rauch, John, colourist. | Pruett, Adam O., letterer.
Title: Last stop on the red line / story, Paul Maybury ; art, Sam Lotfi ; color, John Rauch ; letters, Adam Pruett
Description: First edition. | Milwaukie, OR : Dark Horse Books, 2019. | "Collects Last Stop on the Red Line #1-#4." | Summary: "Detective Migdalia Torres investigates a vicious strangling on a Boston subway car with no feasible leads. As potential evidence produces dead ends, Migdalia inadvertently takes in a vagrant named Yusef who may have a supernatural connection to the crime at hand. While Yusef's plagued by visions and seemingly false memories, both suspect and detective struggle to discover the identity of the phantom killer that stalks the Boston Metro"-- Provided by publisher.
Identifiers: LCCN 2019022528 | ISBN 9781506713397 (trade paperback) | ISBN 9781506713403 (ebook)
Subjects: LCSH: Comic books, strips, etc.
Classification: LCC PN6728.L365 M39 2019 | DDC 741.5/973--dc23
LC record available at https://lccn.loc.gov/2019022528

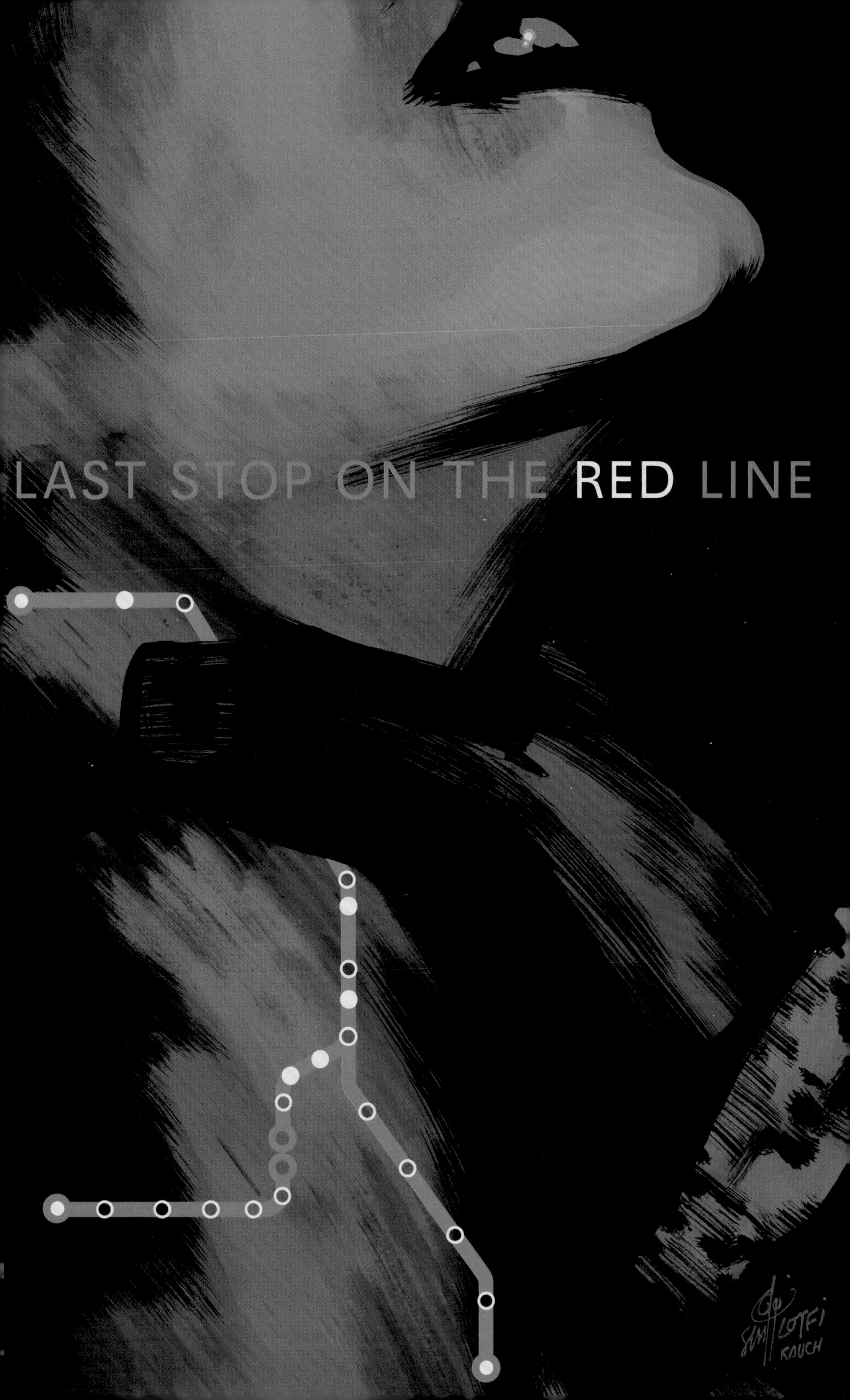
LAST STOP ON THE RED LINE

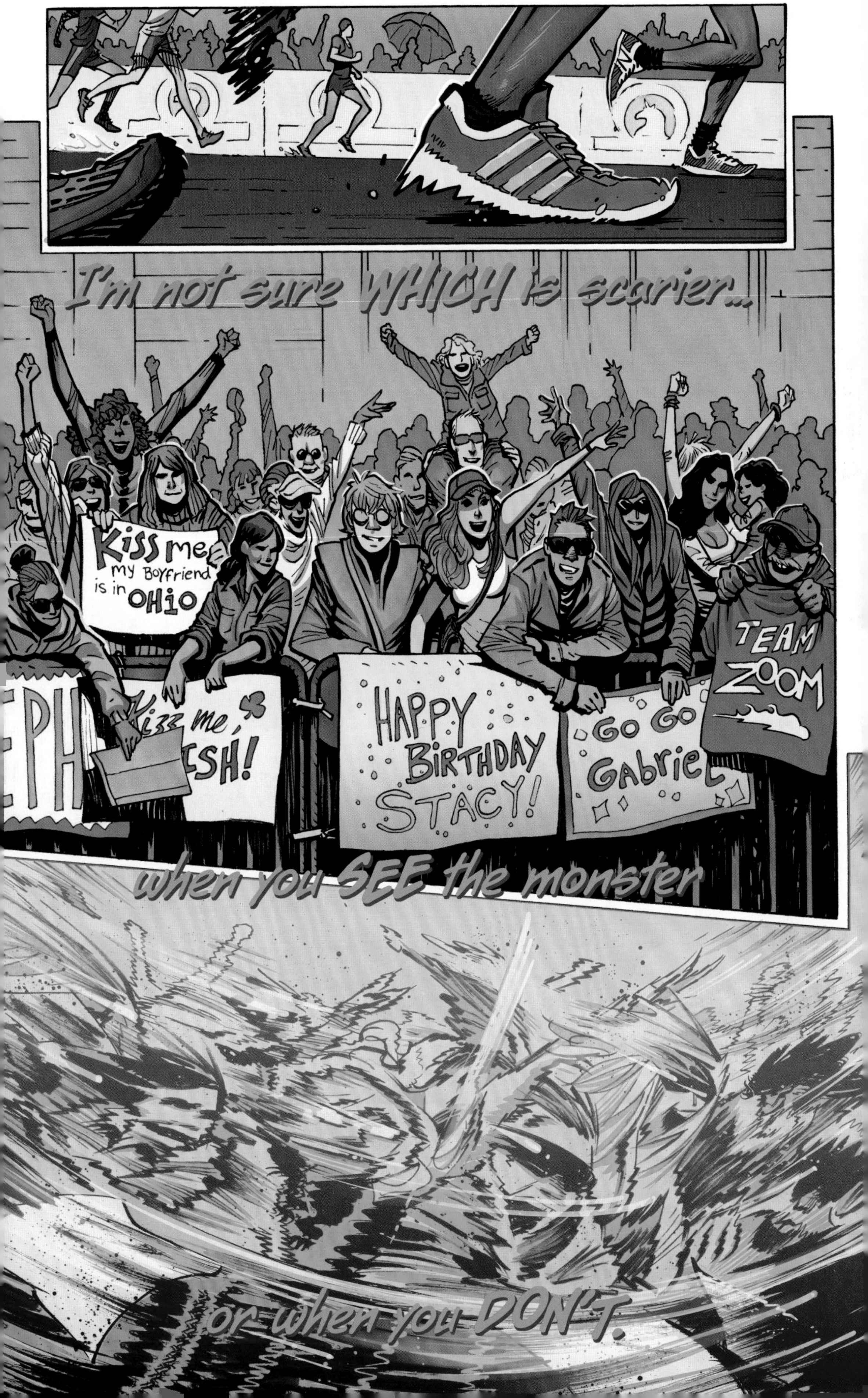
I'm not sure WHICH is scarier...
Kiss me my Boyfriend is in OHIO
EPH
Kiss me, ...ISH!
HAPPY BIRTHDAY STACY!
GO GO Gabriel
TEAM ZOOM
when you SEE the monster
or when you DON'T.

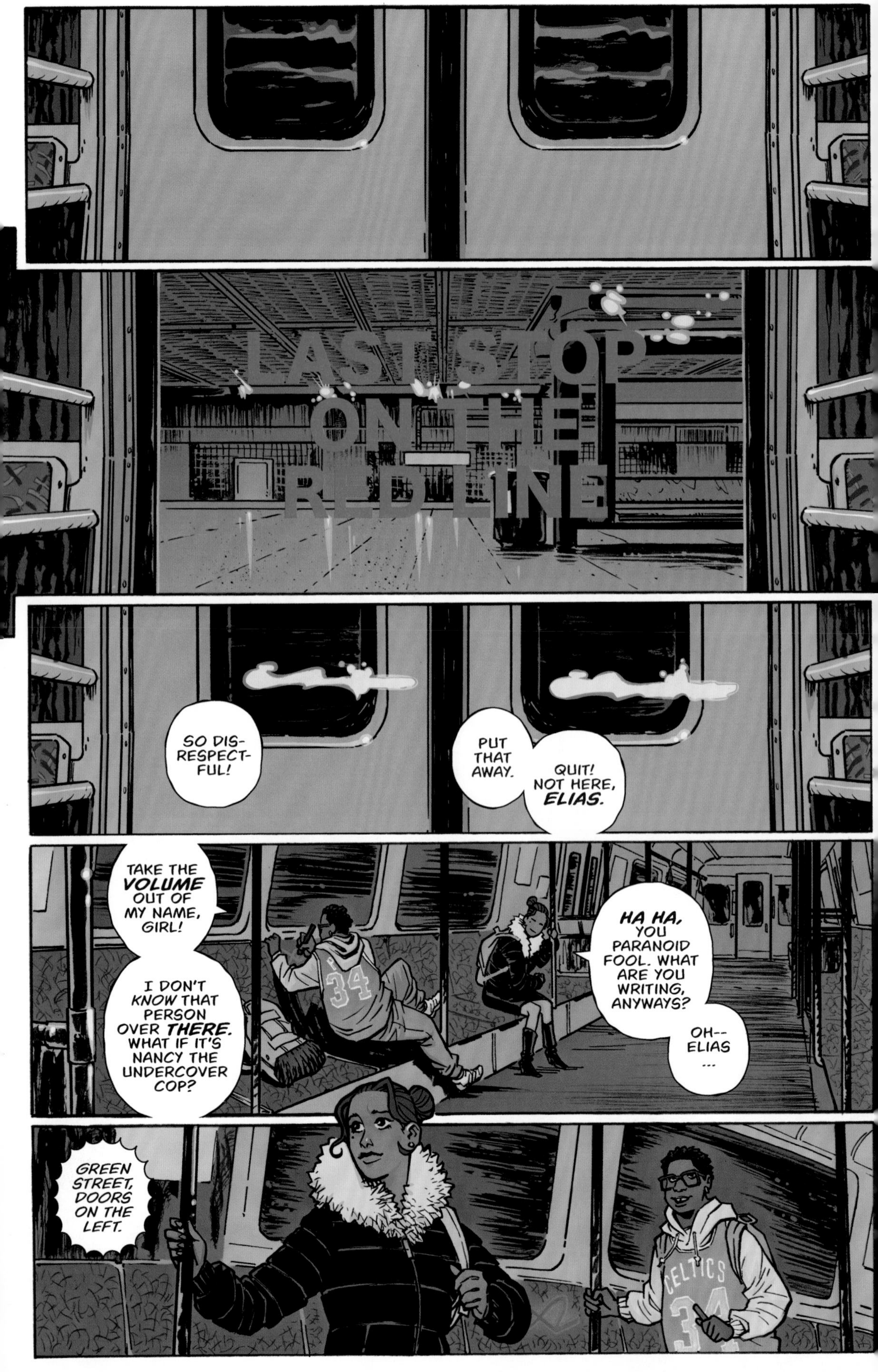
LAST STOP ON THE RED LINE
SO DIS-RESPECT-FUL!
PUT THAT AWAY.
QUIT! NOT HERE, ELIAS.
TAKE THE VOLUME OUT OF MY NAME, GIRL!
I DON'T KNOW THAT PERSON OVER THERE. WHAT IF IT'S NANCY THE UNDERCOVER COP?
HA HA, YOU PARANOID FOOL. WHAT ARE YOU WRITING, ANYWAYS?
OH-- ELIAS ...
GREEN STREET, DOORS ON THE LEFT.
CELTICS 34

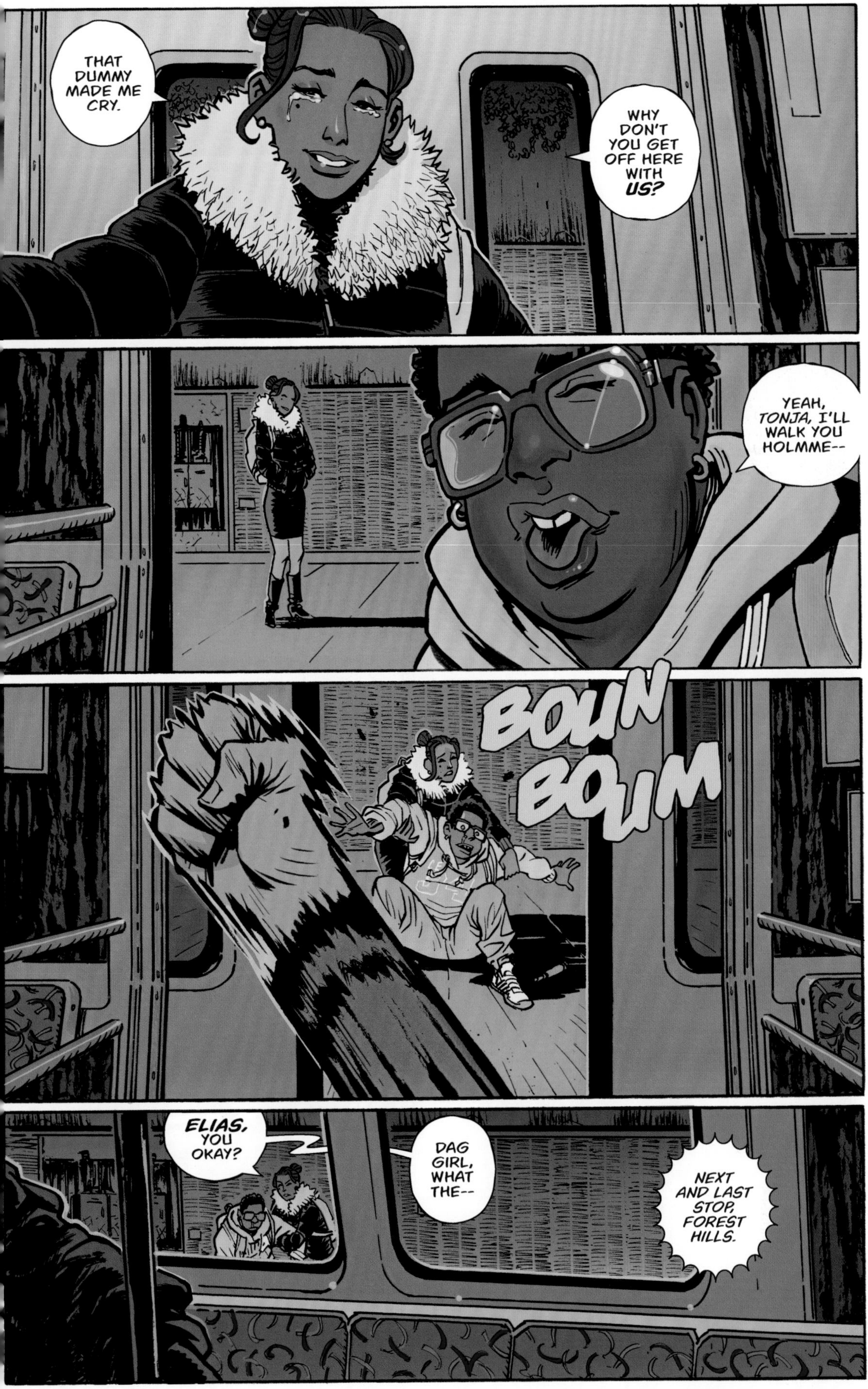
THAT DUMMY MADE ME CRY.
WHY DON'T YOU GET OFF HERE WITH *US?*
YEAH, *TONJA,* I'LL WALK YOU HOLMME--
BOUN BOUM
ELIAS, YOU OKAY?
DAG GIRL, WHAT THE--
NEXT AND LAST STOP, FOREST HILLS.

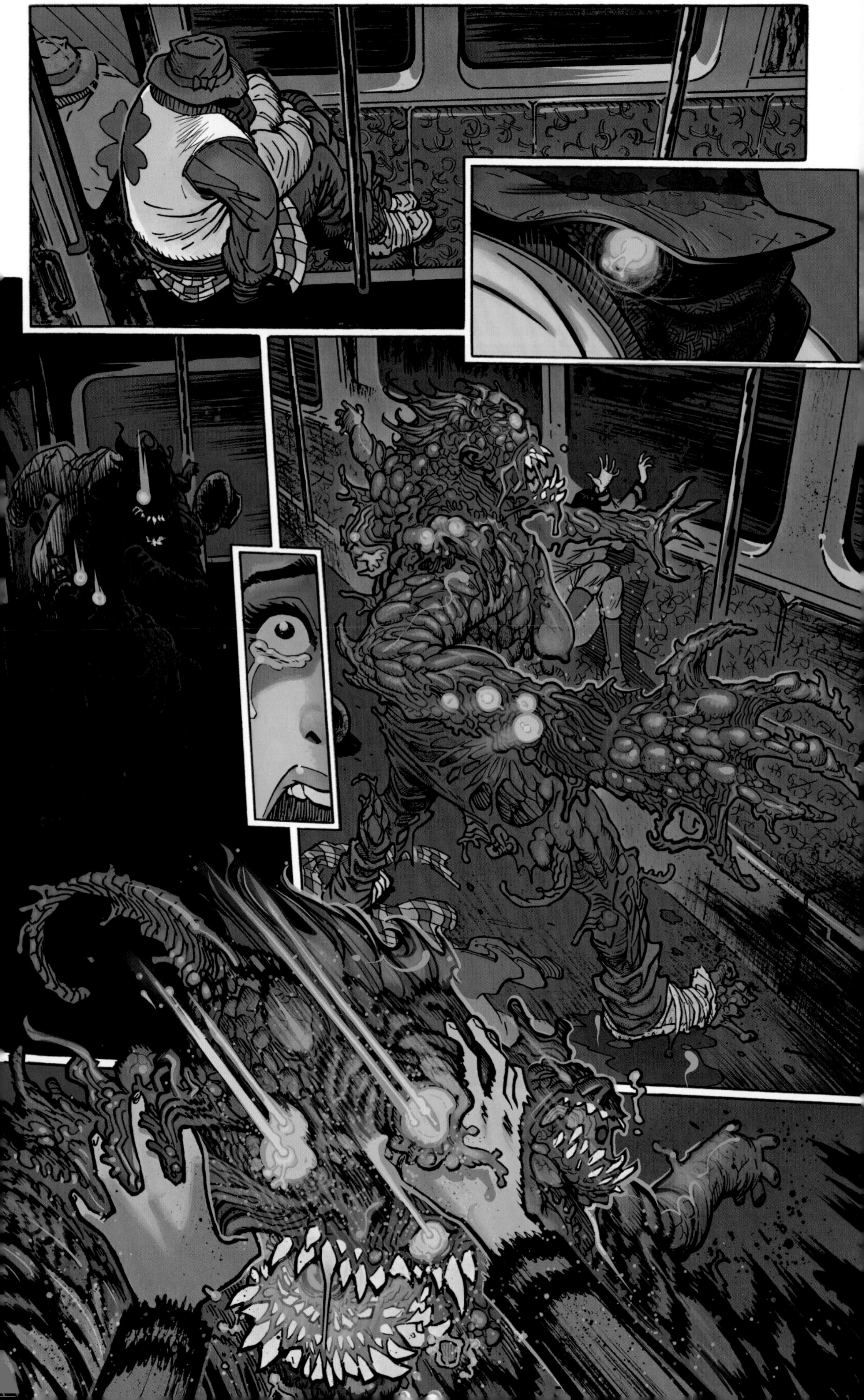

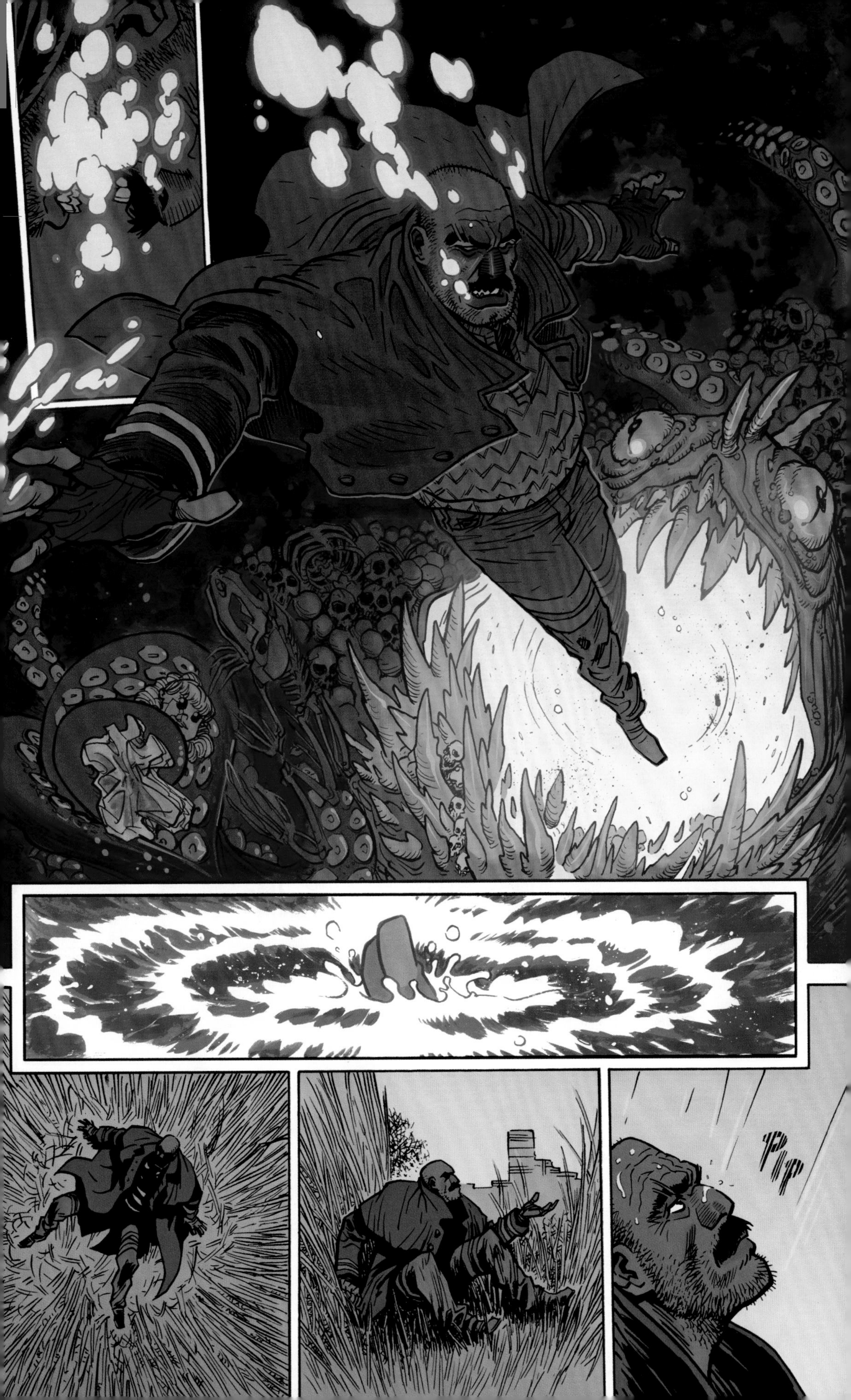

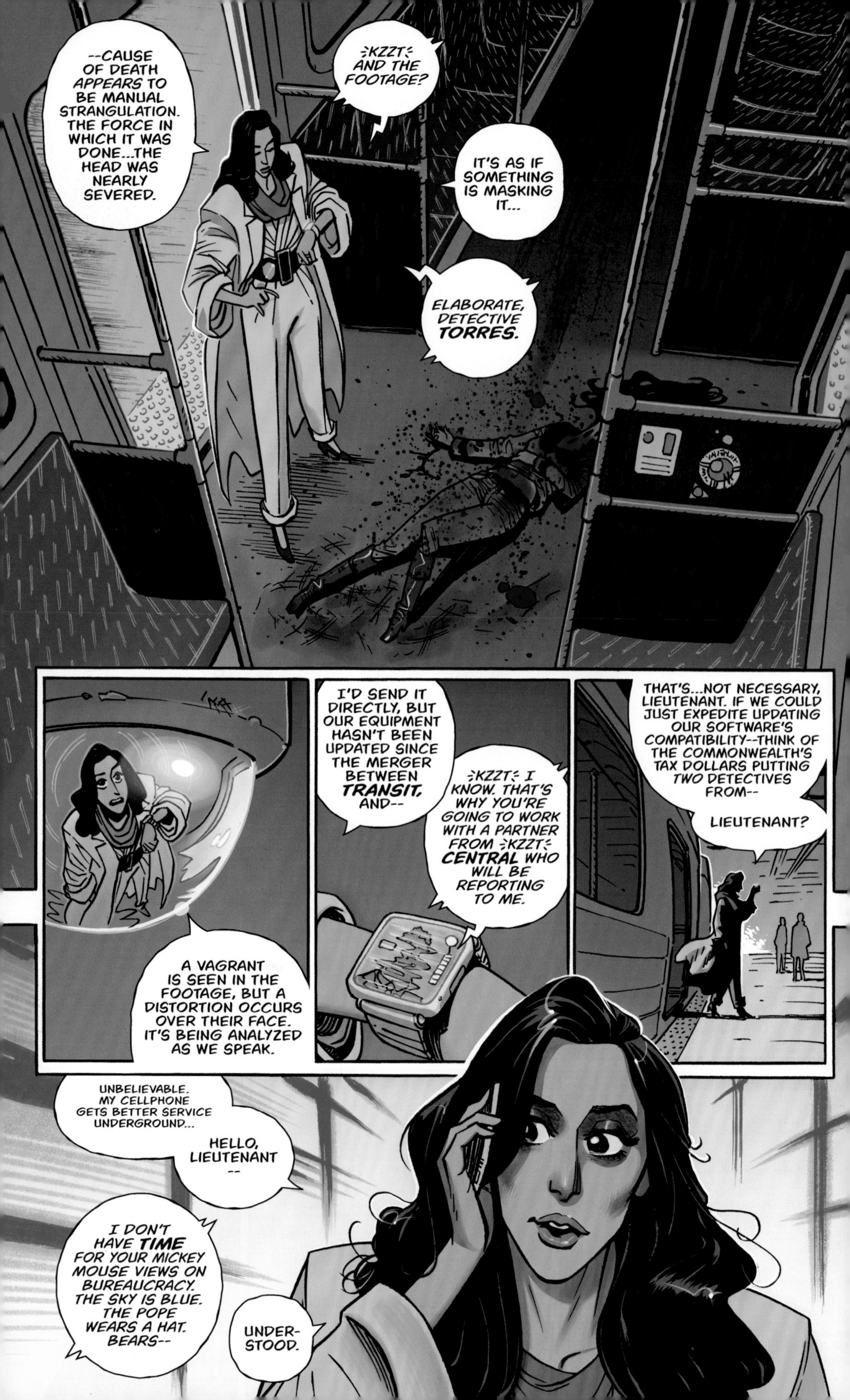
--CAUSE OF DEATH APPEARS TO BE MANUAL STRANGULATION. THE FORCE IN WHICH IT WAS DONE...THE HEAD WAS NEARLY SEVERED.
⫶KZZT⫶ AND THE FOOTAGE?
IT'S AS IF SOMETHING IS MASKING IT...
ELABORATE, DETECTIVE TORRES.
A VAGRANT IS SEEN IN THE FOOTAGE, BUT A DISTORTION OCCURS OVER THEIR FACE. IT'S BEING ANALYZED AS WE SPEAK.
I'D SEND IT DIRECTLY, BUT OUR EQUIPMENT HASN'T BEEN UPDATED SINCE THE MERGER BETWEEN TRANSIT, AND--
⫶KZZT⫶ I KNOW. THAT'S WHY YOU'RE GOING TO WORK WITH A PARTNER FROM ⫶KZZT⫶ CENTRAL WHO WILL BE REPORTING TO ME.
THAT'S...NOT NECESSARY, LIEUTENANT. IF WE COULD JUST EXPEDITE UPDATING OUR SOFTWARE'S COMPATIBILITY--THINK OF THE COMMONWEALTH'S TAX DOLLARS PUTTING TWO DETECTIVES FROM--
LIEUTENANT?
UNBELIEVABLE. MY CELLPHONE GETS BETTER SERVICE UNDERGROUND...
HELLO, LIEUTENANT --
I DON'T HAVE TIME FOR YOUR MICKEY MOUSE VIEWS ON BUREAUCRACY. THE SKY IS BLUE. THE POPE WEARS A HAT. BEARS--
UNDER-STOOD.

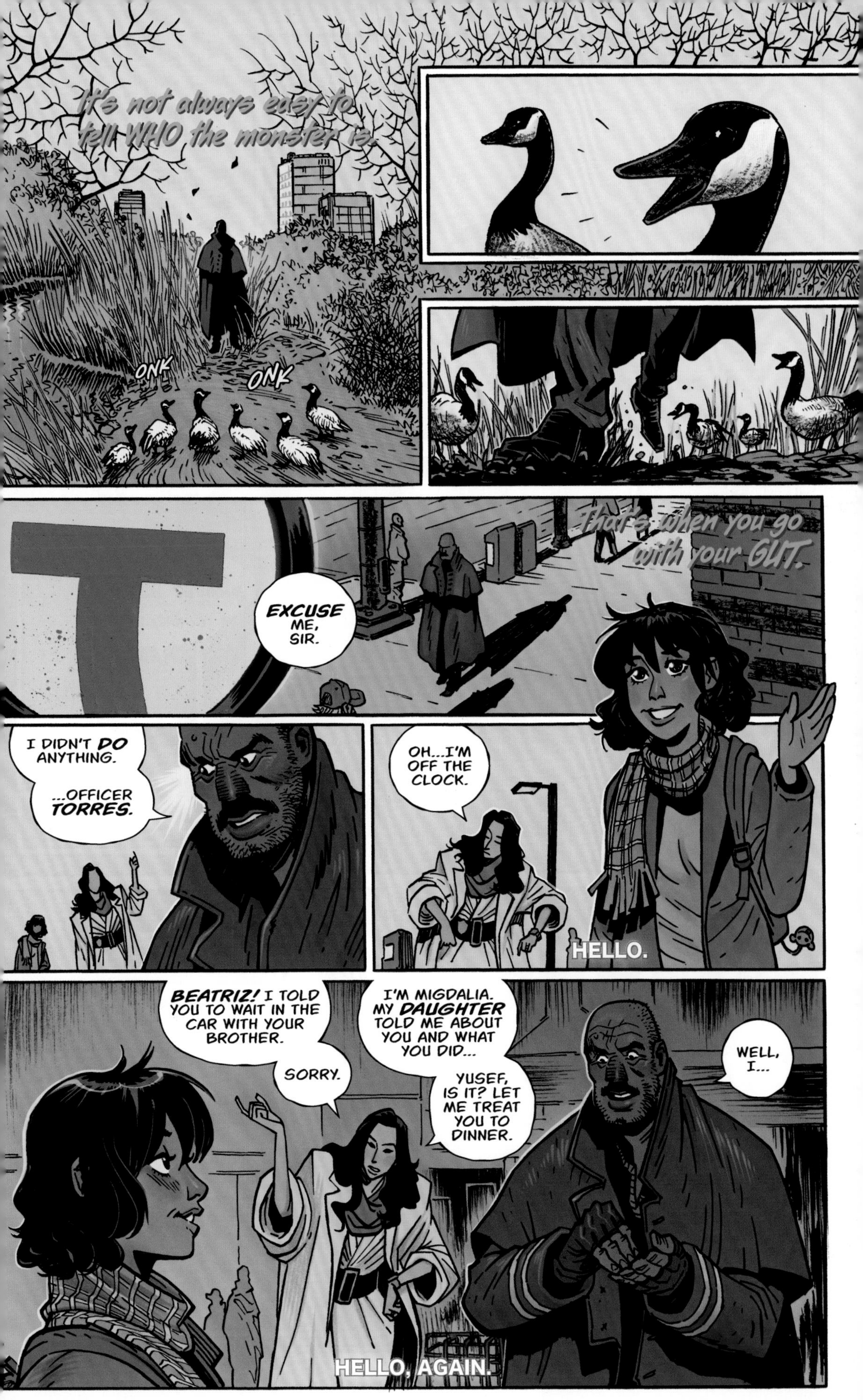

It's not always easy to tell WHO the monster is.
ONK
ONK
That's when you go with your GUT.
EXCUSE ME, SIR.
I DIDN'T DO ANYTHING.
...OFFICER TORRES.
OH...I'M OFF THE CLOCK.
HELLO.
BEATRIZ! I TOLD YOU TO WAIT IN THE CAR WITH YOUR BROTHER.
SORRY.
I'M MIGDALIA. MY DAUGHTER TOLD ME ABOUT YOU AND WHAT YOU DID...
YUSEF, IS IT? LET ME TREAT YOU TO DINNER.
WELL, I...
HELLO, AGAIN.

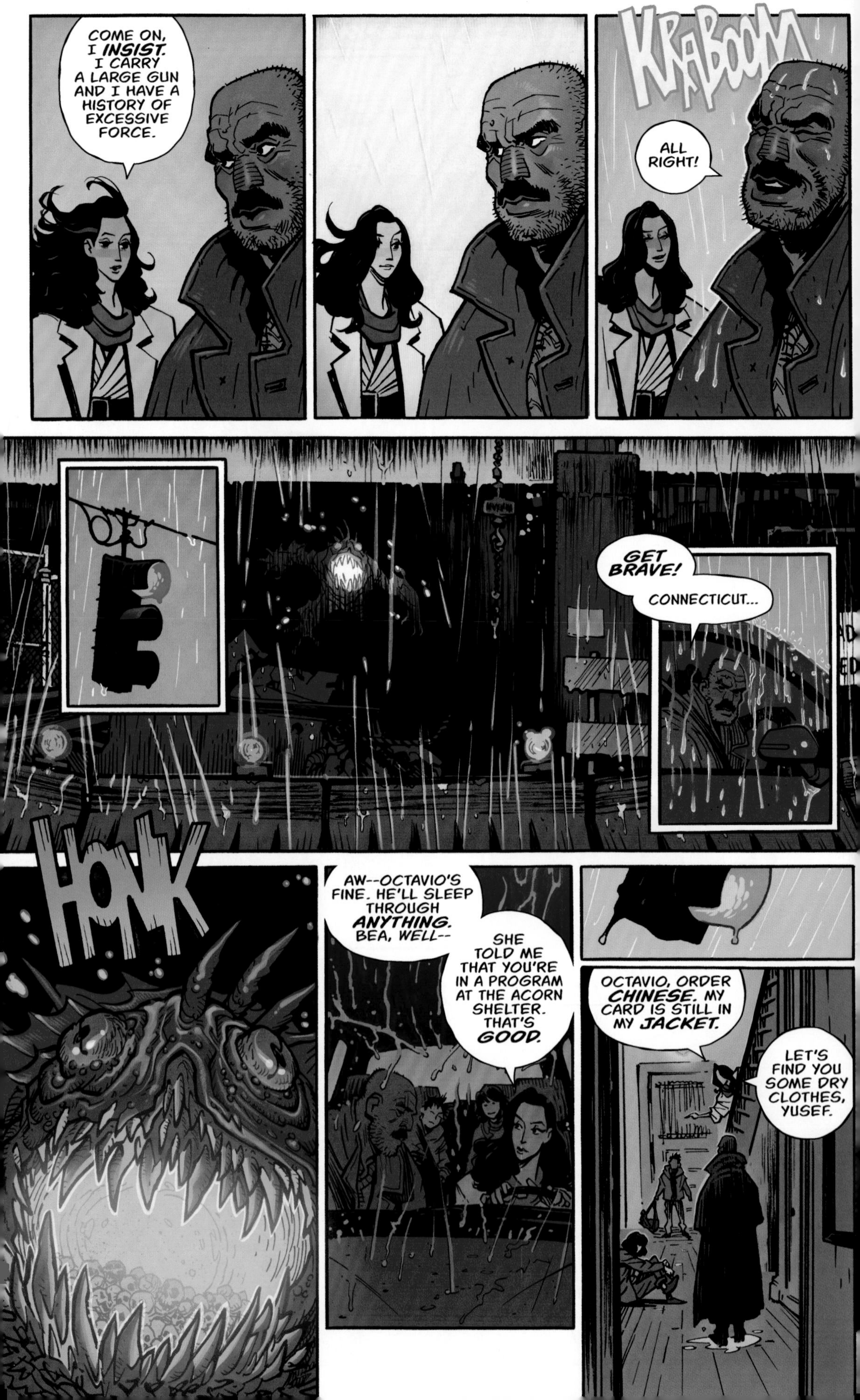
COME ON, I INSIST. I CARRY A LARGE GUN AND I HAVE A HISTORY OF EXCESSIVE FORCE.
KRABOOM
ALL RIGHT!
GET BRAVE!
CONNECTICUT...
HONK
AW--OCTAVIO'S FINE. HE'LL SLEEP THROUGH ANYTHING. BEA, WELL--
SHE TOLD ME THAT YOU'RE IN A PROGRAM AT THE ACORN SHELTER. THAT'S GOOD.
OCTAVIO, ORDER CHINESE. MY CARD IS STILL IN MY JACKET.
LET'S FIND YOU SOME DRY CLOTHES, YUSEF.

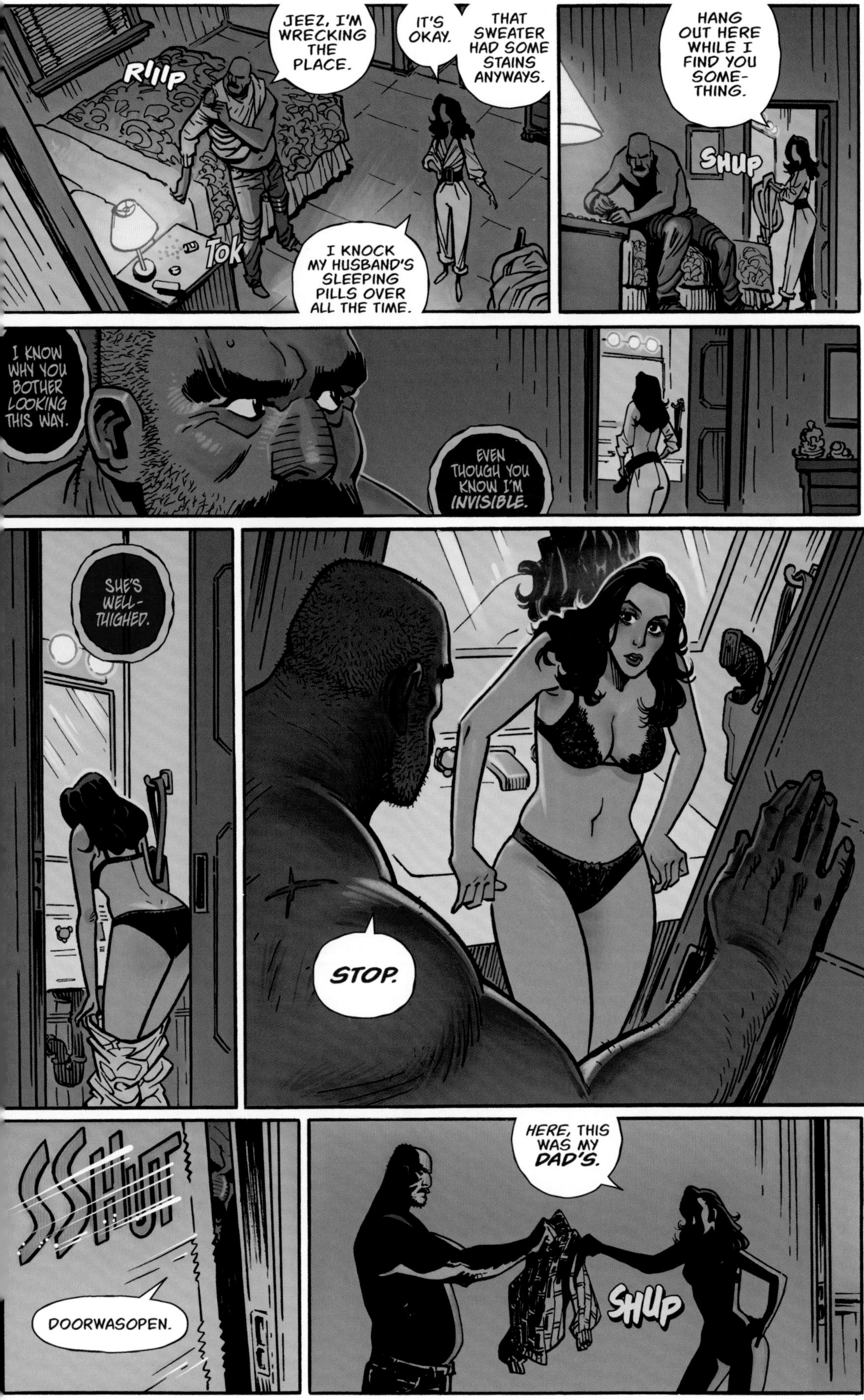
RIIIP
JEEZ, I'M WRECKING THE PLACE.
TOK
IT'S OKAY.
THAT SWEATER HAD SOME STAINS ANYWAYS.
I KNOCK MY HUSBAND'S SLEEPING PILLS OVER ALL THE TIME.
HANG OUT HERE WHILE I FIND YOU SOMETHING.
SHUP
I KNOW WHY YOU BOTHER LOOKING THIS WAY.
EVEN THOUGH YOU KNOW I'M INVISIBLE.
SHE'S WELL-THIGHED.
STOP.
SSHUT
DOORWASOPEN.
HERE, THIS WAS MY DAD'S.
SHUP

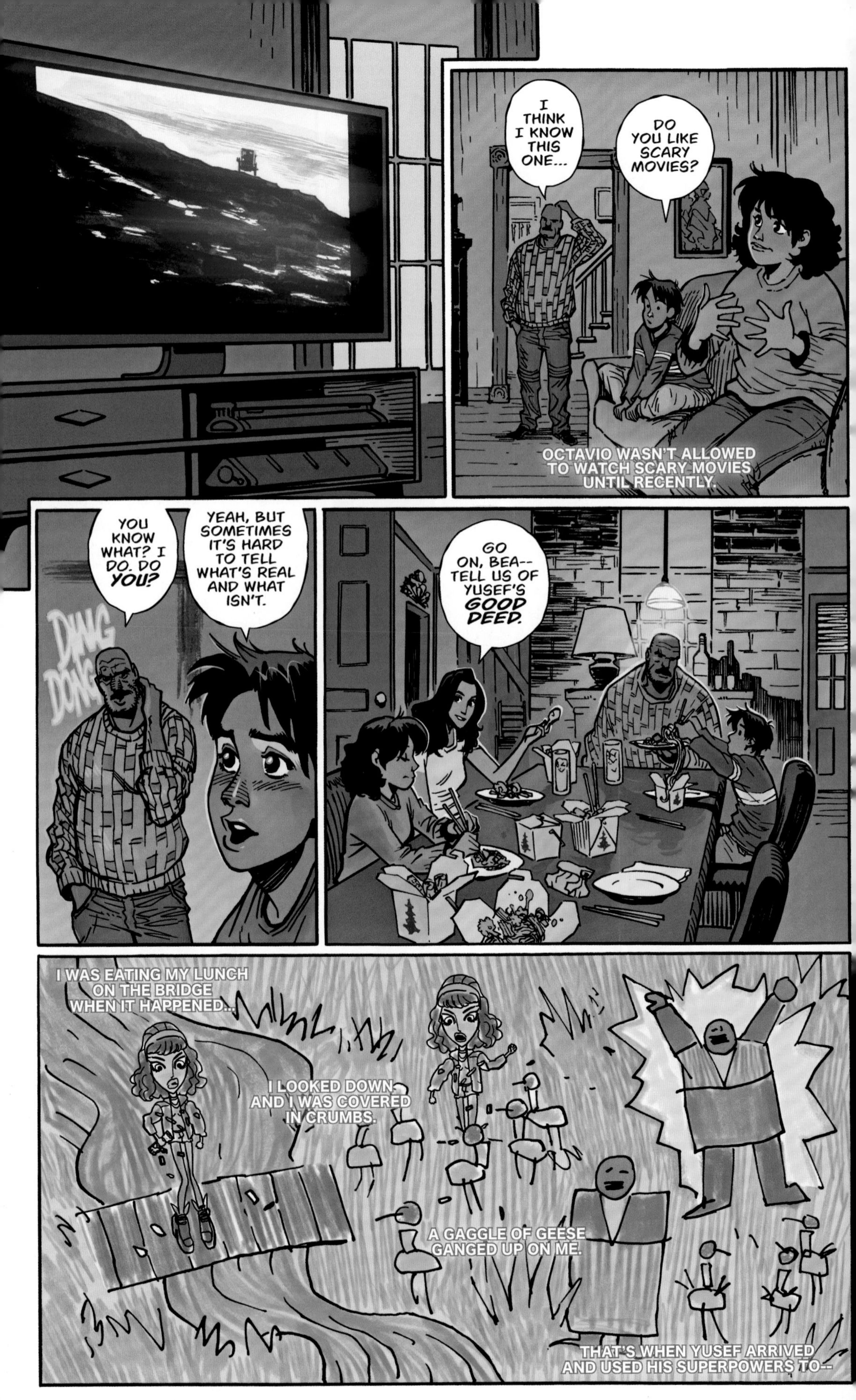
I THINK I KNOW THIS ONE...
DO YOU LIKE SCARY MOVIES?
OCTAVIO WASN'T ALLOWED TO WATCH SCARY MOVIES UNTIL RECENTLY.
YOU KNOW WHAT? I DO. DO YOU?
YEAH, BUT SOMETIMES IT'S HARD TO TELL WHAT'S REAL AND WHAT ISN'T.
DING DONG
GO ON, BEA-- TELL US OF YUSEF'S GOOD DEED.
I WAS EATING MY LUNCH ON THE BRIDGE WHEN IT HAPPENED...
I LOOKED DOWN AND I WAS COVERED IN CRUMBS.
A GAGGLE OF GEESE GANGED UP ON ME.
THAT'S WHEN YUSEF ARRIVED AND USED HIS SUPERPOWERS TO--

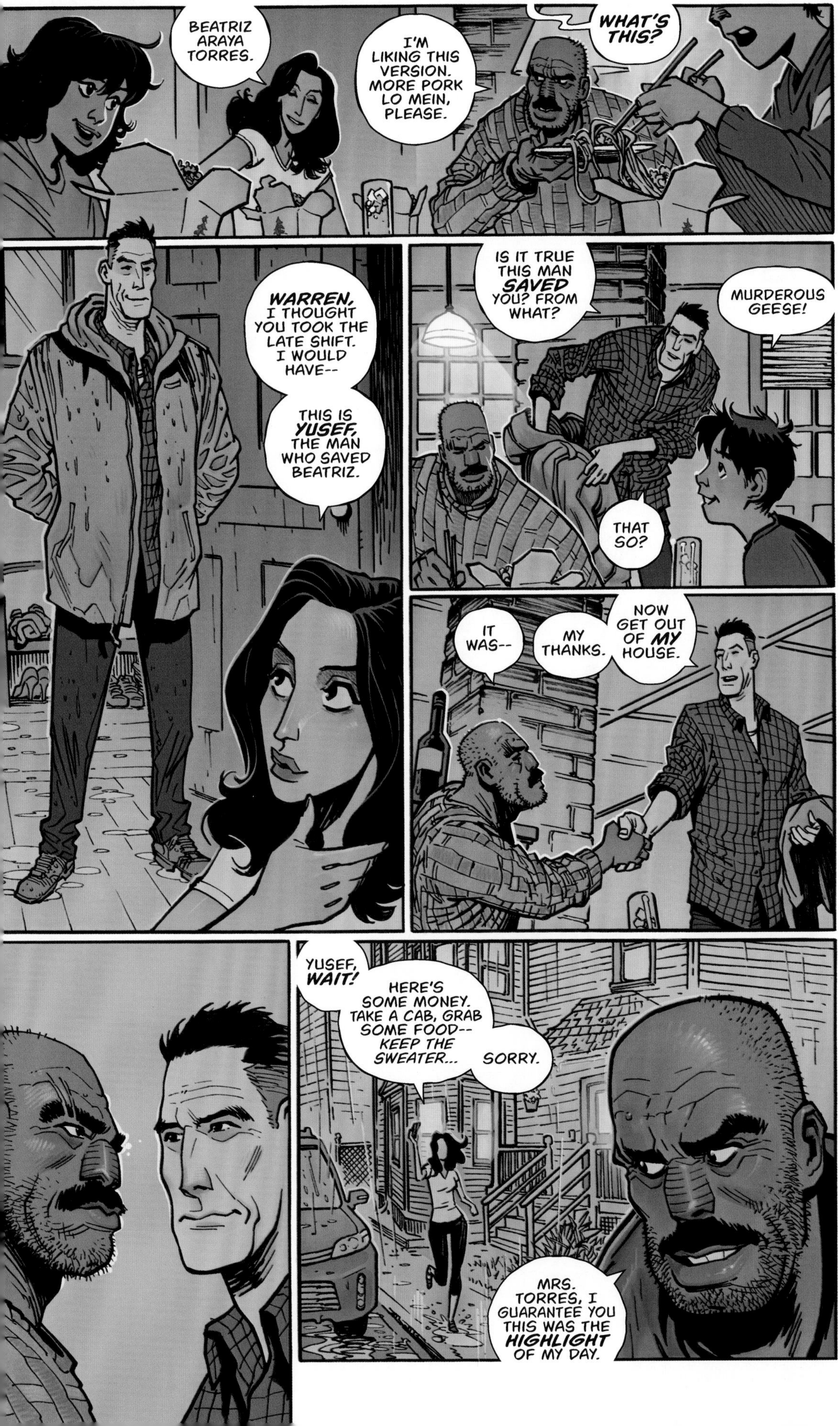

BEATRIZ ARAYA TORRES.
I'M LIKING THIS VERSION. MORE PORK LO MEIN, PLEASE.
WHAT'S THIS?
WARREN, I THOUGHT YOU TOOK THE LATE SHIFT. I WOULD HAVE--
THIS IS YUSEF, THE MAN WHO SAVED BEATRIZ.
IS IT TRUE THIS MAN SAVED YOU? FROM WHAT?
MURDEROUS GEESE!
THAT SO?
IT WAS--
MY THANKS.
NOW GET OUT OF MY HOUSE.
YUSEF, WAIT!
HERE'S SOME MONEY. TAKE A CAB, GRAB SOME FOOD-- KEEP THE SWEATER...
SORRY.
MRS. TORRES, I GUARANTEE YOU THIS WAS THE HIGHLIGHT OF MY DAY.

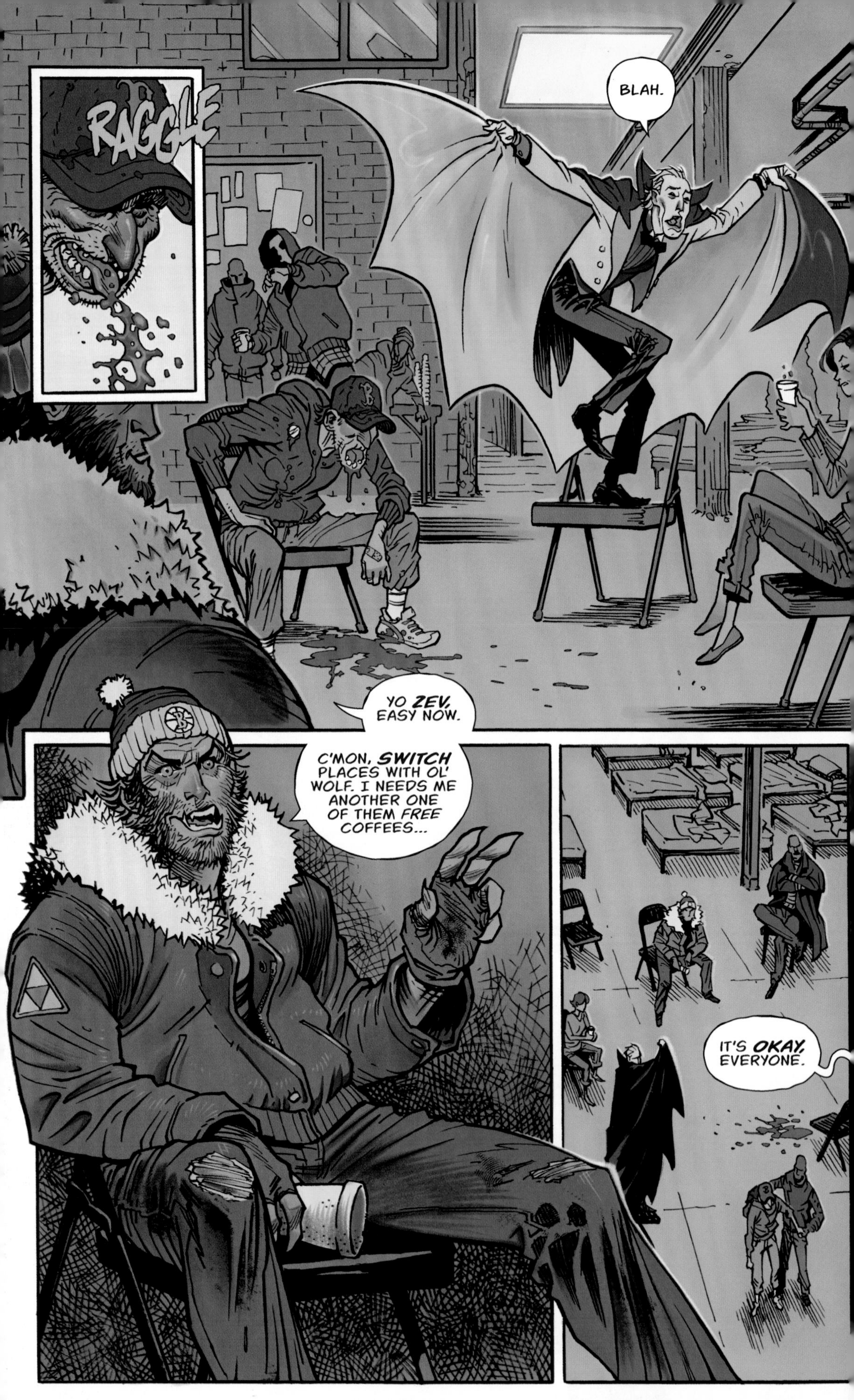
RAGGLE
BLAH.
YO ZEV, EASY NOW.
C'MON, SWITCH PLACES WITH OL' WOLF. I NEEDS ME ANOTHER ONE OF THEM FREE COFFEES...
IT'S OKAY, EVERYONE.

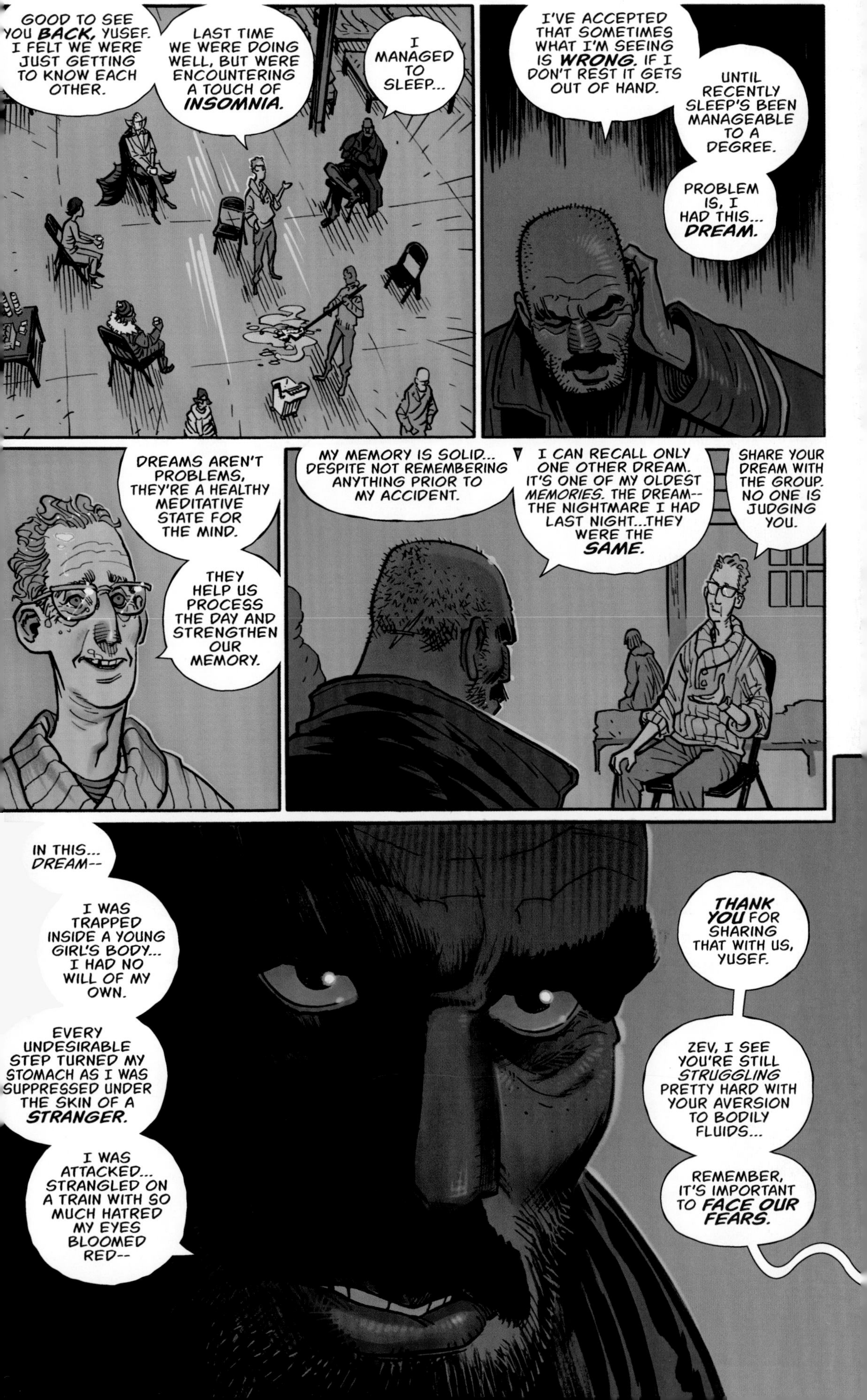
GOOD TO SEE YOU BACK, YUSEF. I FELT WE WERE JUST GETTING TO KNOW EACH OTHER.
LAST TIME WE WERE DOING WELL, BUT WERE ENCOUNTERING A TOUCH OF INSOMNIA.
I MANAGED TO SLEEP...
I'VE ACCEPTED THAT SOMETIMES WHAT I'M SEEING IS WRONG. IF I DON'T REST IT GETS OUT OF HAND.
UNTIL RECENTLY SLEEP'S BEEN MANAGEABLE TO A DEGREE.
PROBLEM IS, I HAD THIS... DREAM.
DREAMS AREN'T PROBLEMS, THEY'RE A HEALTHY MEDITATIVE STATE FOR THE MIND.
THEY HELP US PROCESS THE DAY AND STRENGTHEN OUR MEMORY.
MY MEMORY IS SOLID... DESPITE NOT REMEMBERING ANYTHING PRIOR TO MY ACCIDENT.
I CAN RECALL ONLY ONE OTHER DREAM. IT'S ONE OF MY OLDEST MEMORIES. THE DREAM-- THE NIGHTMARE I HAD LAST NIGHT...THEY WERE THE SAME.
SHARE YOUR DREAM WITH THE GROUP. NO ONE IS JUDGING YOU.
IN THIS... DREAM--
I WAS TRAPPED INSIDE A YOUNG GIRL'S BODY... I HAD NO WILL OF MY OWN.
EVERY UNDESIRABLE STEP TURNED MY STOMACH AS I WAS SUPPRESSED UNDER THE SKIN OF A STRANGER.
I WAS ATTACKED... STRANGLED ON A TRAIN WITH SO MUCH HATRED MY EYES BLOOMED RED--
THANK YOU FOR SHARING THAT WITH US, YUSEF.
ZEV, I SEE YOU'RE STILL STRUGGLING PRETTY HARD WITH YOUR AVERSION TO BODILY FLUIDS...
REMEMBER, IT'S IMPORTANT TO FACE OUR FEARS.

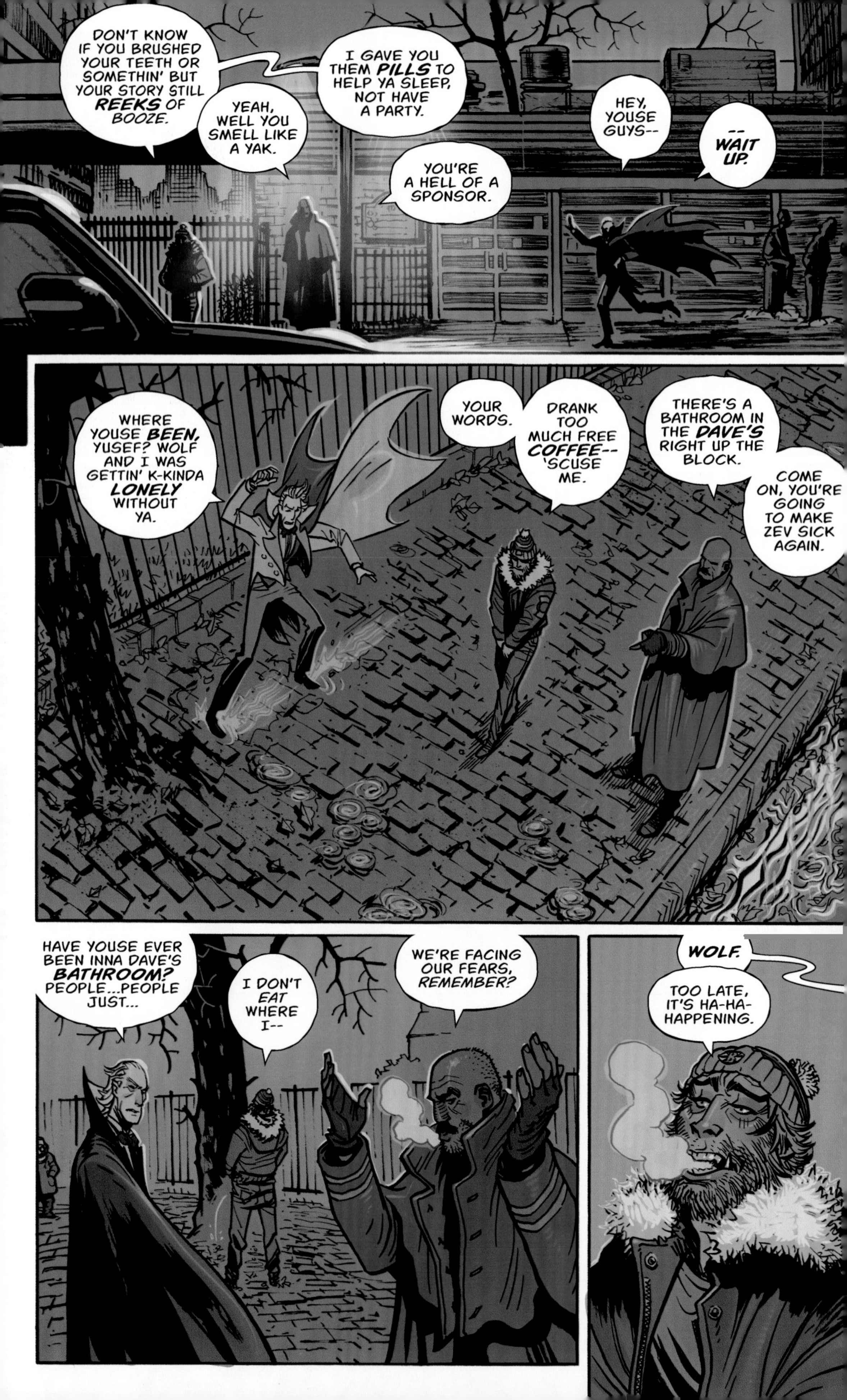
DON'T KNOW IF YOU BRUSHED YOUR TEETH OR SOMETHIN' BUT YOUR STORY STILL REEKS OF BOOZE.
YEAH, WELL YOU SMELL LIKE A YAK.
I GAVE YOU THEM PILLS TO HELP YA SLEEP, NOT HAVE A PARTY.
YOU'RE A HELL OF A SPONSOR.
HEY, YOUSE GUYS--
--WAIT UP.
WHERE YOUSE BEEN, YUSEF? WOLF AND I WAS GETTIN' K-KINDA LONELY WITHOUT YA.
YOUR WORDS.
DRANK TOO MUCH FREE COFFEE-- 'SCUSE ME.
THERE'S A BATHROOM IN THE DAVE'S RIGHT UP THE BLOCK.
COME ON, YOU'RE GOING TO MAKE ZEV SICK AGAIN.
HAVE YOUSE EVER BEEN INNA DAVE'S BATHROOM? PEOPLE...PEOPLE JUST...
I DON'T EAT WHERE I--
WE'RE FACING OUR FEARS, REMEMBER?
WOLF.
TOO LATE, IT'S HA-HA-HAPPENING.

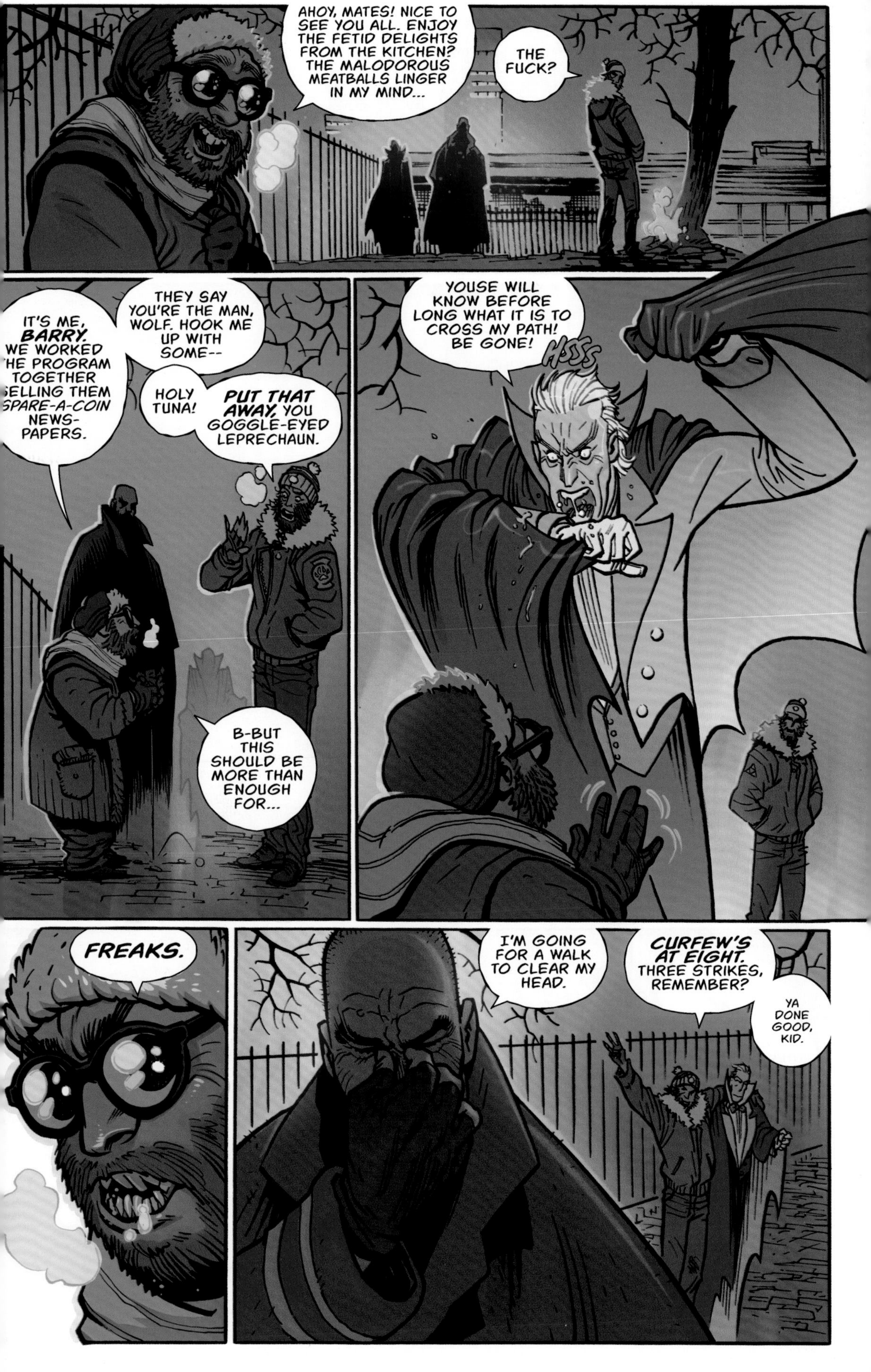
AHOY, MATES! NICE TO SEE YOU ALL. ENJOY THE FETID DELIGHTS FROM THE KITCHEN? THE MALODOROUS MEATBALLS LINGER IN MY MIND...
THE FUCK?
IT'S ME, BARRY. WE WORKED THE PROGRAM TOGETHER SELLING THEM SPARE-A-COIN NEWS-PAPERS.
THEY SAY YOU'RE THE MAN, WOLF. HOOK ME UP WITH SOME--
HOLY TUNA!
PUT THAT AWAY, YOU GOGGLE-EYED LEPRECHAUN.
B-BUT THIS SHOULD BE MORE THAN ENOUGH FOR...
YOUSE WILL KNOW BEFORE LONG WHAT IT IS TO CROSS MY PATH! BE GONE!
HSSS
FREAKS.
I'M GOING FOR A WALK TO CLEAR MY HEAD.
CURFEW'S AT EIGHT. THREE STRIKES, REMEMBER?
YA DONE GOOD, KID.

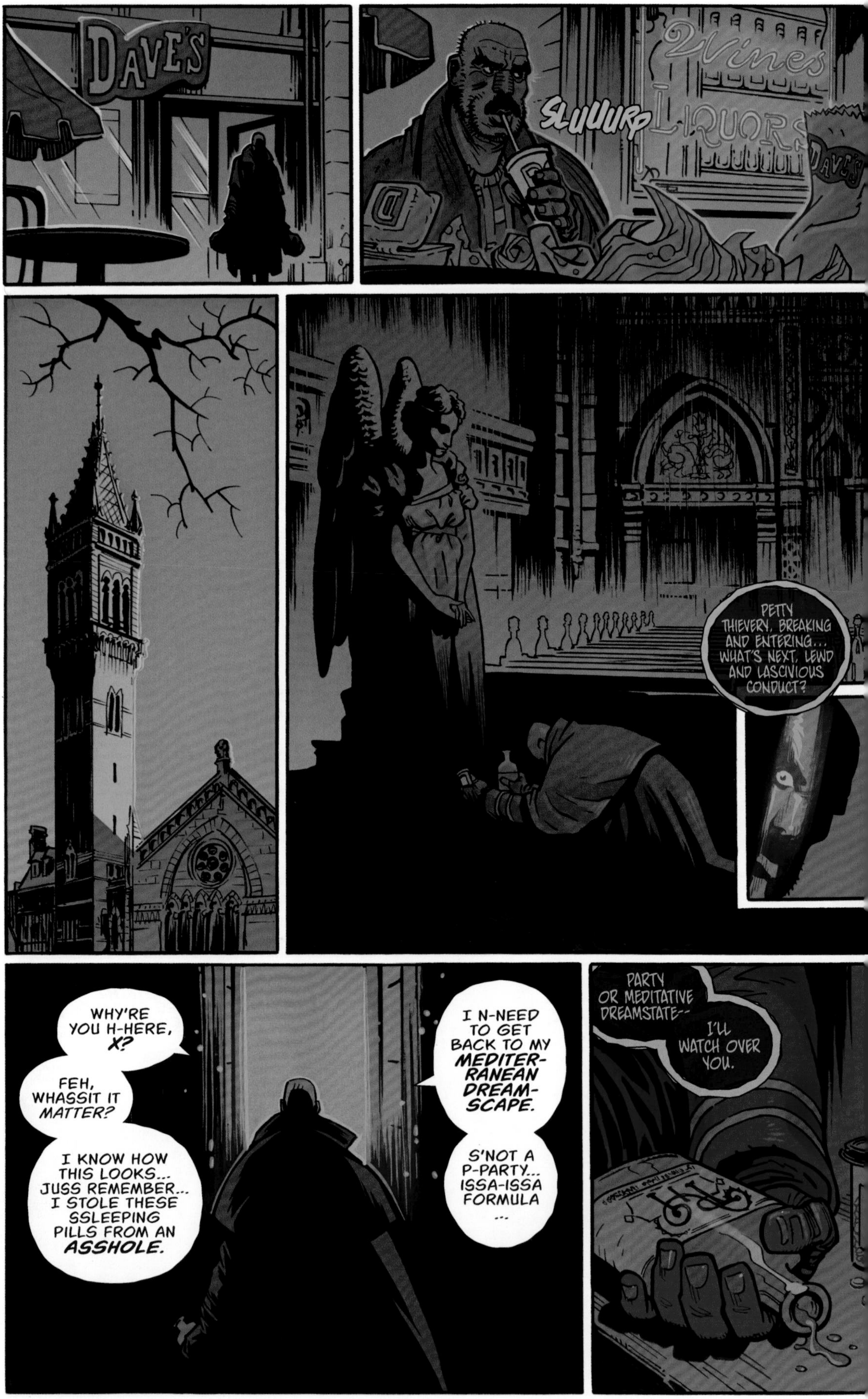
DAVE'S
SLUUURP
2Vines
LIQUORS
DAVE'S
PETTY THIEVERY, BREAKING AND ENTERING... WHAT'S NEXT, LEWD AND LASCIVIOUS CONDUCT?
WHY'RE YOU H-HERE, X?
FEH, WHASSIT IT MATTER?
I KNOW HOW THIS LOOKS... JUSS REMEMBER... I STOLE THESE SSLEEPING PILLS FROM AN ASSHOLE.
I N-NEED TO GET BACK TO MY MEDITER-RANEAN DREAM-SCAPE.
S'NOT A P-PARTY... ISSA-ISSA FORMULA ...
PARTY OR MEDITATIVE DREAMSTATE--
I'LL WATCH OVER YOU.

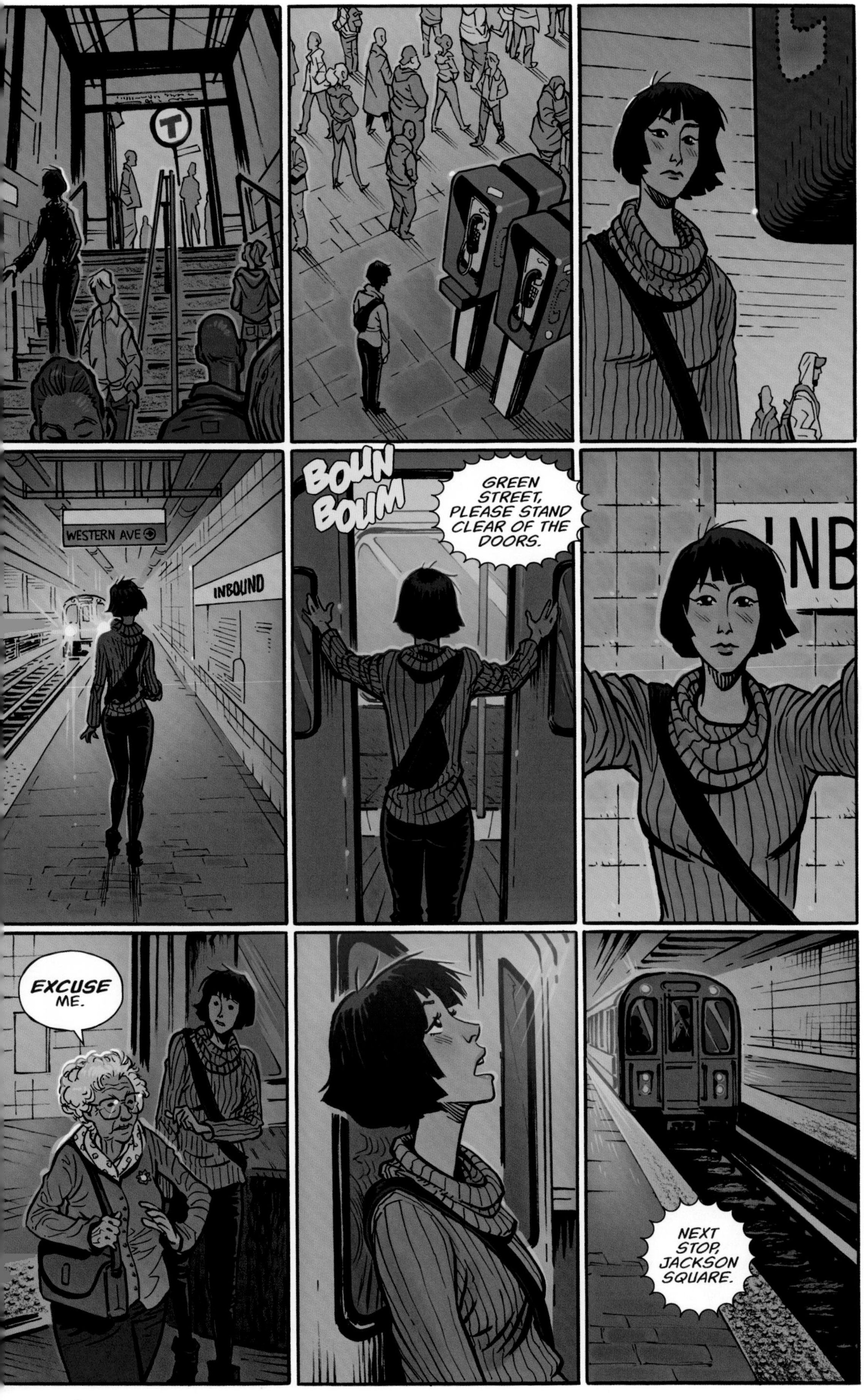
WESTERN AVE
INBOUND
BOUN BOUM
GREEN STREET, PLEASE STAND CLEAR OF THE DOORS.
INB
EXCUSE ME.
NEXT STOP, JACKSON SQUARE.

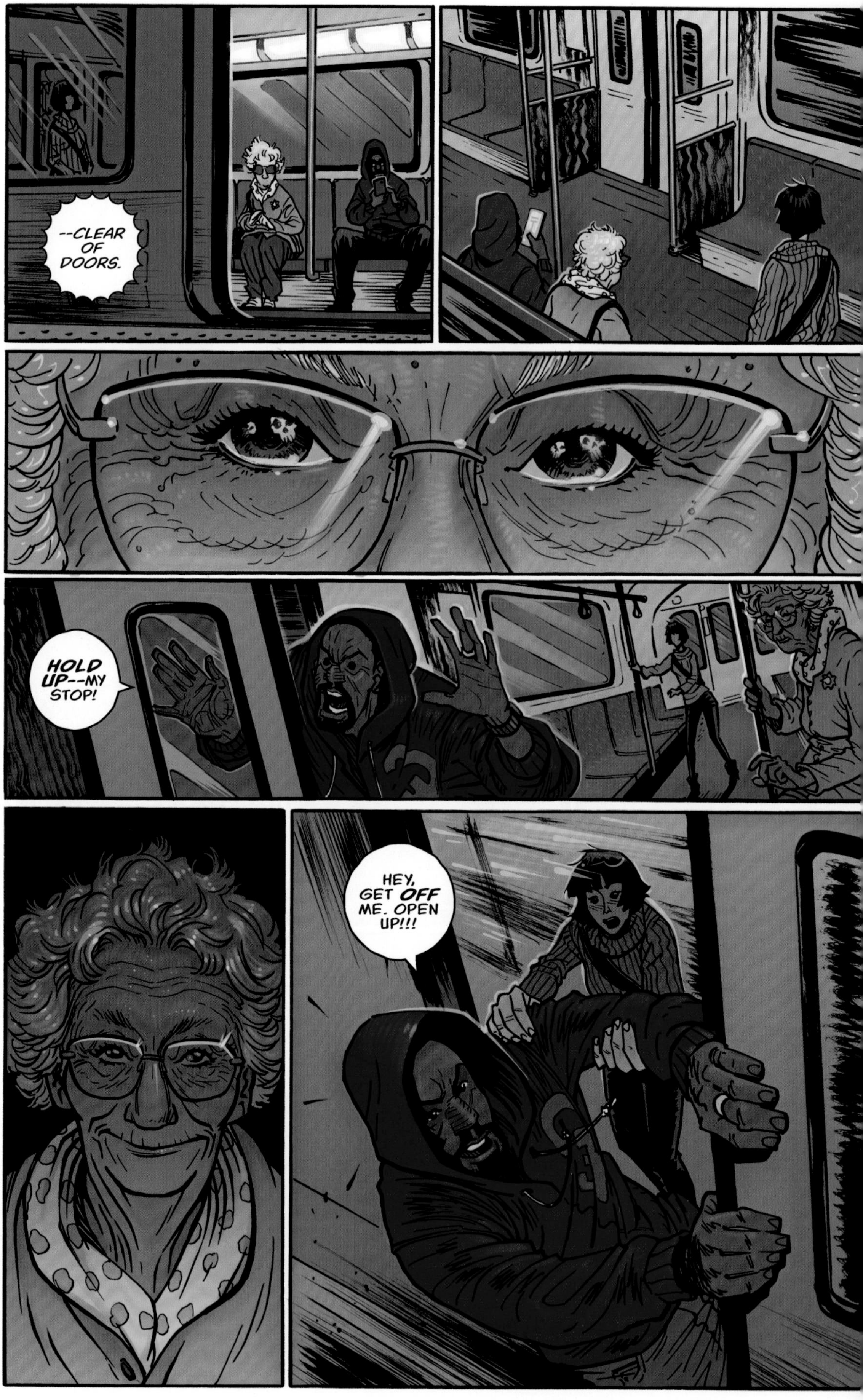
--CLEAR OF DOORS.
HOLD UP--MY STOP!
HEY, GET OFF ME. OPEN UP!!!

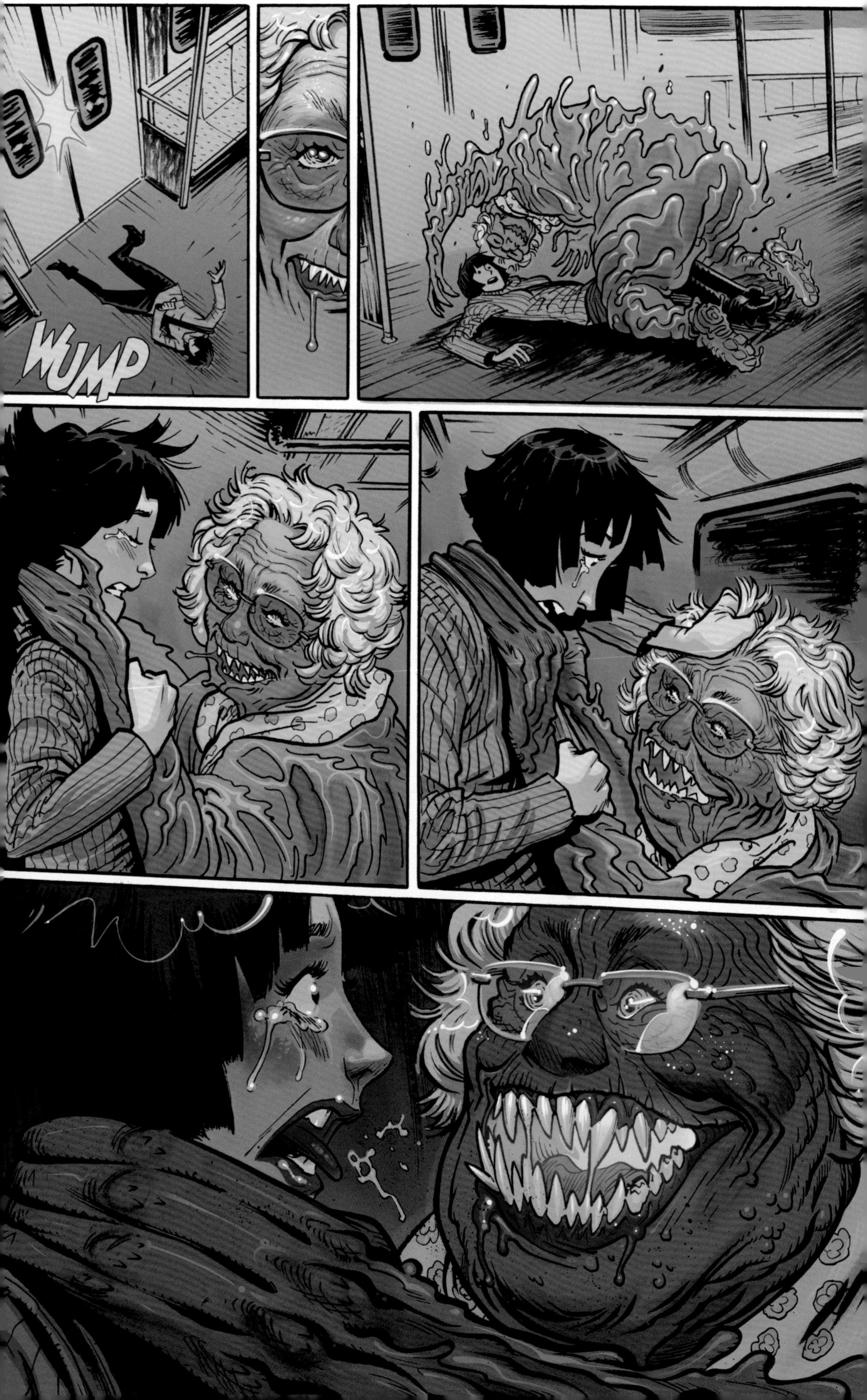
WUMP

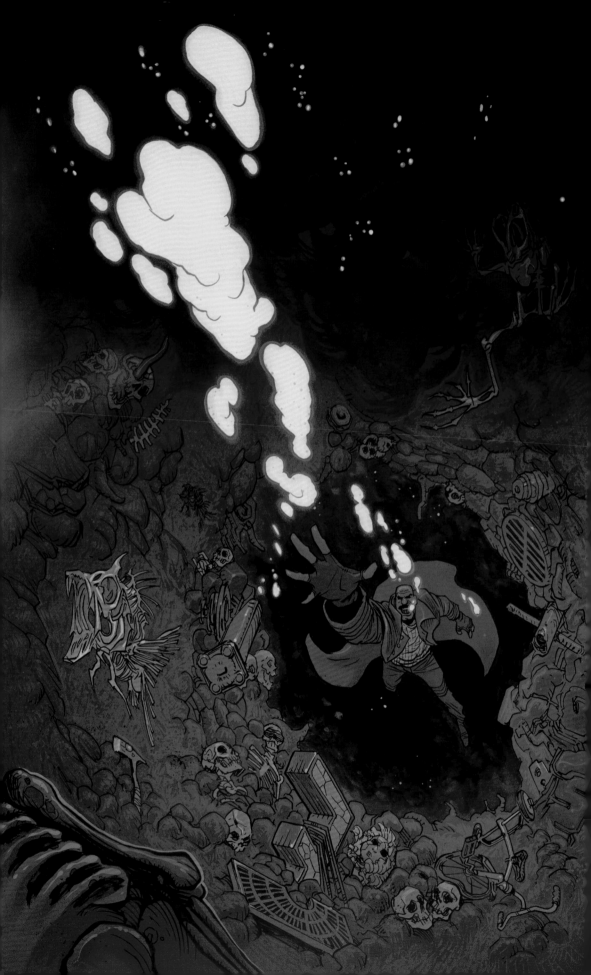

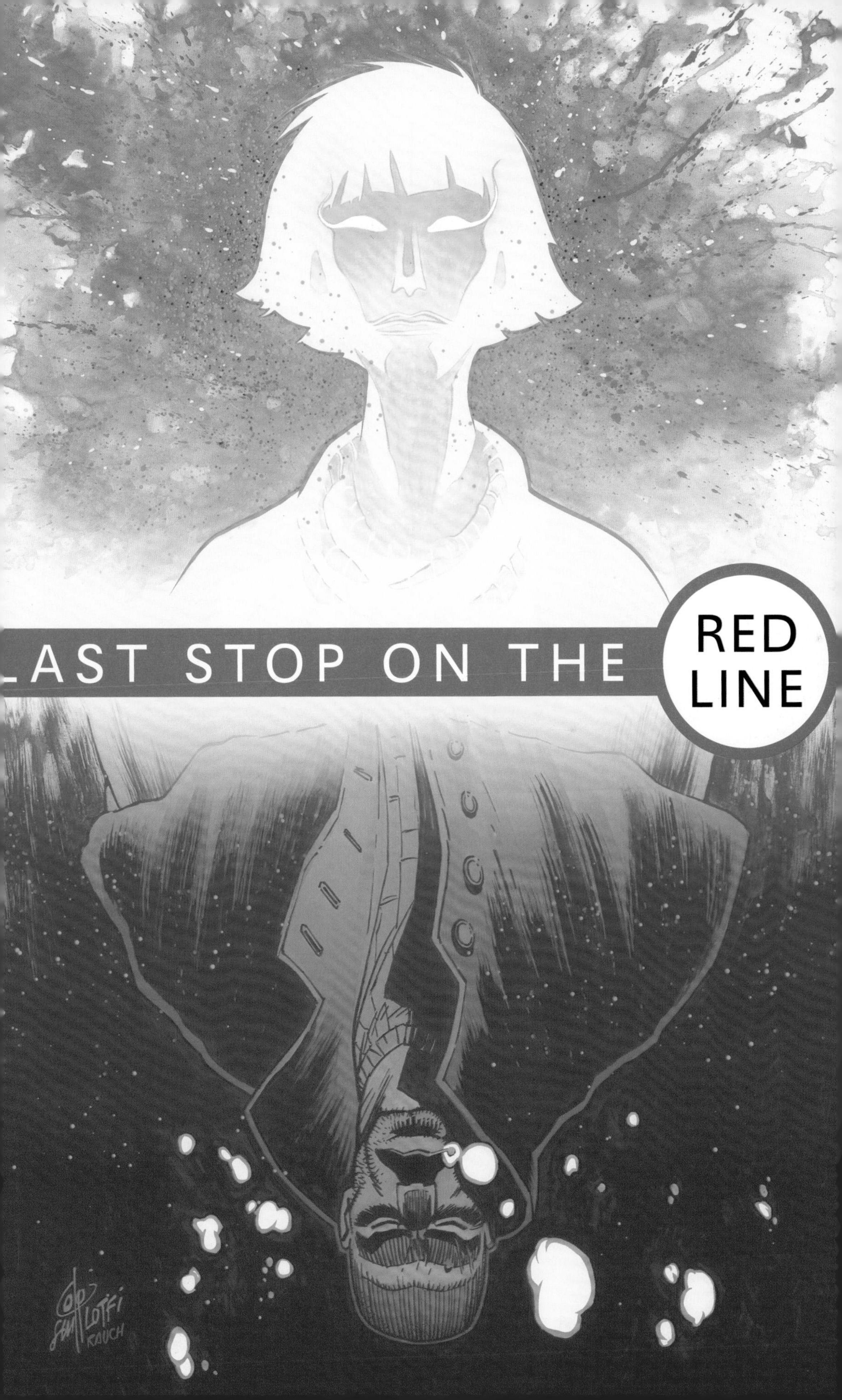
LAST STOP ON THE
RED LINE
LOTFI
RAUCH

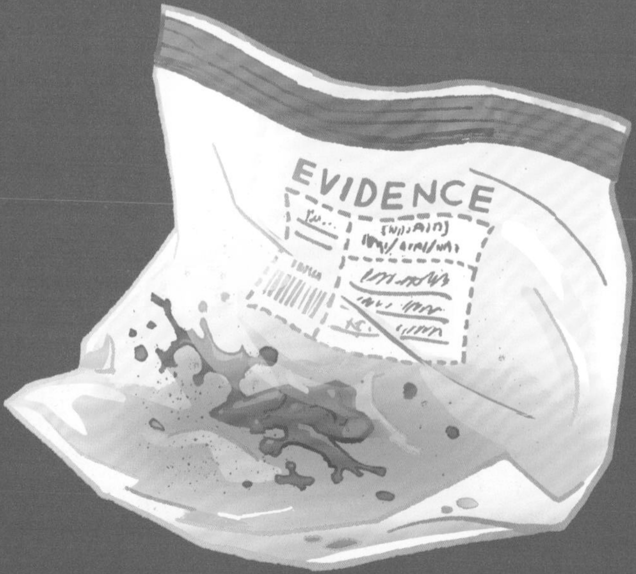
EVIDENCE

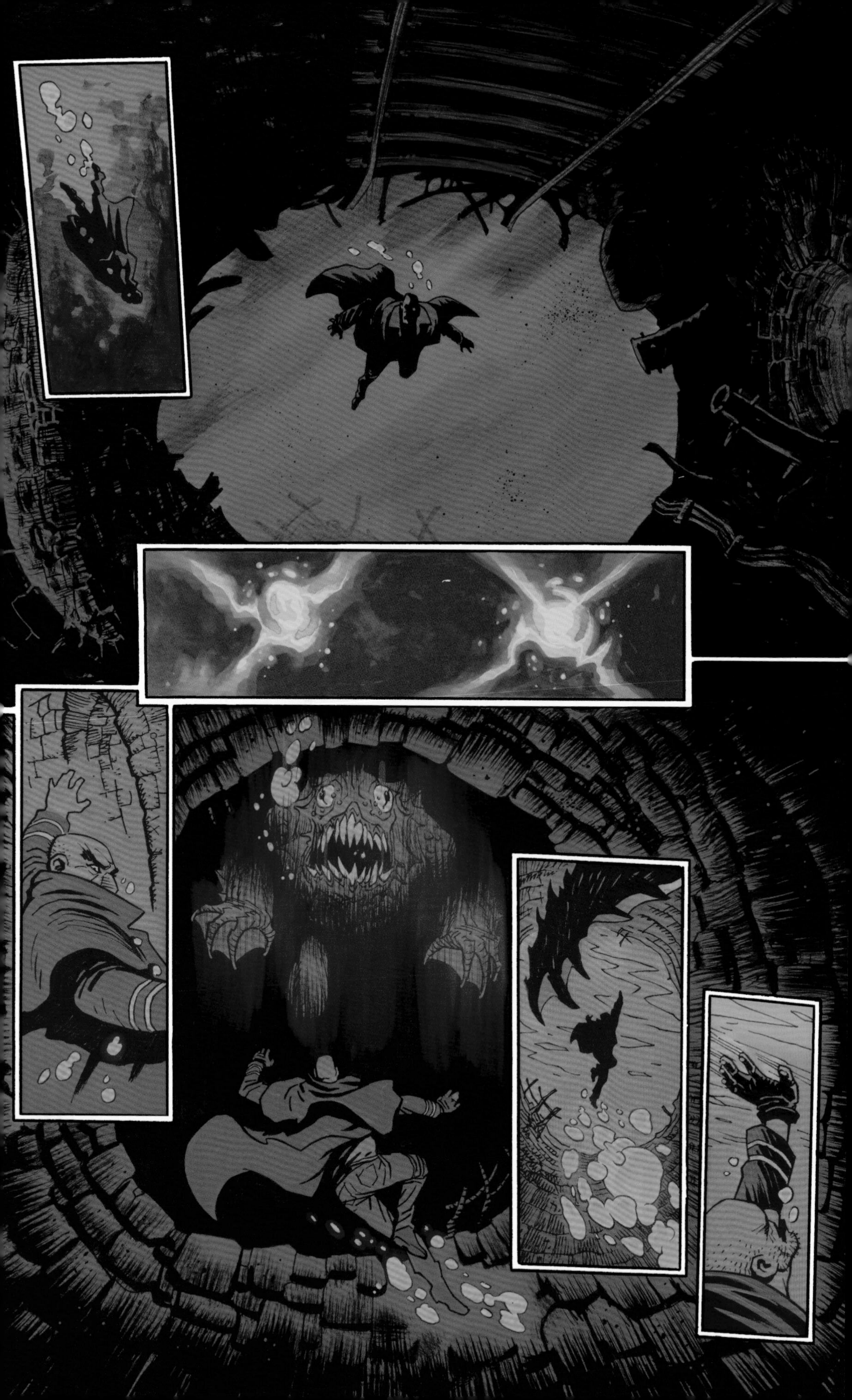

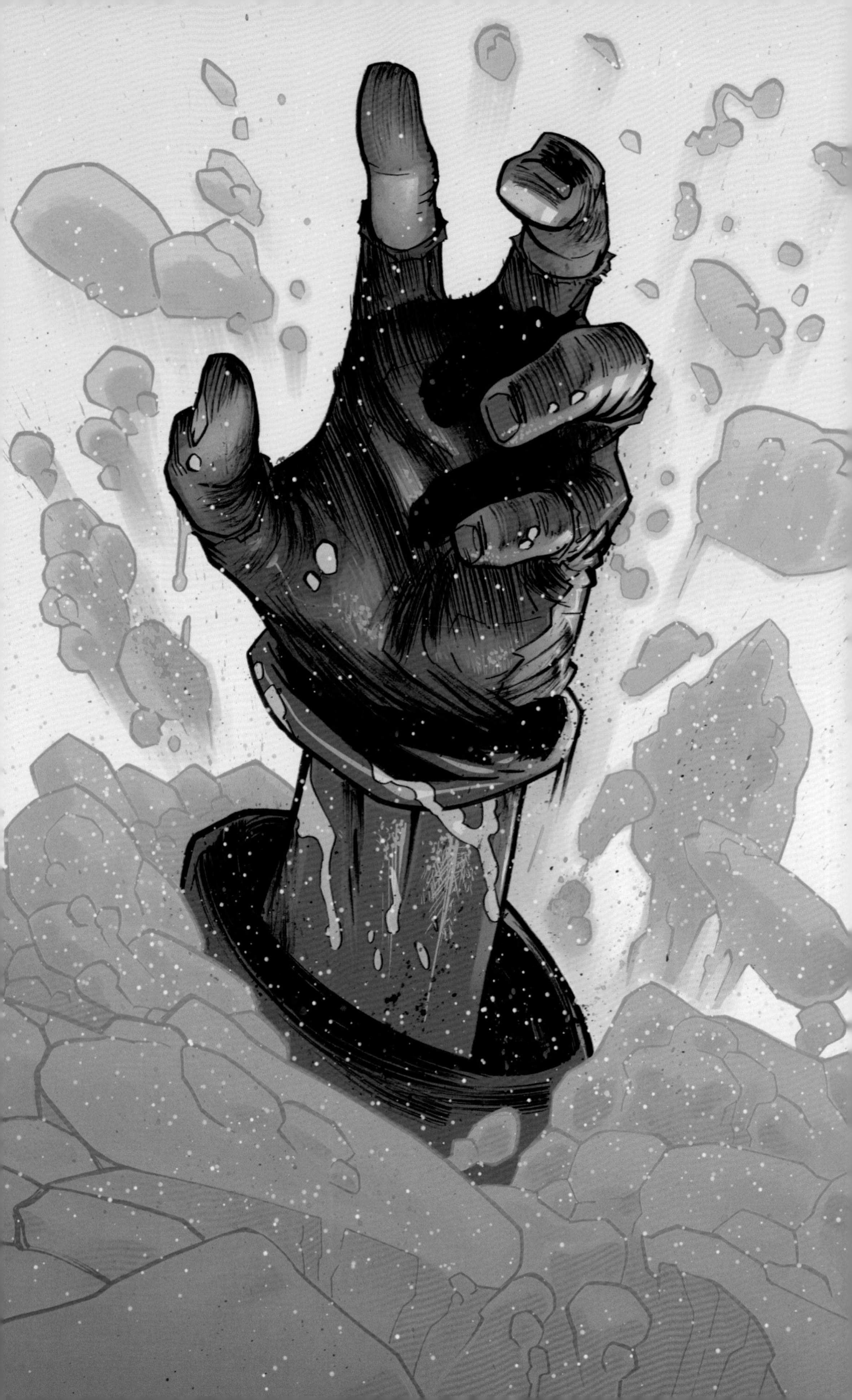

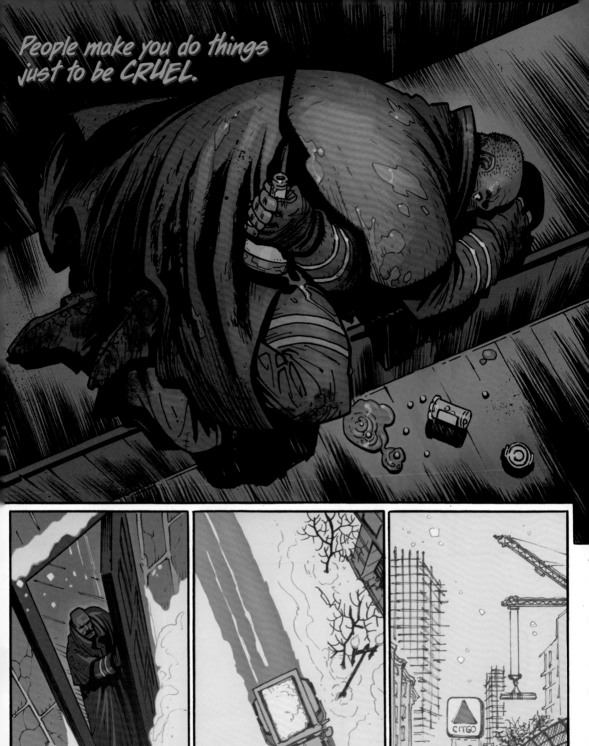

People make you do things just to be CRUEL.

They make you feel humiliated and powerless.

That's how they feed their own power.

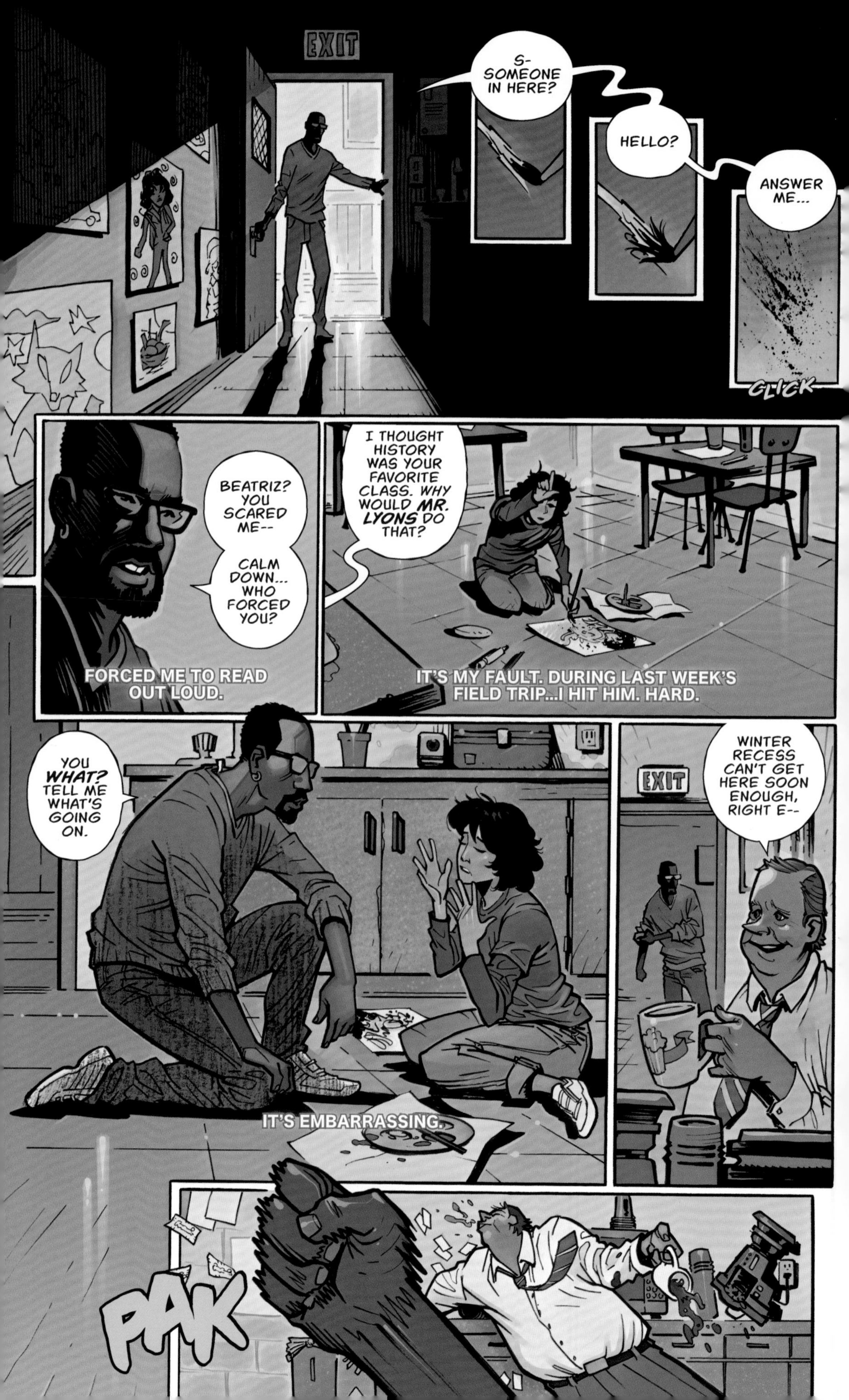
EXIT
S-SOMEONE IN HERE?
HELLO?
ANSWER ME...
CLICK
BEATRIZ? YOU SCARED ME--
CALM DOWN... WHO FORCED YOU?
FORCED ME TO READ OUT LOUD.
I THOUGHT HISTORY WAS YOUR FAVORITE CLASS. WHY WOULD MR. LYONS DO THAT?
IT'S MY FAULT. DURING LAST WEEK'S FIELD TRIP...I HIT HIM. HARD.
YOU WHAT? TELL ME WHAT'S GOING ON.
IT'S EMBARRASSING.
EXIT
WINTER RECESS CAN'T GET HERE SOON ENOUGH, RIGHT E--
PAK

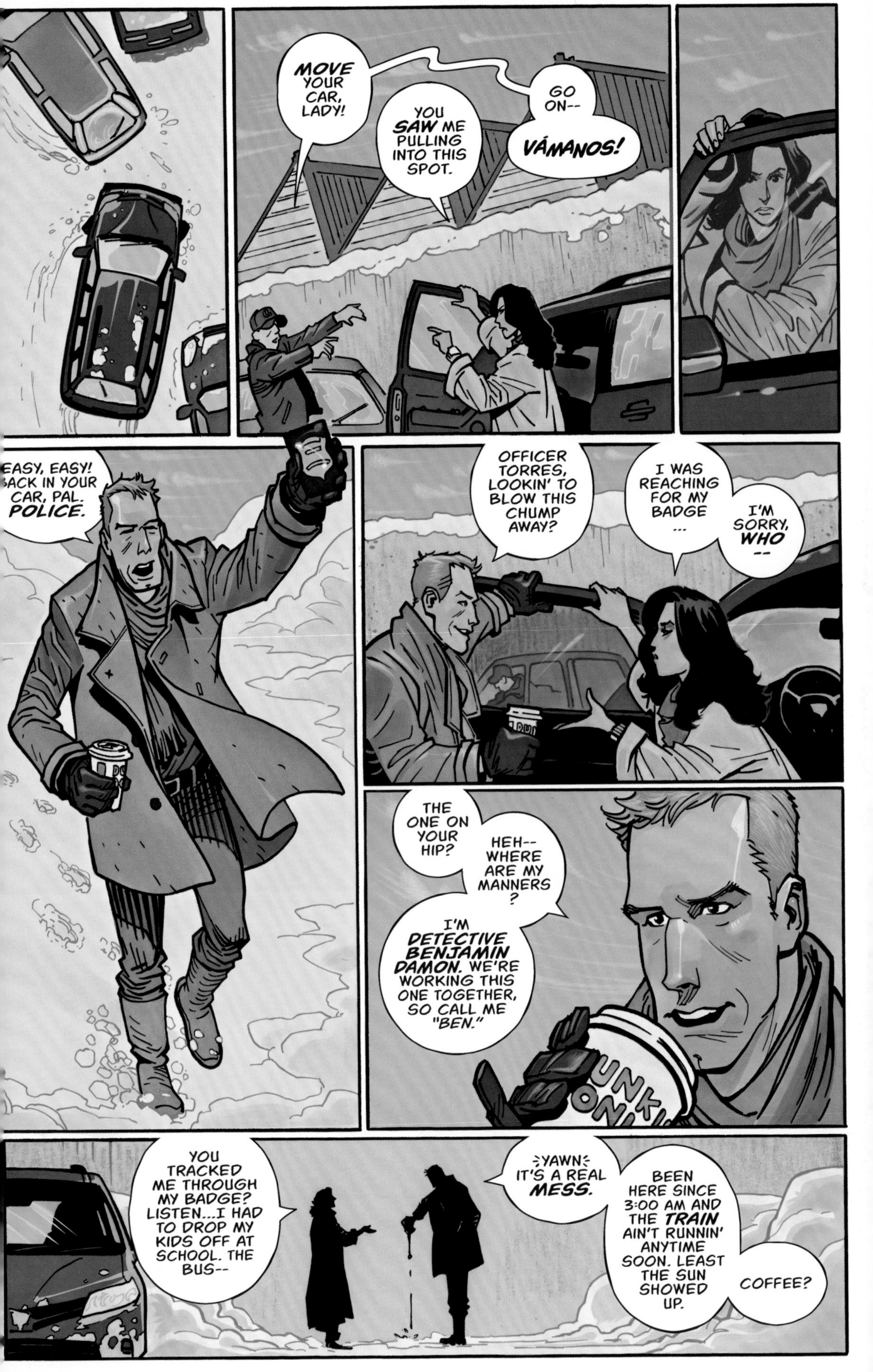
MOVE YOUR CAR, LADY!
YOU SAW ME PULLING INTO THIS SPOT.
GO ON--
VÁMANOS!
EASY, EASY! BACK IN YOUR CAR, PAL. POLICE.
OFFICER TORRES, LOOKIN' TO BLOW THIS CHUMP AWAY?
I WAS REACHING FOR MY BADGE ...
I'M SORRY, WHO --
THE ONE ON YOUR HIP?
HEH--WHERE ARE MY MANNERS ?
I'M DETECTIVE BENJAMIN DAMON. WE'RE WORKING THIS ONE TOGETHER, SO CALL ME "BEN."
YOU TRACKED ME THROUGH MY BADGE? LISTEN...I HAD TO DROP MY KIDS OFF AT SCHOOL. THE BUS--
YAWN IT'S A REAL MESS.
BEEN HERE SINCE 3:00 AM AND THE TRAIN AIN'T RUNNIN' ANYTIME SOON. LEAST THE SUN SHOWED UP.
COFFEE?

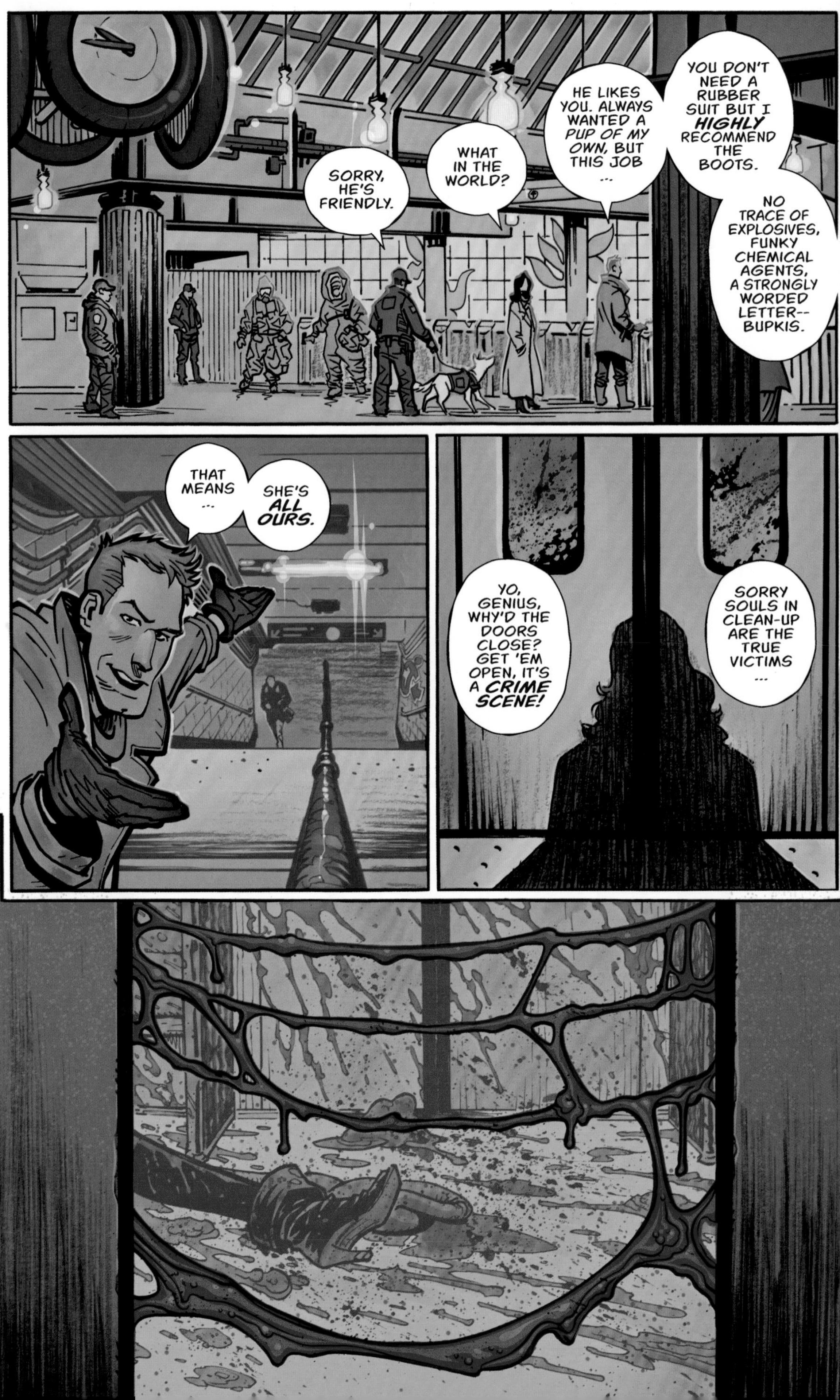
SORRY, HE'S FRIENDLY.
WHAT IN THE WORLD?
HE LIKES YOU. ALWAYS WANTED A PUP OF MY OWN, BUT THIS JOB ...
YOU DON'T NEED A RUBBER SUIT BUT I HIGHLY RECOMMEND THE BOOTS.
NO TRACE OF EXPLOSIVES, FUNKY CHEMICAL AGENTS, A STRONGLY WORDED LETTER-- BUPKIS.
THAT MEANS ...
SHE'S ALL OURS.
YO, GENIUS, WHY'D THE DOORS CLOSE? GET 'EM OPEN, IT'S A CRIME SCENE!
SORRY SOULS IN CLEAN-UP ARE THE TRUE VICTIMS ...

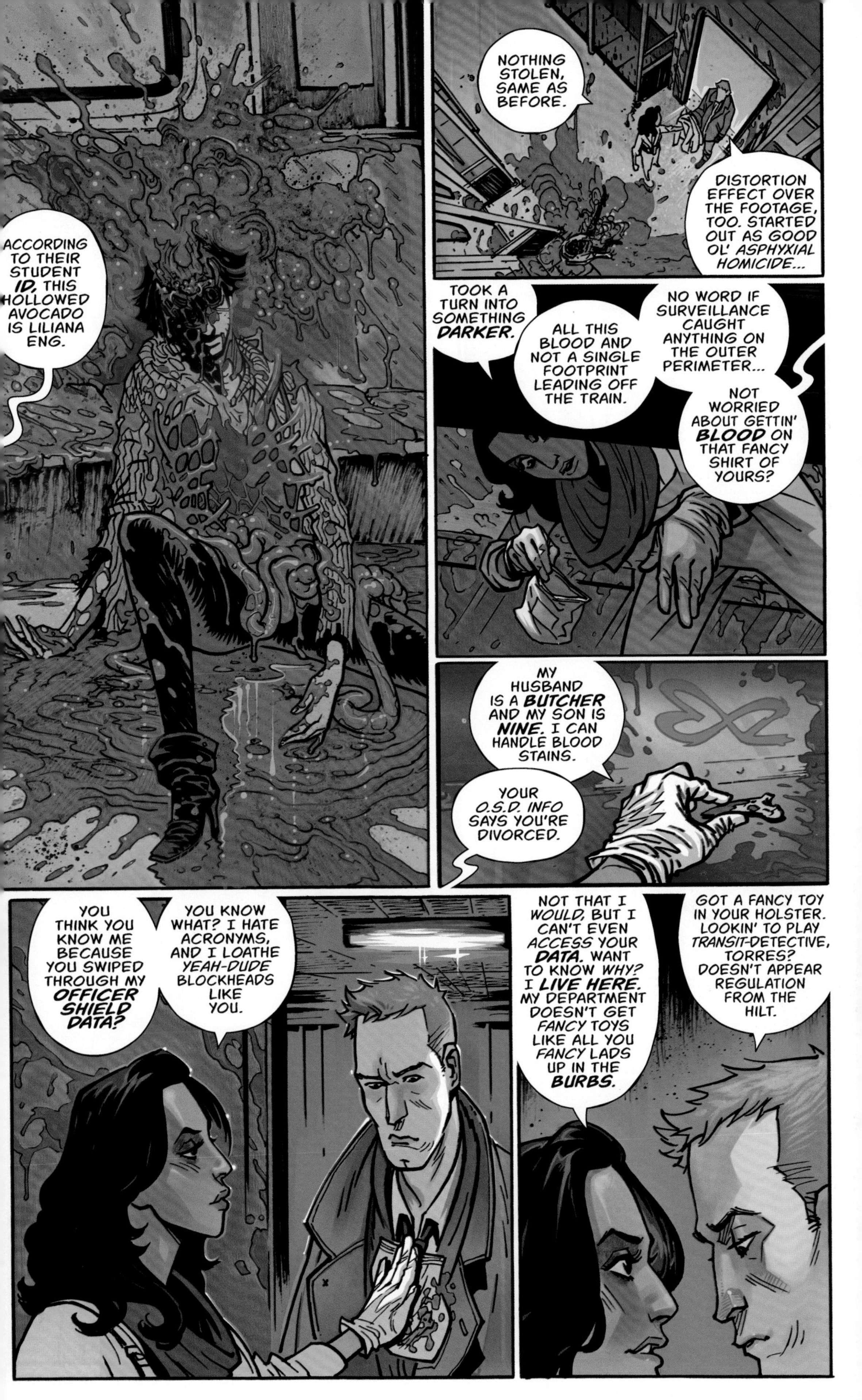
ACCORDING TO THEIR STUDENT ID, THIS HOLLOWED AVOCADO IS LILIANA ENG.
NOTHING STOLEN, SAME AS BEFORE.
DISTORTION EFFECT OVER THE FOOTAGE, TOO. STARTED OUT AS GOOD OL' ASPHYXIAL HOMICIDE...
TOOK A TURN INTO SOMETHING DARKER.
ALL THIS BLOOD AND NOT A SINGLE FOOTPRINT LEADING OFF THE TRAIN.
NO WORD IF SURVEILLANCE CAUGHT ANYTHING ON THE OUTER PERIMETER...
NOT WORRIED ABOUT GETTIN' BLOOD ON THAT FANCY SHIRT OF YOURS?
MY HUSBAND IS A BUTCHER AND MY SON IS NINE. I CAN HANDLE BLOOD STAINS.
YOUR O.S.D. INFO SAYS YOU'RE DIVORCED.
YOU THINK YOU KNOW ME BECAUSE YOU SWIPED THROUGH MY OFFICER SHIELD DATA?
YOU KNOW WHAT? I HATE ACRONYMS, AND I LOATHE YEAH-DUDE BLOCKHEADS LIKE YOU.
NOT THAT I WOULD, BUT I CAN'T EVEN ACCESS YOUR DATA. WANT TO KNOW WHY? I LIVE HERE. MY DEPARTMENT DOESN'T GET FANCY TOYS LIKE ALL YOU FANCY LADS UP IN THE BURBS.
GOT A FANCY TOY IN YOUR HOLSTER. LOOKIN' TO PLAY TRANSIT-DETECTIVE, TORRES? DOESN'T APPEAR REGULATION FROM THE HILT.

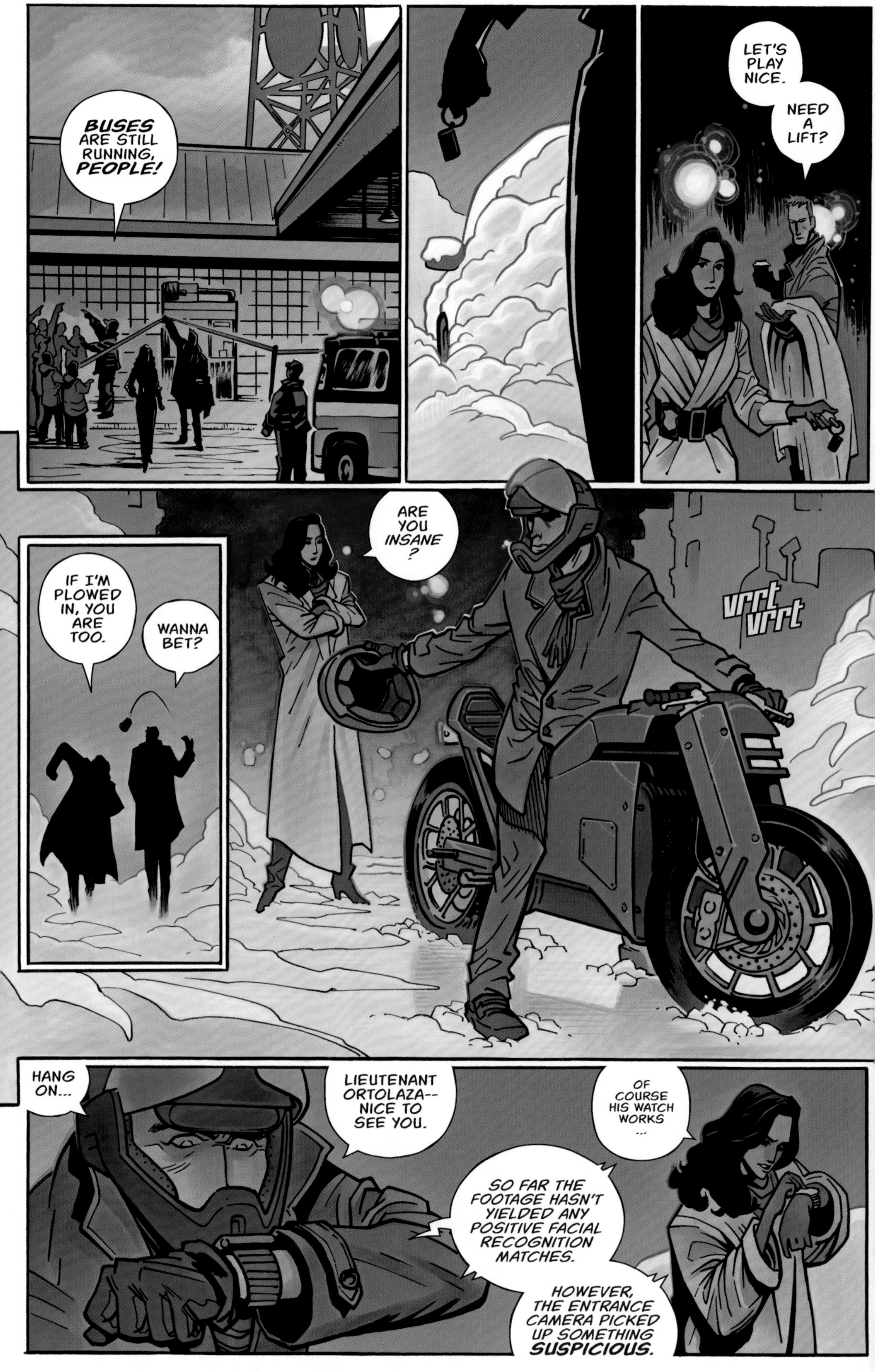
BUSES ARE STILL RUNNING, PEOPLE!
LET'S PLAY NICE.
NEED A LIFT?
IF I'M PLOWED IN, YOU ARE TOO.
WANNA BET?
ARE YOU INSANE?
vrrt vrrt
HANG ON...
LIEUTENANT ORTOLAZA-- NICE TO SEE YOU.
OF COURSE HIS WATCH WORKS...
SO FAR THE FOOTAGE HASN'T YIELDED ANY POSITIVE FACIAL RECOGNITION MATCHES.
HOWEVER, THE ENTRANCE CAMERA PICKED UP SOMETHING SUSPICIOUS.

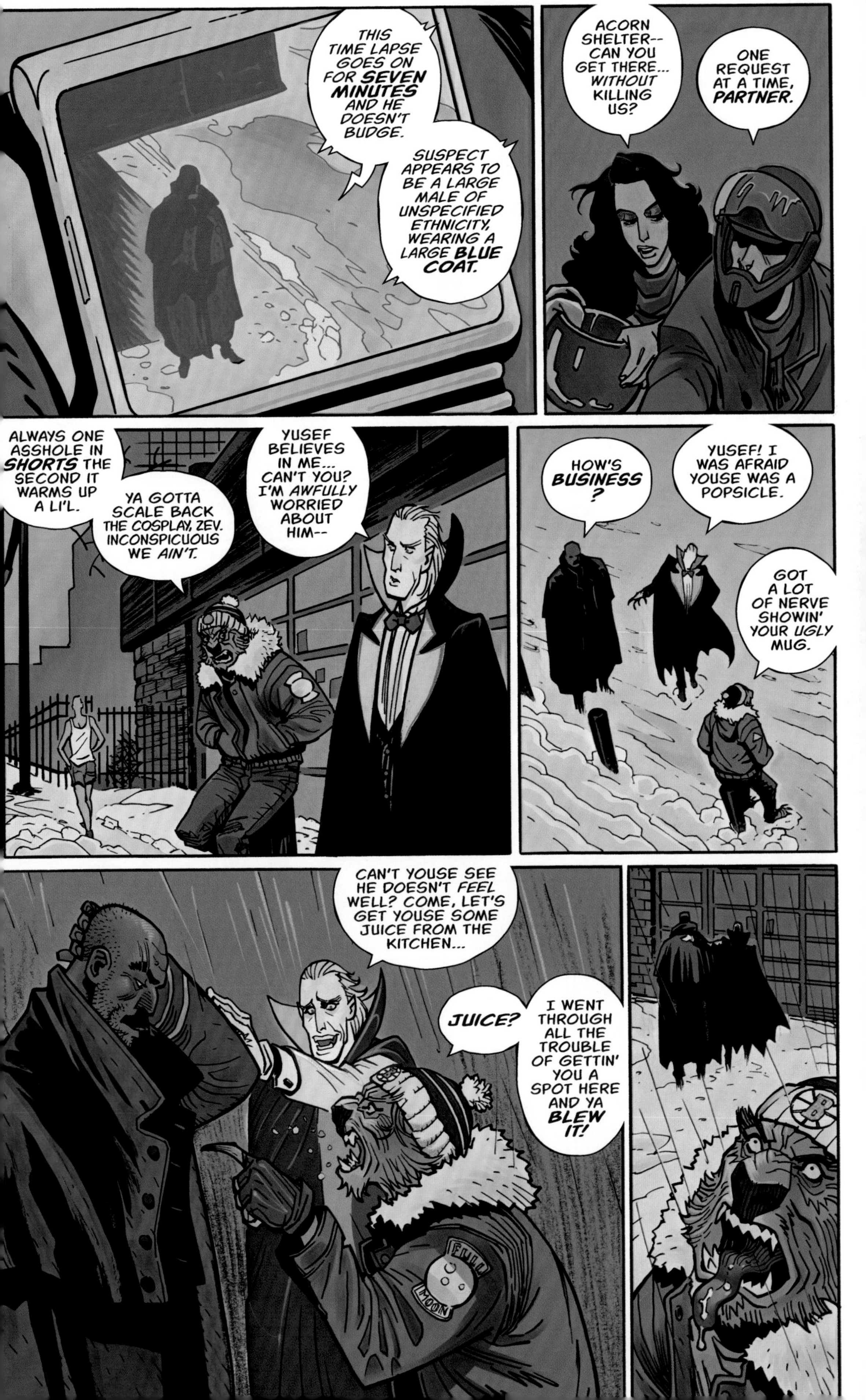
THIS TIME LAPSE GOES ON FOR SEVEN MINUTES AND HE DOESN'T BUDGE.
SUSPECT APPEARS TO BE A LARGE MALE OF UNSPECIFIED ETHNICITY, WEARING A LARGE BLUE COAT.
ACORN SHELTER-- CAN YOU GET THERE... WITHOUT KILLING US?
ONE REQUEST AT A TIME, PARTNER.
ALWAYS ONE ASSHOLE IN SHORTS THE SECOND IT WARMS UP A LI'L.
YA GOTTA SCALE BACK THE COSPLAY, ZEV. INCONSPICUOUS WE AIN'T.
YUSEF BELIEVES IN ME... CAN'T YOU? I'M AWFULLY WORRIED ABOUT HIM--
HOW'S BUSINESS?
YUSEF! I WAS AFRAID YOUSE WAS A POPSICLE.
GOT A LOT OF NERVE SHOWIN' YOUR UGLY MUG.
CAN'T YOUSE SEE HE DOESN'T FEEL WELL? COME, LET'S GET YOUSE SOME JUICE FROM THE KITCHEN...
JUICE?
I WENT THROUGH ALL THE TROUBLE OF GETTIN' YOU A SPOT HERE AND YA BLEW IT!
FULL MOON

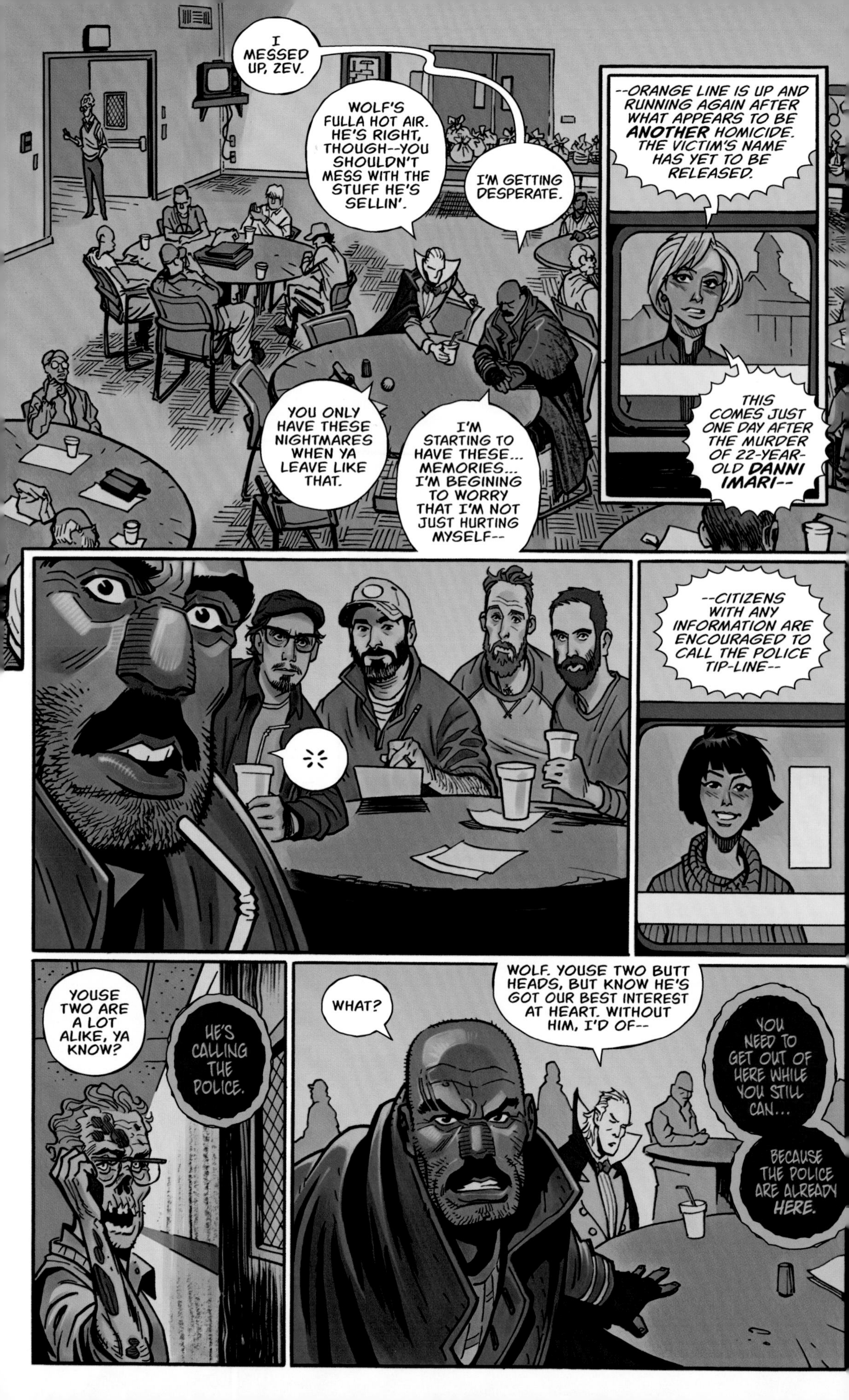
I MESSED UP, ZEV.
WOLF'S FULLA HOT AIR. HE'S RIGHT, THOUGH--YOU SHOULDN'T MESS WITH THE STUFF HE'S SELLIN'.
I'M GETTING DESPERATE.
--ORANGE LINE IS UP AND RUNNING AGAIN AFTER WHAT APPEARS TO BE ANOTHER HOMICIDE. THE VICTIM'S NAME HAS YET TO BE RELEASED.
YOU ONLY HAVE THESE NIGHTMARES WHEN YA LEAVE LIKE THAT.
I'M STARTING TO HAVE THESE... MEMORIES... I'M BEGINING TO WORRY THAT I'M NOT JUST HURTING MYSELF--
THIS COMES JUST ONE DAY AFTER THE MURDER OF 22-YEAR-OLD DANNI IMARI--
--CITIZENS WITH ANY INFORMATION ARE ENCOURAGED TO CALL THE POLICE TIP-LINE--
YOUSE TWO ARE A LOT ALIKE, YA KNOW?
HE'S CALLING THE POLICE.
WHAT?
WOLF. YOUSE TWO BUTT HEADS, BUT KNOW HE'S GOT OUR BEST INTEREST AT HEART. WITHOUT HIM, I'D OF--
YOU NEED TO GET OUT OF HERE WHILE YOU STILL CAN...
BECAUSE THE POLICE ARE ALREADY HERE.

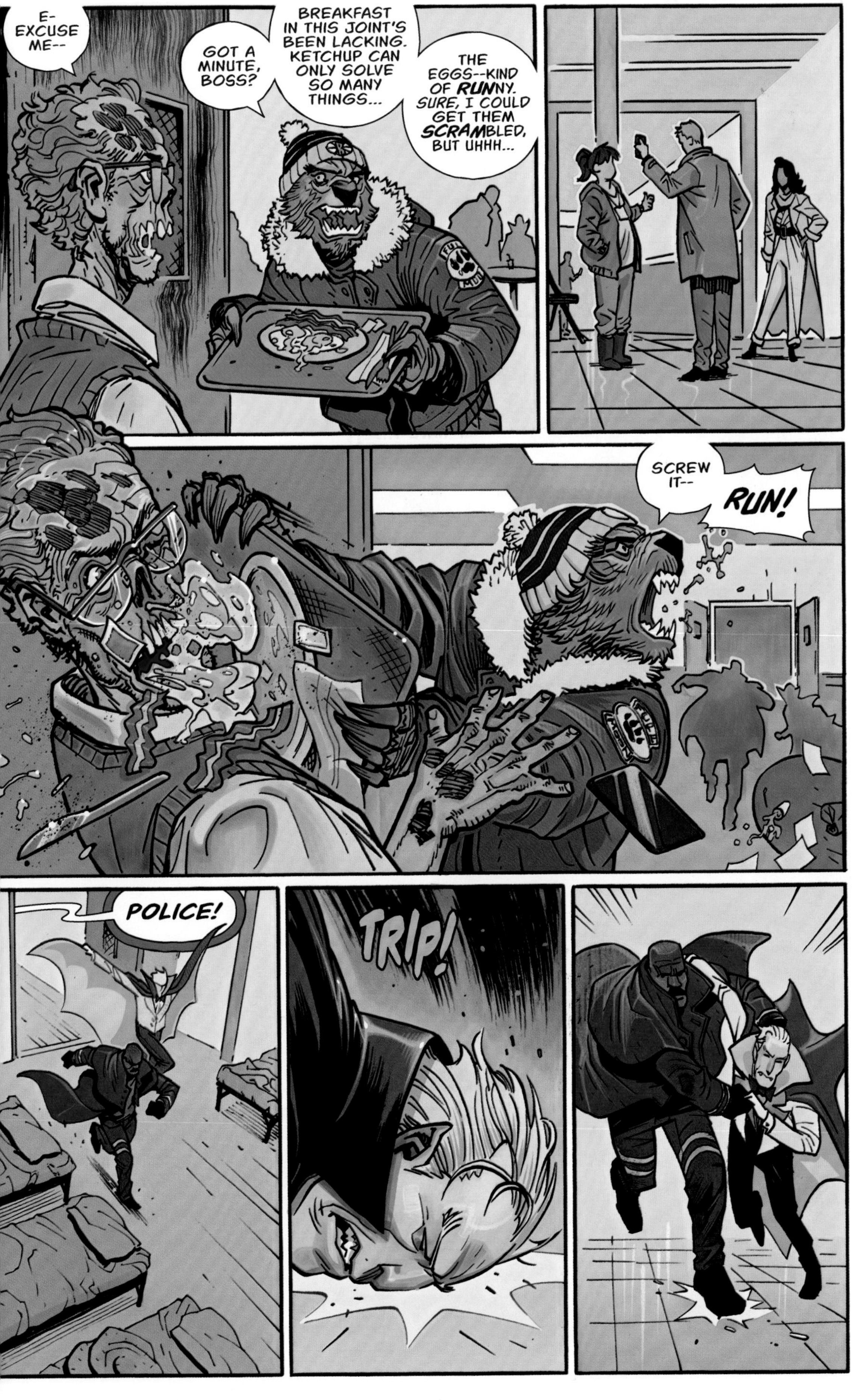
E-EXCUSE ME--
GOT A MINUTE, BOSS?
BREAKFAST IN THIS JOINT'S BEEN LACKING. KETCHUP CAN ONLY SOLVE SO MANY THINGS...
THE EGGS--KIND OF RUNNY. SURE, I COULD GET THEM SCRAMBLED, BUT UHHH...
SCREW IT--
RUN!
POLICE!
TRIP!

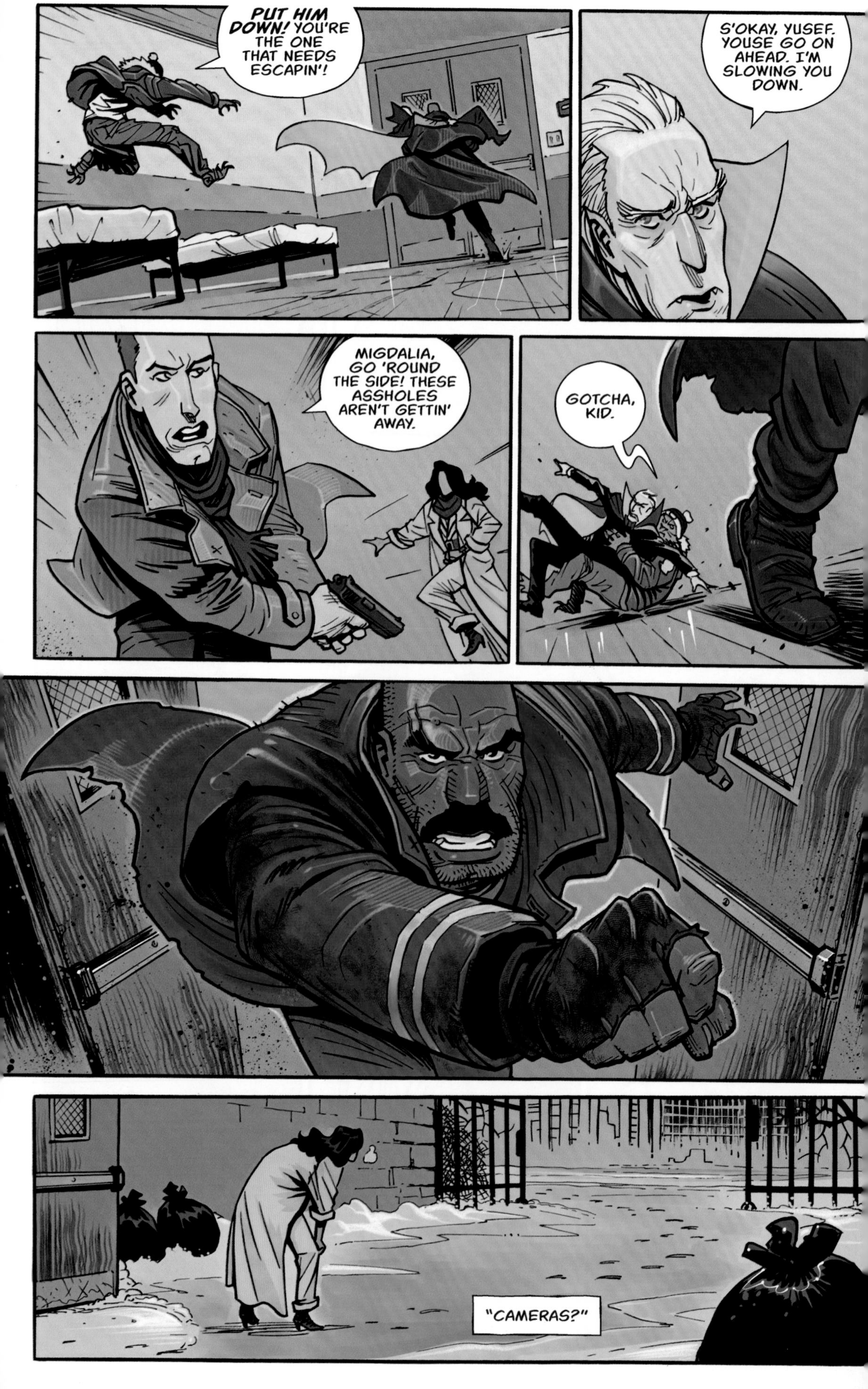
PUT HIM DOWN! YOU'RE THE ONE THAT NEEDS ESCAPIN'!
S'OKAY, YUSEF. YOUSE GO ON AHEAD. I'M SLOWING YOU DOWN.
MIGDALIA, GO 'ROUND THE SIDE! THESE ASSHOLES AREN'T GETTIN' AWAY.
GOTCHA, KID.
"CAMERAS?"

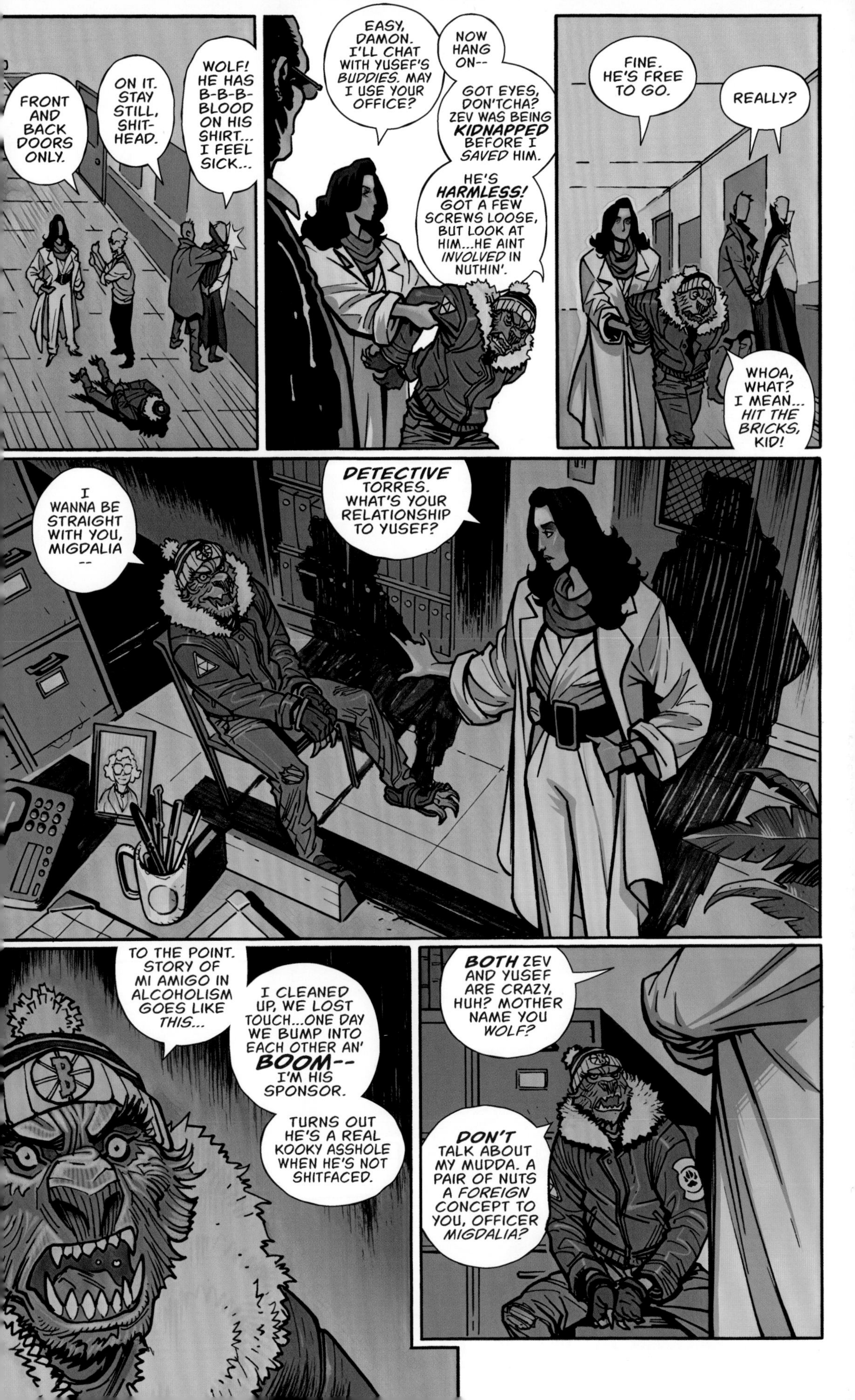
FRONT AND BACK DOORS ONLY.
ON IT. STAY STILL, SHIT-HEAD.
WOLF! HE HAS B-B-B-BLOOD ON HIS SHIRT... I FEEL SICK...
EASY, DAMON. I'LL CHAT WITH YUSEF'S BUDDIES. MAY I USE YOUR OFFICE?
NOW HANG ON--
GOT EYES, DON'TCHA? ZEV WAS BEING KIDNAPPED BEFORE I SAVED HIM.
HE'S HARMLESS! GOT A FEW SCREWS LOOSE, BUT LOOK AT HIM...HE AINT INVOLVED IN NUTHIN'.
FINE. HE'S FREE TO GO.
REALLY?
WHOA, WHAT? I MEAN... HIT THE BRICKS, KID!
I WANNA BE STRAIGHT WITH YOU, MIGDALIA --
DETECTIVE TORRES. WHAT'S YOUR RELATIONSHIP TO YUSEF?
TO THE POINT. STORY OF MI AMIGO IN ALCOHOLISM GOES LIKE THIS...
I CLEANED UP, WE LOST TOUCH...ONE DAY WE BUMP INTO EACH OTHER AN' BOOM-- I'M HIS SPONSOR.
TURNS OUT HE'S A REAL KOOKY ASSHOLE WHEN HE'S NOT SHITFACED.
BOTH ZEV AND YUSEF ARE CRAZY, HUH? MOTHER NAME YOU WOLF?
DON'T TALK ABOUT MY MUDDA. A PAIR OF NUTS A FOREIGN CONCEPT TO YOU, OFFICER MIGDALIA?

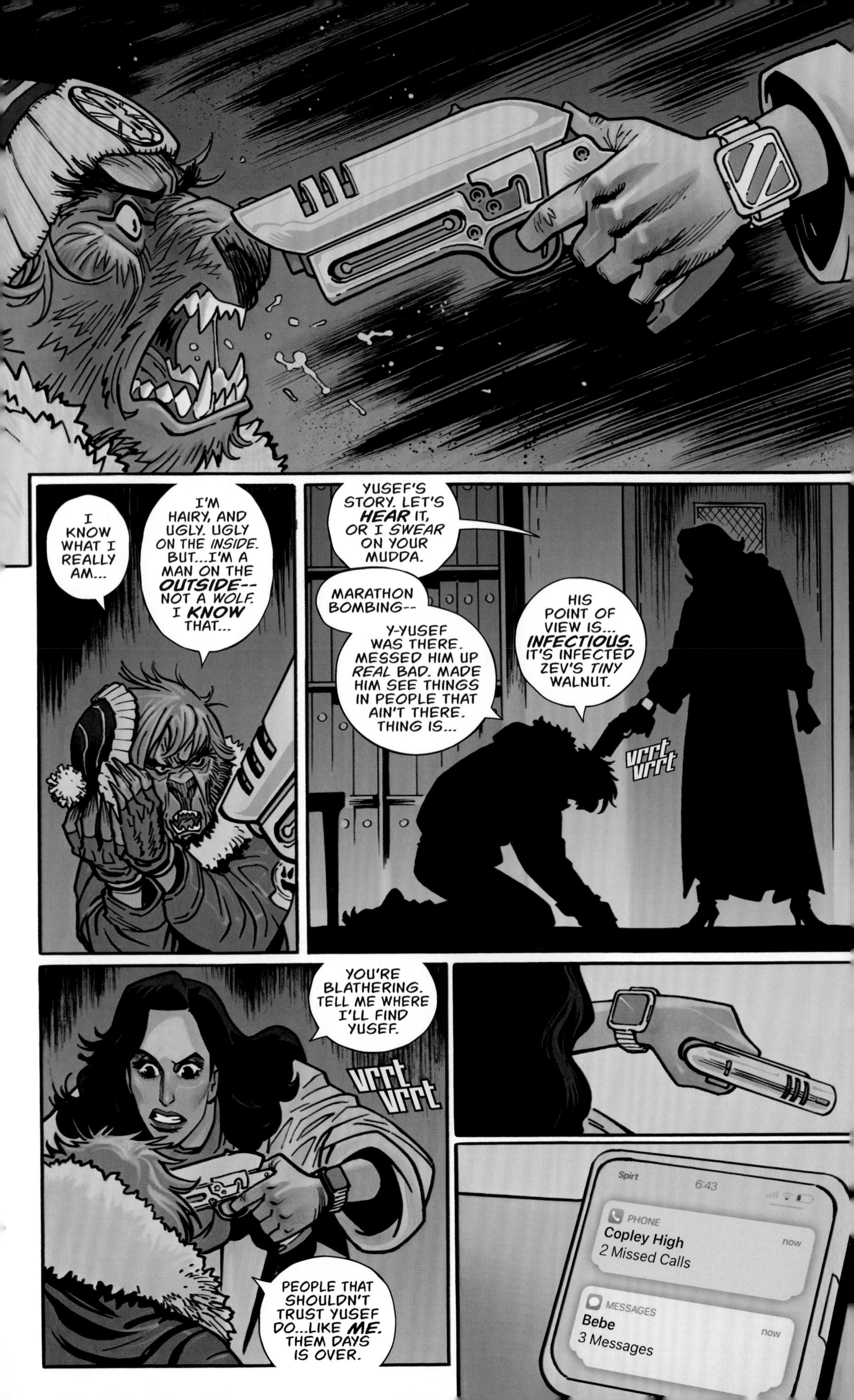

I KNOW WHAT I REALLY AM...
I'M HAIRY, AND UGLY. UGLY ON THE *INSIDE.* BUT...I'M A MAN ON THE **OUTSIDE--** NOT A *WOLF.* I **KNOW** THAT...
YUSEF'S STORY. LET'S **HEAR** IT, OR I *SWEAR* ON YOUR MUDDA.
MARATHON BOMBING--
Y-YUSEF WAS THERE. MESSED HIM UP *REAL* BAD. MADE HIM SEE THINGS IN PEOPLE THAT AIN'T THERE. THING IS...
HIS POINT OF VIEW IS... **INFECTIOUS.** IT'S INFECTED ZEV'S *TINY* WALNUT.
vrrt vrrt
YOU'RE BLATHERING. TELL ME WHERE I'LL FIND YUSEF.
vrrt vrrt
PEOPLE THAT SHOULDN'T TRUST YUSEF DO...LIKE **ME.** THEM DAYS IS OVER.
Spirt
6:43
PHONE
Copley High
now
2 Missed Calls
MESSAGES
Bebe
now
3 Messages

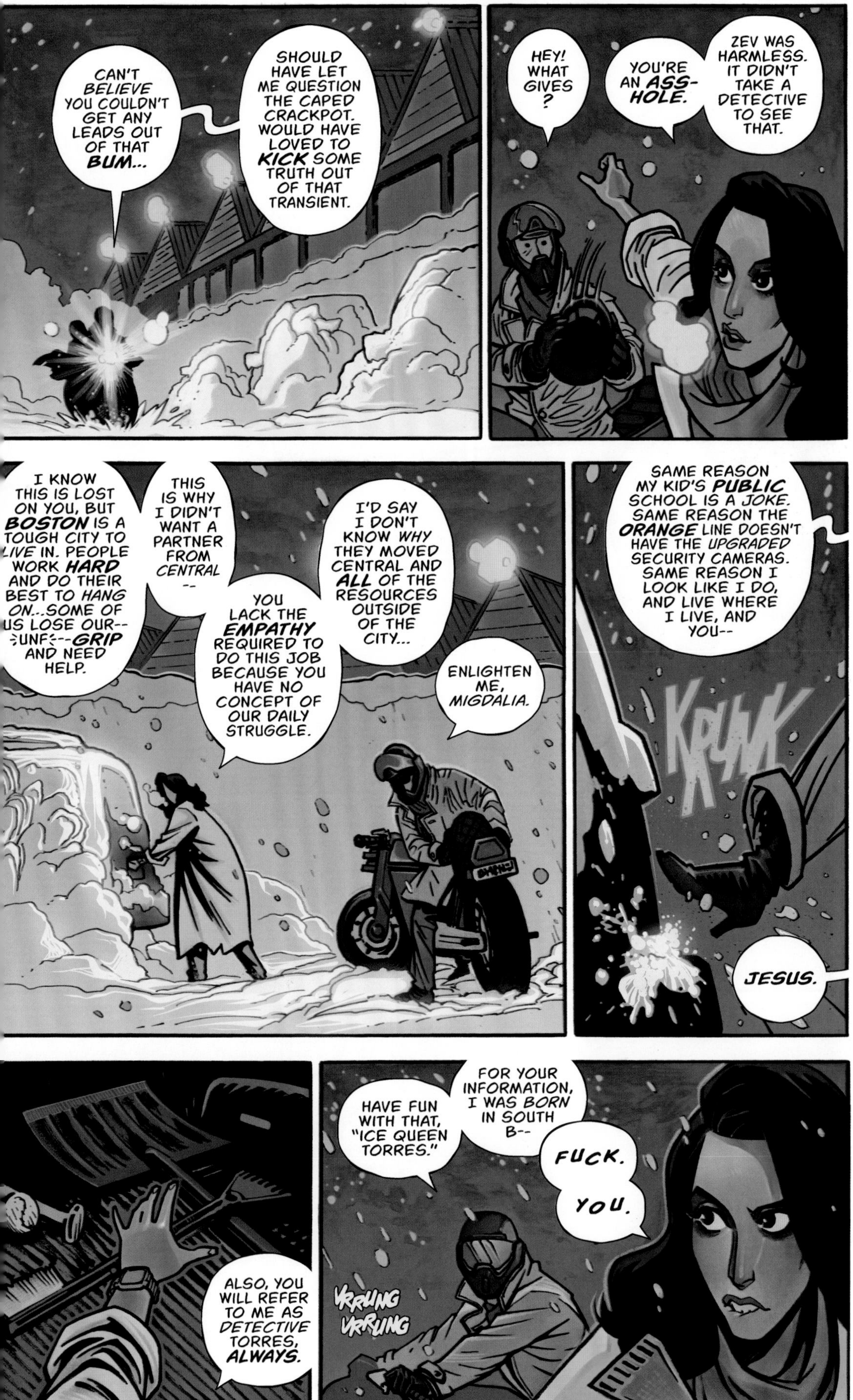

CAN'T BELIEVE YOU COULDN'T GET ANY LEADS OUT OF THAT BUM...
SHOULD HAVE LET ME QUESTION THE CAPED CRACKPOT. WOULD HAVE LOVED TO KICK SOME TRUTH OUT OF THAT TRANSIENT.
HEY! WHAT GIVES?
YOU'RE AN ASS-HOLE.
ZEV WAS HARMLESS. IT DIDN'T TAKE A DETECTIVE TO SEE THAT.
I KNOW THIS IS LOST ON YOU, BUT BOSTON IS A TOUGH CITY TO LIVE IN. PEOPLE WORK HARD AND DO THEIR BEST TO HANG ON...SOME OF US LOSE OUR-- UNF--GRIP AND NEED HELP.
THIS IS WHY I DIDN'T WANT A PARTNER FROM CENTRAL --
YOU LACK THE EMPATHY REQUIRED TO DO THIS JOB BECAUSE YOU HAVE NO CONCEPT OF OUR DAILY STRUGGLE.
I'D SAY I DON'T KNOW WHY THEY MOVED CENTRAL AND ALL OF THE RESOURCES OUTSIDE OF THE CITY...
ENLIGHTEN ME, MIGDALIA.
SAME REASON MY KID'S PUBLIC SCHOOL IS A JOKE. SAME REASON THE ORANGE LINE DOESN'T HAVE THE UPGRADED SECURITY CAMERAS. SAME REASON I LOOK LIKE I DO, AND LIVE WHERE I LIVE, AND YOU--
KRUNK
JESUS.
ALSO, YOU WILL REFER TO ME AS DETECTIVE TORRES, ALWAYS.
HAVE FUN WITH THAT, "ICE QUEEN TORRES."
FOR YOUR INFORMATION, I WAS BORN IN SOUTH B--
FUCK.
YOU.
VRRUNG
VRRUNG

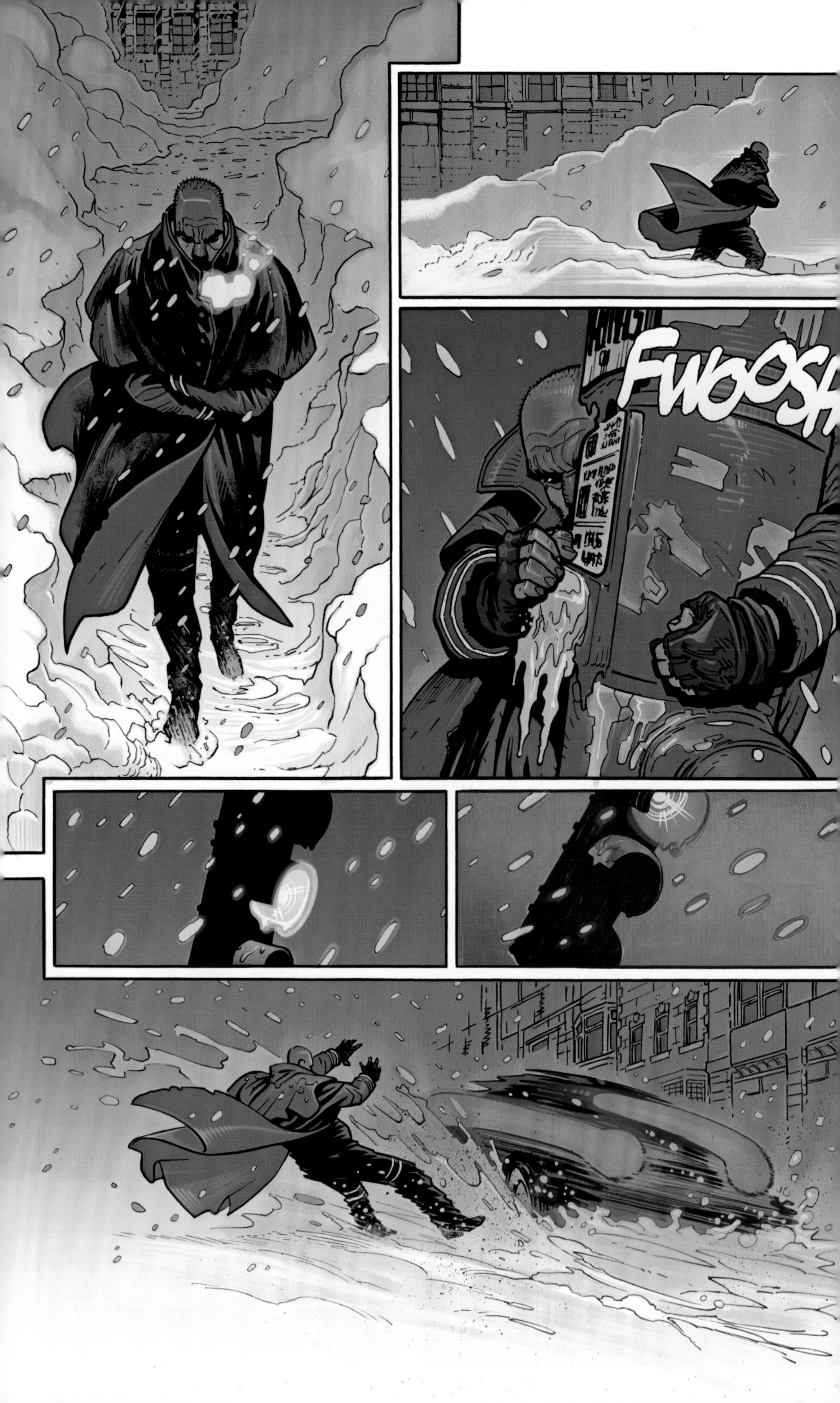
FWOOSH

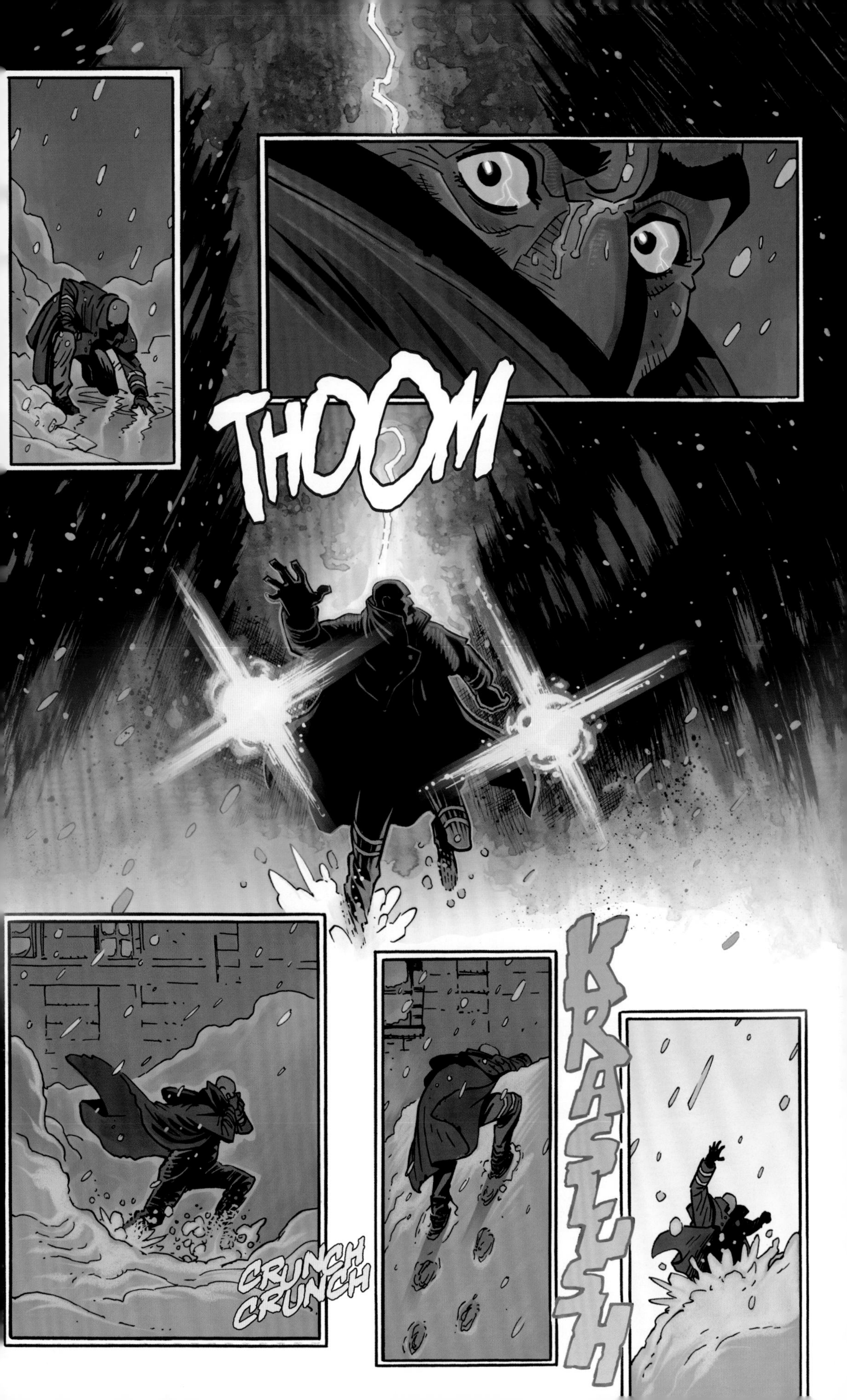
THOOM
CRUNCH
CRUNCH
KRASSH

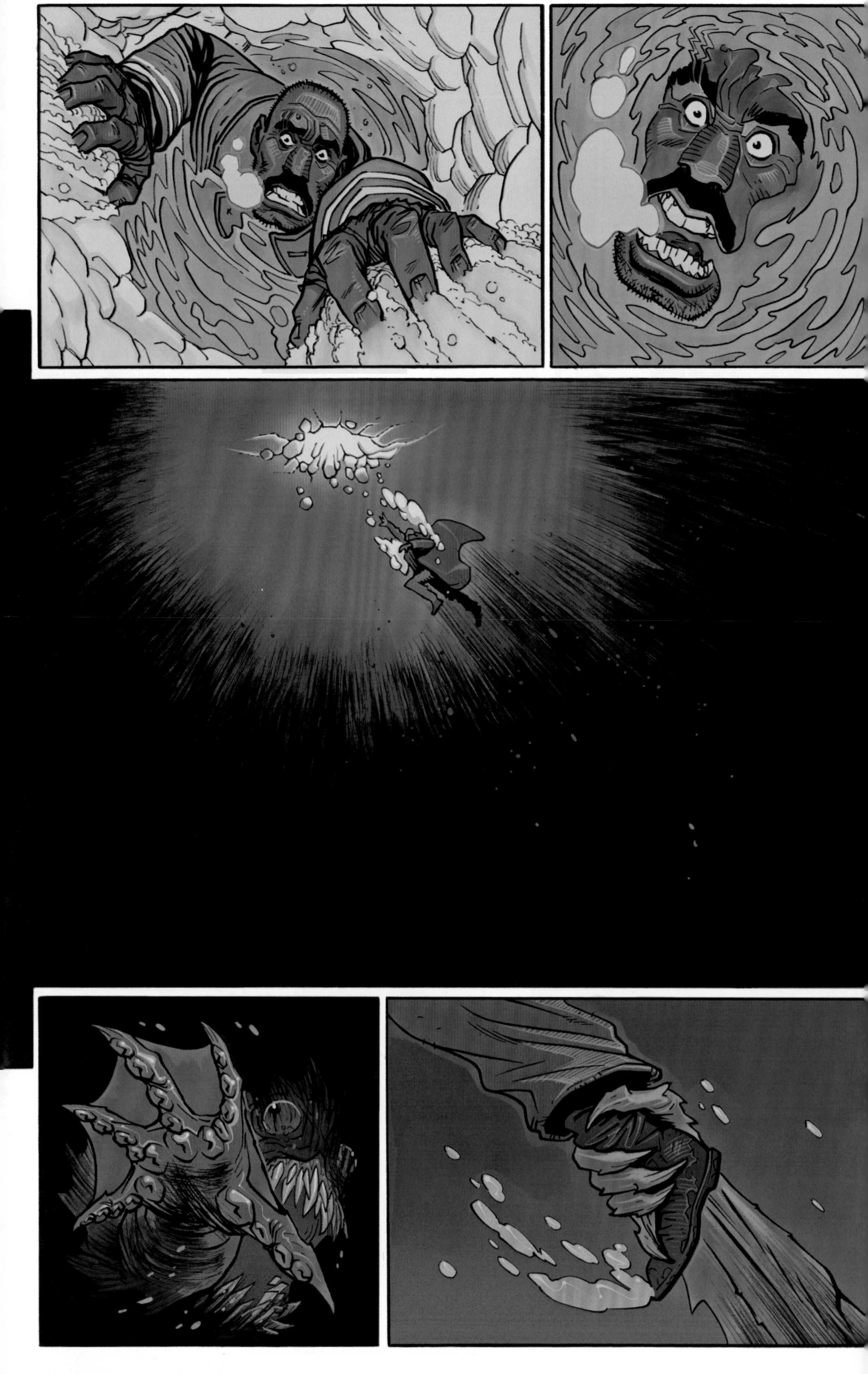

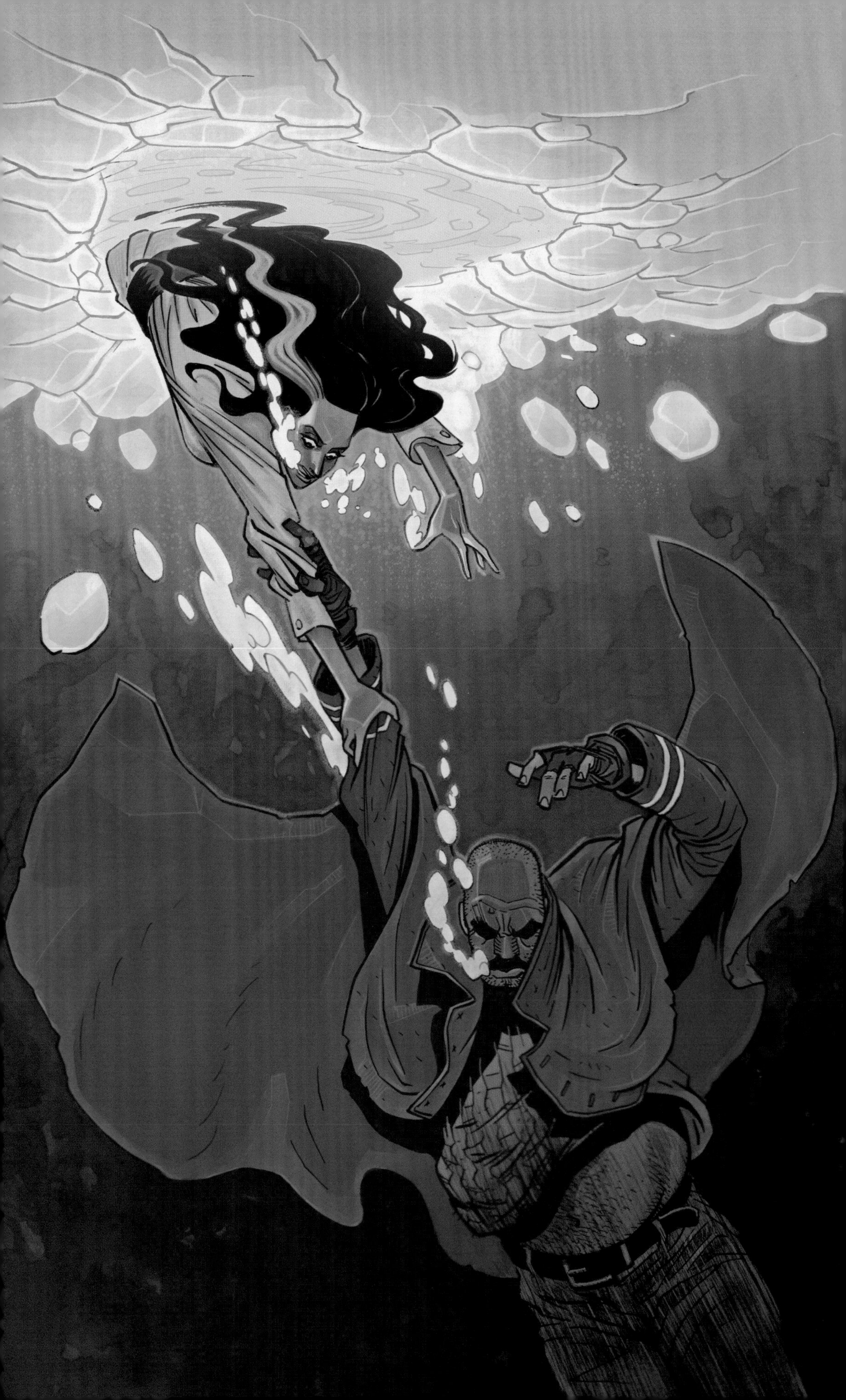

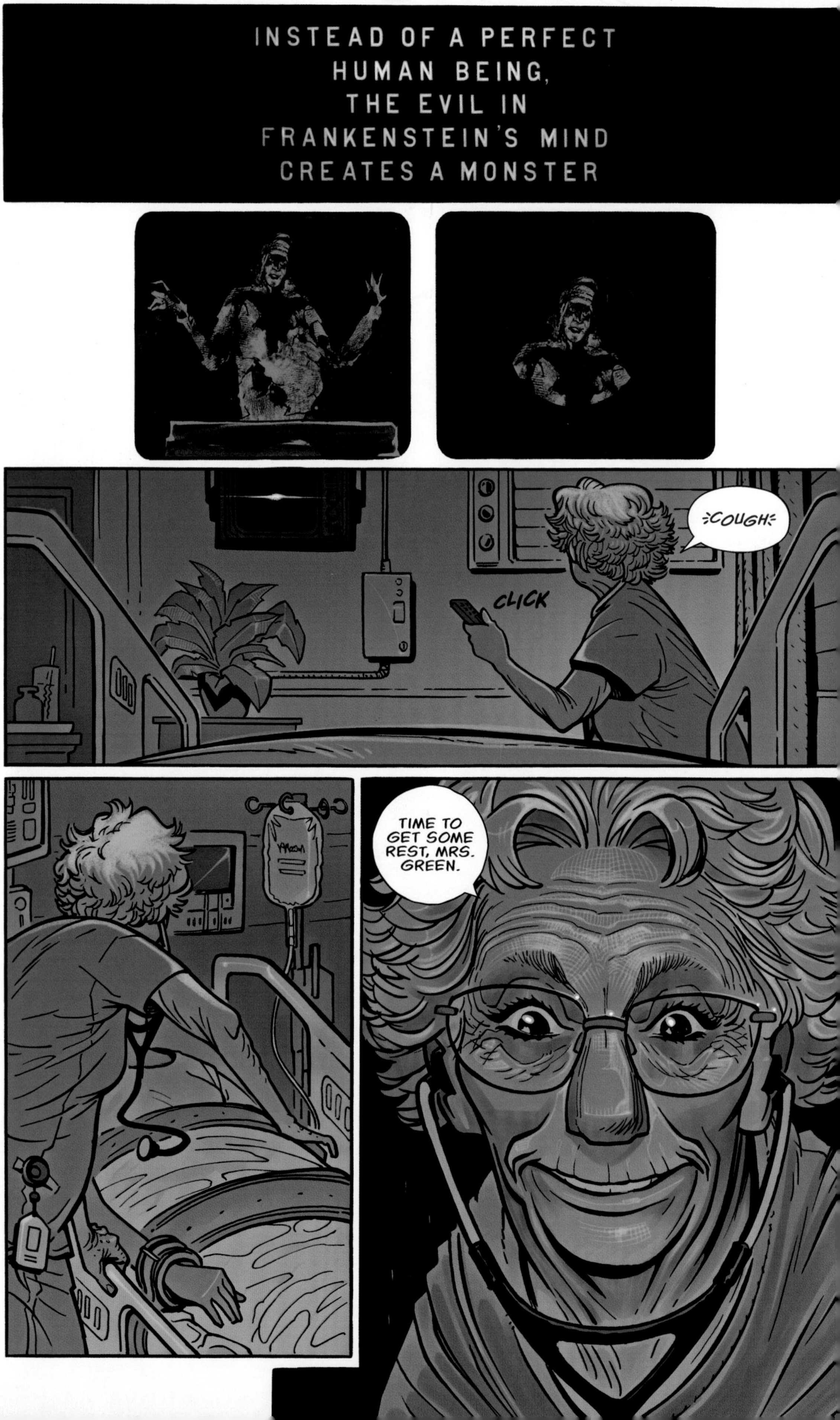
INSTEAD OF A PERFECT HUMAN BEING, THE EVIL IN FRANKENSTEIN'S MIND CREATES A MONSTER
COUGH
CLICK
TIME TO GET SOME REST, MRS. GREEN.

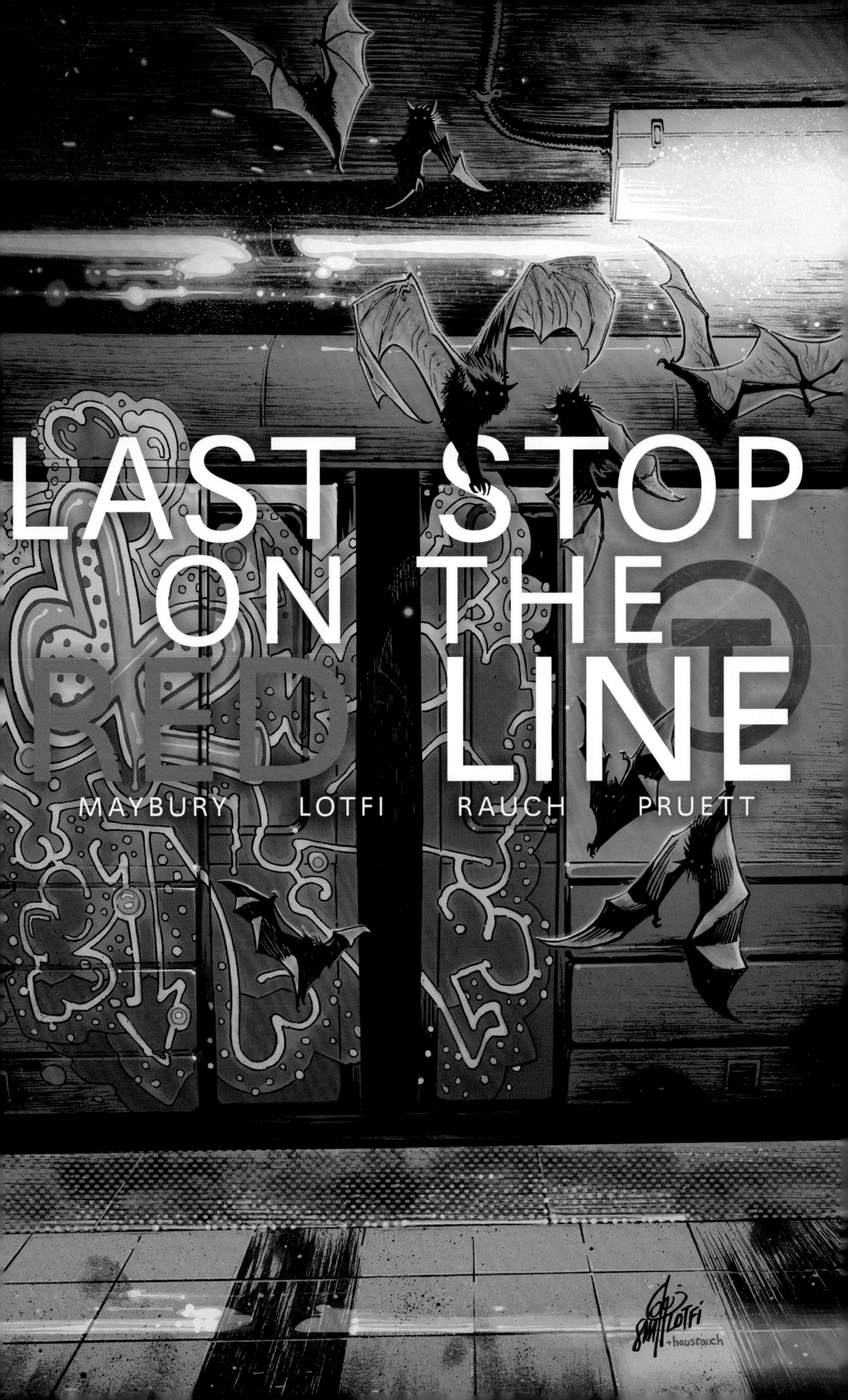
LAST STOP
ON THE
RED LINE
MAYBURY LOTFI RAUCH PRUETT

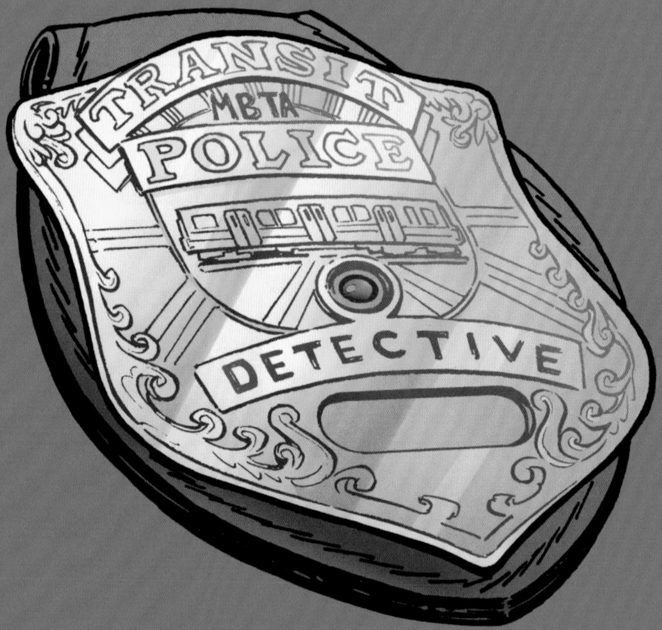
TRANSIT
MBTA
POLICE
DETECTIVE

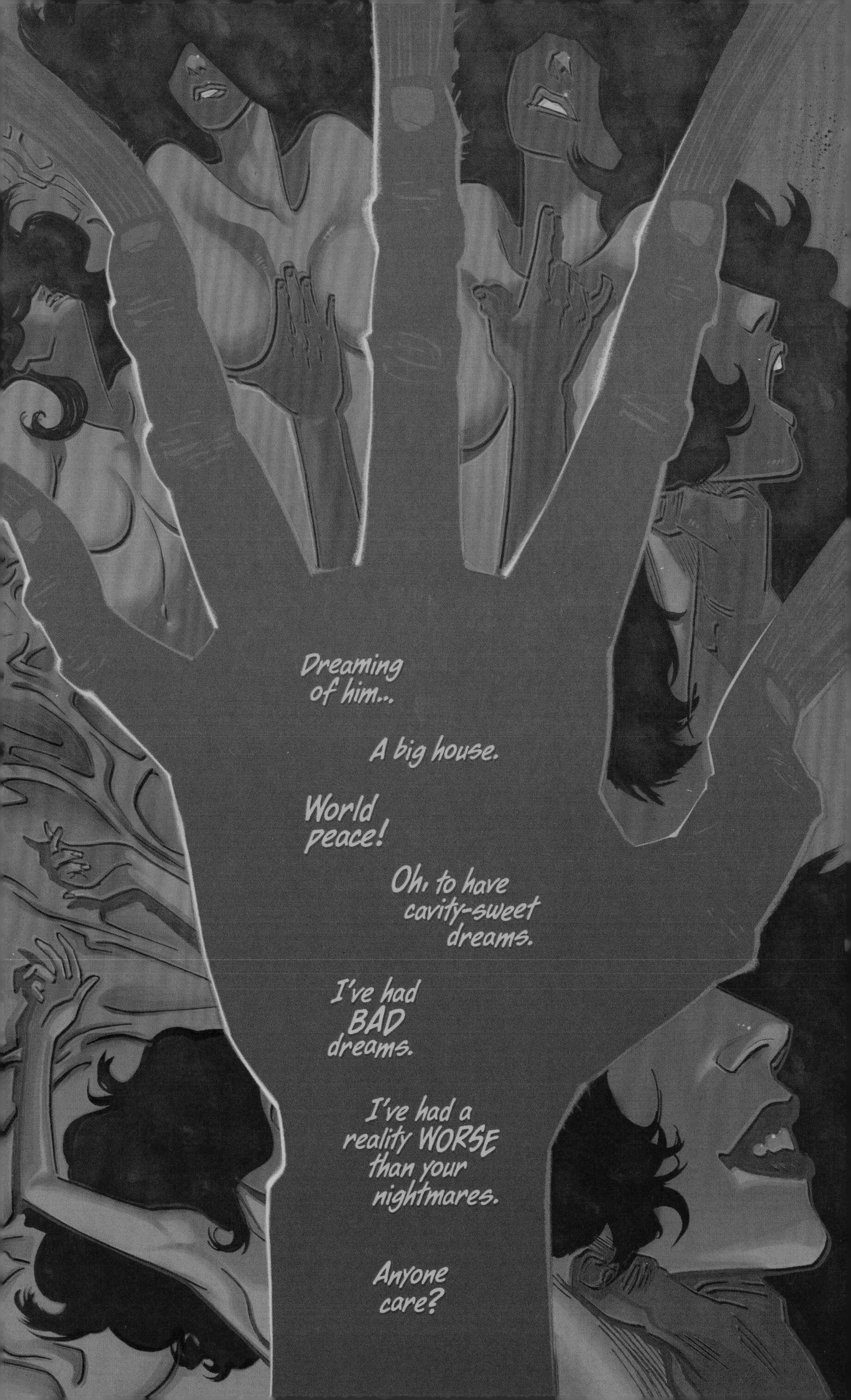
Dreaming of him...
A big house.
World peace!
Oh, to have cavity-sweet dreams.
I've had BAD dreams.
I've had a reality WORSE than your nightmares.
Anyone care?

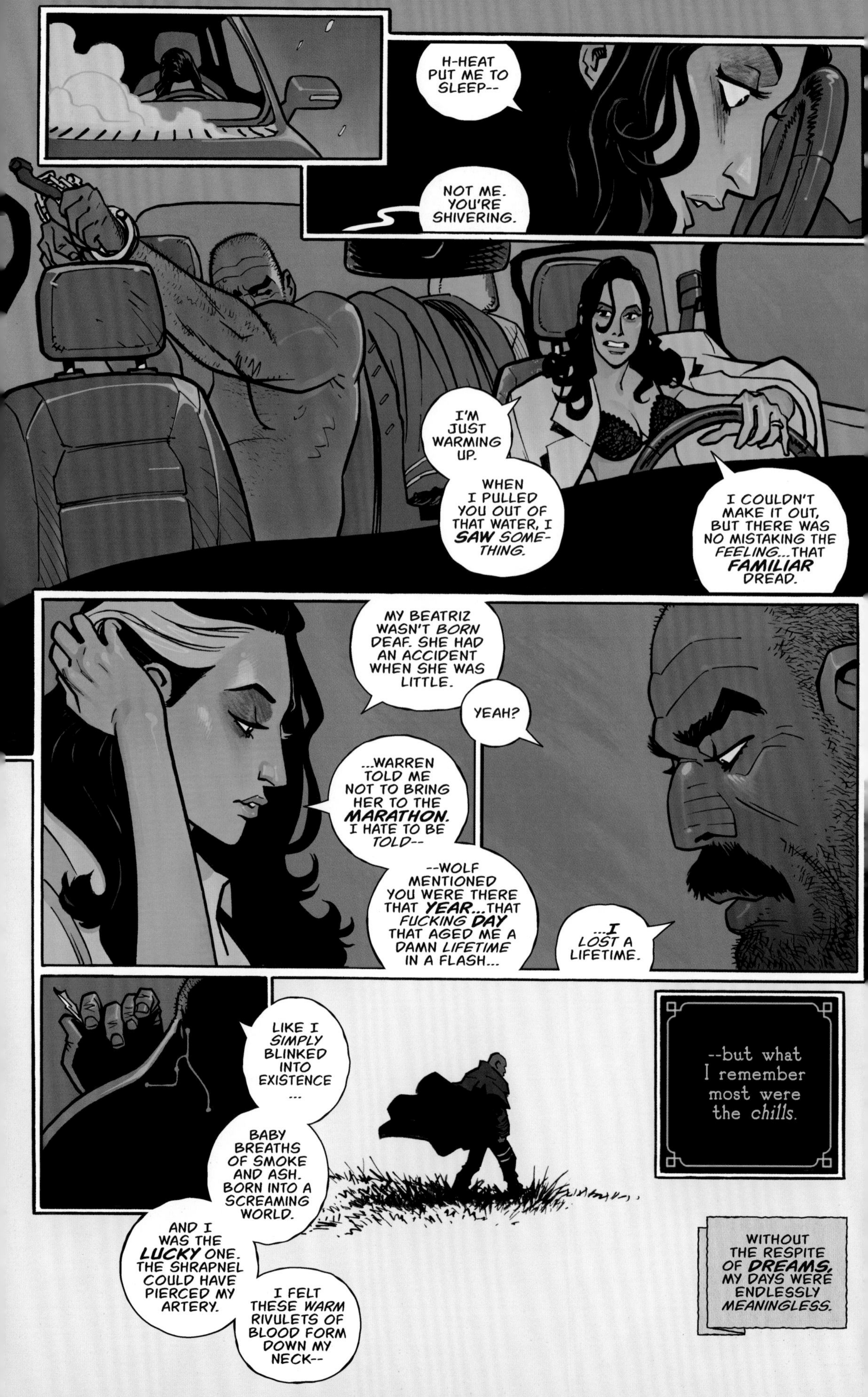
H-HEAT PUT ME TO SLEEP--
NOT ME. YOU'RE SHIVERING.
I'M JUST WARMING UP.
WHEN I PULLED YOU OUT OF THAT WATER, I SAW SOME-THING.
I COULDN'T MAKE IT OUT, BUT THERE WAS NO MISTAKING THE FEELING...THAT FAMILIAR DREAD.
MY BEATRIZ WASN'T BORN DEAF. SHE HAD AN ACCIDENT WHEN SHE WAS LITTLE.
YEAH?
...WARREN TOLD ME NOT TO BRING HER TO THE MARATHON. I HATE TO BE TOLD--
--WOLF MENTIONED YOU WERE THERE THAT YEAR...THAT FUCKING DAY THAT AGED ME A DAMN LIFETIME IN A FLASH...
...I LOST A LIFETIME.
LIKE I SIMPLY BLINKED INTO EXISTENCE ...
BABY BREATHS OF SMOKE AND ASH. BORN INTO A SCREAMING WORLD.
AND I WAS THE LUCKY ONE. THE SHRAPNEL COULD HAVE PIERCED MY ARTERY.
I FELT THESE WARM RIVULETS OF BLOOD FORM DOWN MY NECK--
--but what I remember most were the chills.
WITHOUT THE RESPITE OF DREAMS, MY DAYS WERE ENDLESSLY MEANINGLESS.

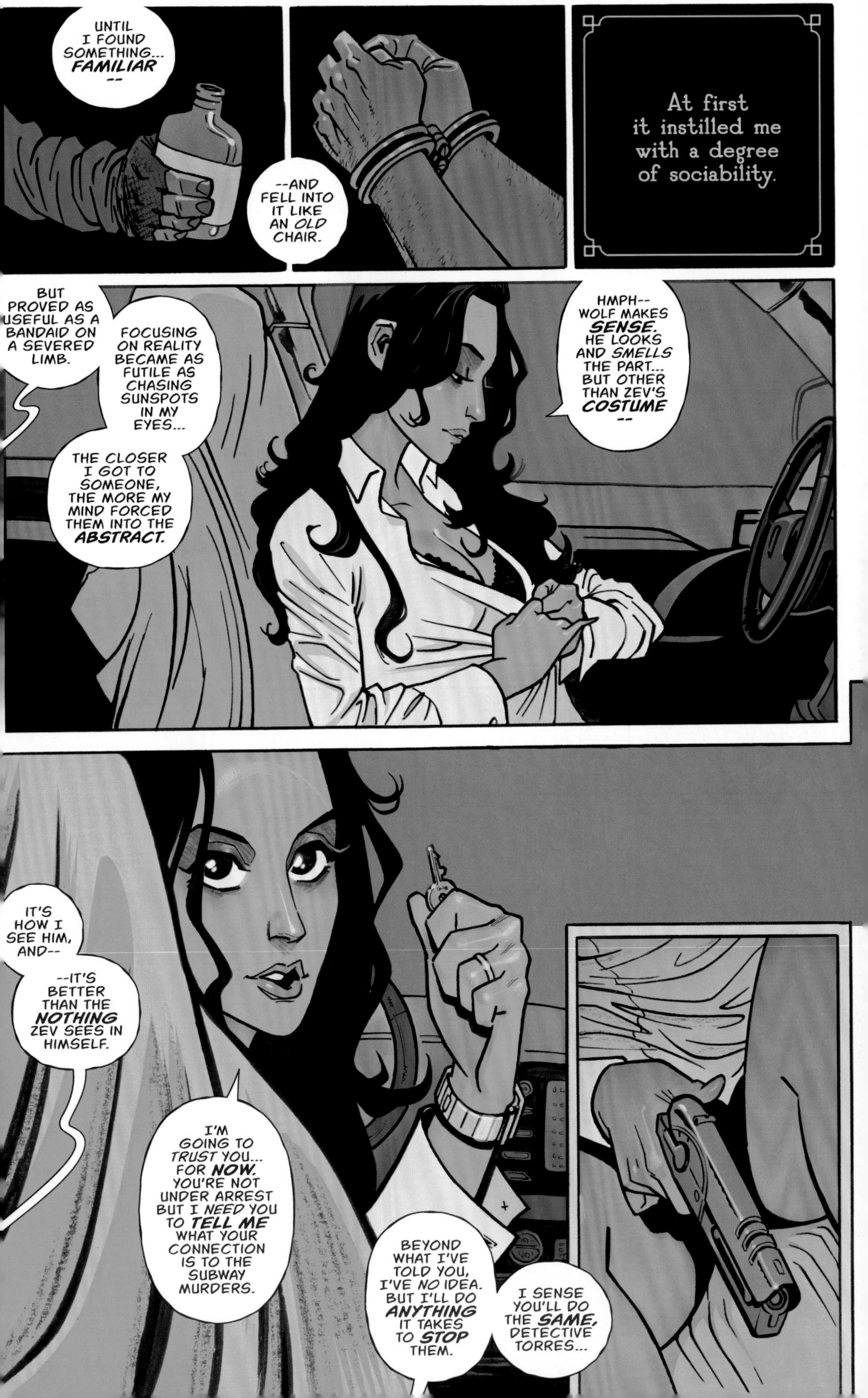
UNTIL I FOUND SOMETHING... FAMILIAR --
--AND FELL INTO IT LIKE AN OLD CHAIR.
At first it instilled me with a degree of sociability.
BUT PROVED AS USEFUL AS A BANDAID ON A SEVERED LIMB.
FOCUSING ON REALITY BECAME AS FUTILE AS CHASING SUNSPOTS IN MY EYES...
THE CLOSER I GOT TO SOMEONE, THE MORE MY MIND FORCED THEM INTO THE ABSTRACT.
HMPH-- WOLF MAKES SENSE. HE LOOKS AND SMELLS THE PART... BUT OTHER THAN ZEV'S COSTUME --
IT'S HOW I SEE HIM, AND--
--IT'S BETTER THAN THE NOTHING ZEV SEES IN HIMSELF.
I'M GOING TO TRUST YOU... FOR NOW. YOU'RE NOT UNDER ARREST BUT I NEED YOU TO TELL ME WHAT YOUR CONNECTION IS TO THE SUBWAY MURDERS.
BEYOND WHAT I'VE TOLD YOU, I'VE NO IDEA. BUT I'LL DO ANYTHING IT TAKES TO STOP THEM.
I SENSE YOU'LL DO THE SAME, DETECTIVE TORRES...

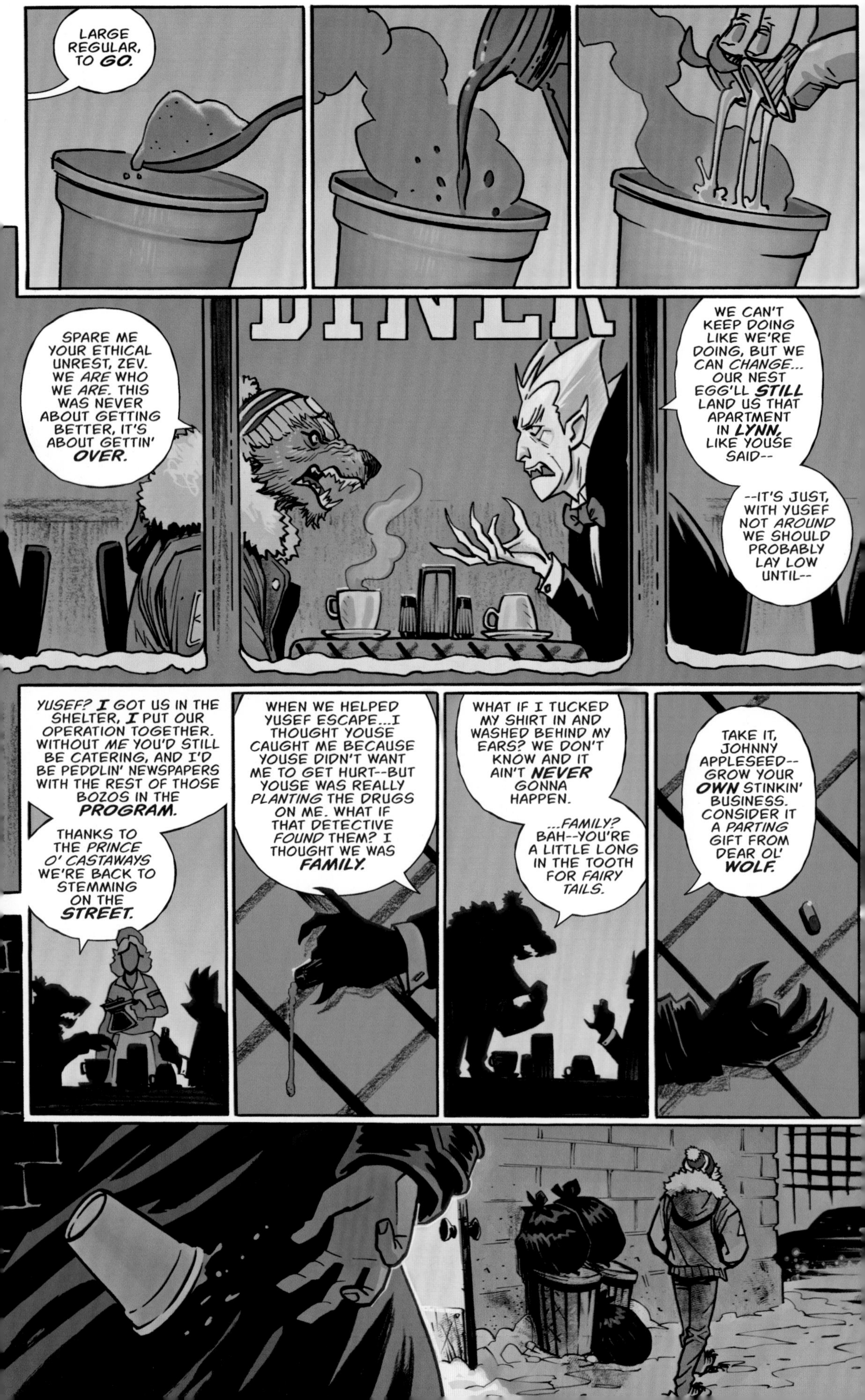
LARGE REGULAR, TO GO.
SPARE ME YOUR ETHICAL UNREST, ZEV. WE ARE WHO WE ARE. THIS WAS NEVER ABOUT GETTING BETTER, IT'S ABOUT GETTIN' OVER.
DINER
WE CAN'T KEEP DOING LIKE WE'RE DOING, BUT WE CAN CHANGE... OUR NEST EGG'LL STILL LAND US THAT APARTMENT IN LYNN, LIKE YOUSE SAID--
--IT'S JUST, WITH YUSEF NOT AROUND WE SHOULD PROBABLY LAY LOW UNTIL--
YUSEF? I GOT US IN THE SHELTER, I PUT OUR OPERATION TOGETHER. WITHOUT ME YOU'D STILL BE CATERING, AND I'D BE PEDDLIN' NEWSPAPERS WITH THE REST OF THOSE BOZOS IN THE PROGRAM.
THANKS TO THE PRINCE O' CASTAWAYS WE'RE BACK TO STEMMING ON THE STREET.
WHEN WE HELPED YUSEF ESCAPE...I THOUGHT YOUSE CAUGHT ME BECAUSE YOUSE DIDN'T WANT ME TO GET HURT--BUT YOUSE WAS REALLY PLANTING THE DRUGS ON ME. WHAT IF THAT DETECTIVE FOUND THEM? I THOUGHT WE WAS FAMILY.
WHAT IF I TUCKED MY SHIRT IN AND WASHED BEHIND MY EARS? WE DON'T KNOW AND IT AIN'T NEVER GONNA HAPPEN.
...FAMILY? BAH--YOU'RE A LITTLE LONG IN THE TOOTH FOR FAIRY TAILS.
TAKE IT, JOHNNY APPLESEED--GROW YOUR OWN STINKIN' BUSINESS. CONSIDER IT A PARTING GIFT FROM DEAR OL' WOLF.

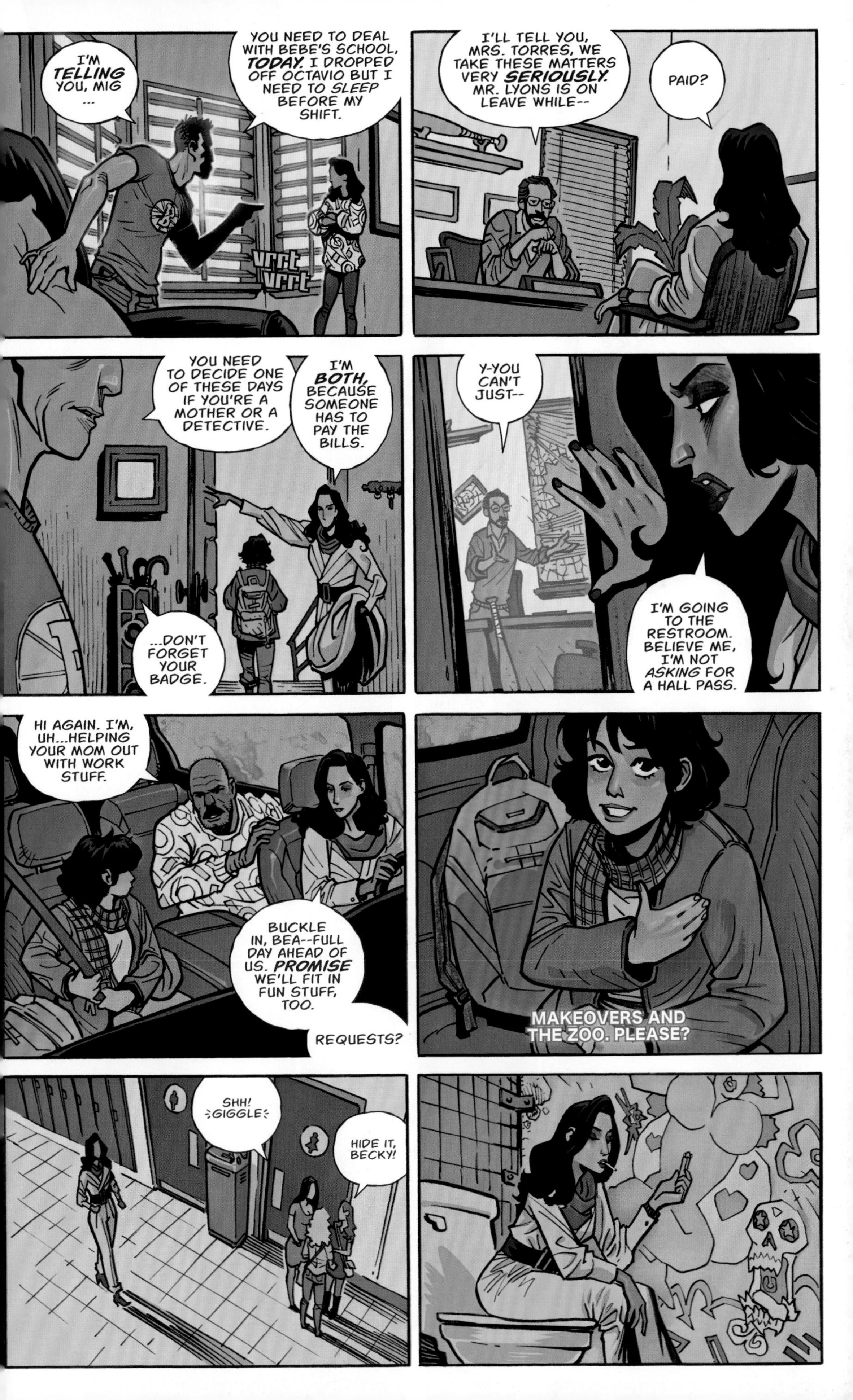
I'M TELLING YOU, MIG ...
YOU NEED TO DEAL WITH BEBE'S SCHOOL, TODAY. I DROPPED OFF OCTAVIO BUT I NEED TO SLEEP BEFORE MY SHIFT.
VRRT VRRT
I'LL TELL YOU, MRS. TORRES, WE TAKE THESE MATTERS VERY SERIOUSLY. MR. LYONS IS ON LEAVE WHILE--
PAID?
YOU NEED TO DECIDE ONE OF THESE DAYS IF YOU'RE A MOTHER OR A DETECTIVE.
I'M BOTH, BECAUSE SOMEONE HAS TO PAY THE BILLS.
...DON'T FORGET YOUR BADGE.
Y-YOU CAN'T JUST--
I'M GOING TO THE RESTROOM. BELIEVE ME, I'M NOT ASKING FOR A HALL PASS.
HI AGAIN. I'M, UH...HELPING YOUR MOM OUT WITH WORK STUFF.
BUCKLE IN, BEA--FULL DAY AHEAD OF US. PROMISE WE'LL FIT IN FUN STUFF, TOO.
REQUESTS?
MAKEOVERS AND THE ZOO. PLEASE?
SHH! GIGGLE
HIDE IT, BECKY!

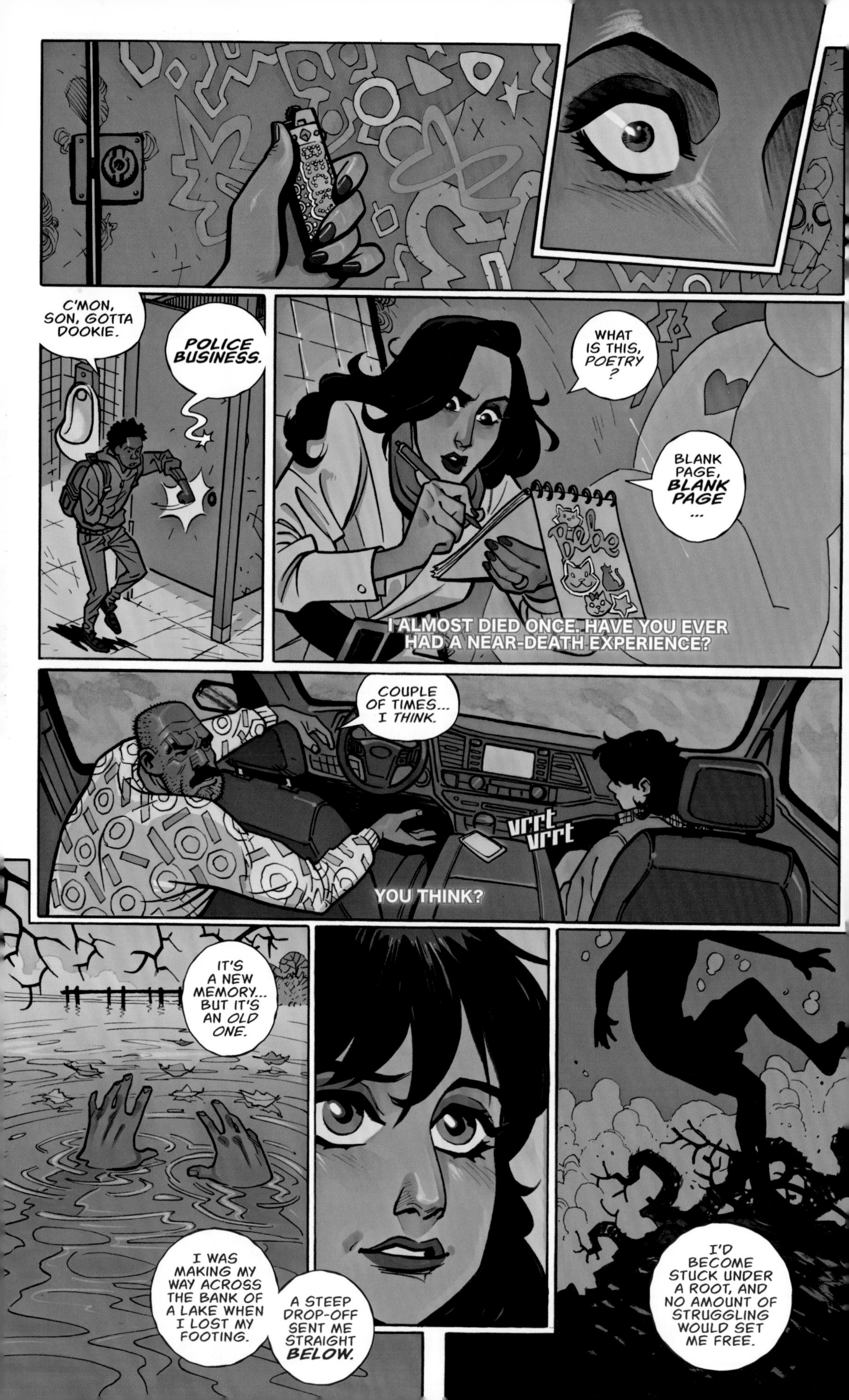
C'MON, SON, GOTTA DOOKIE.
POLICE BUSINESS.
WHAT IS THIS, POETRY?
BLANK PAGE, BLANK PAGE...
Bebe
I ALMOST DIED ONCE. HAVE YOU EVER HAD A NEAR-DEATH EXPERIENCE?
COUPLE OF TIMES... I THINK.
vrrt vrrt
YOU THINK?
IT'S A NEW MEMORY... BUT IT'S AN OLD ONE.
I WAS MAKING MY WAY ACROSS THE BANK OF A LAKE WHEN I LOST MY FOOTING.
A STEEP DROP-OFF SENT ME STRAIGHT BELOW.
I'D BECOME STUCK UNDER A ROOT, AND NO AMOUNT OF STRUGGLING WOULD SET ME FREE.

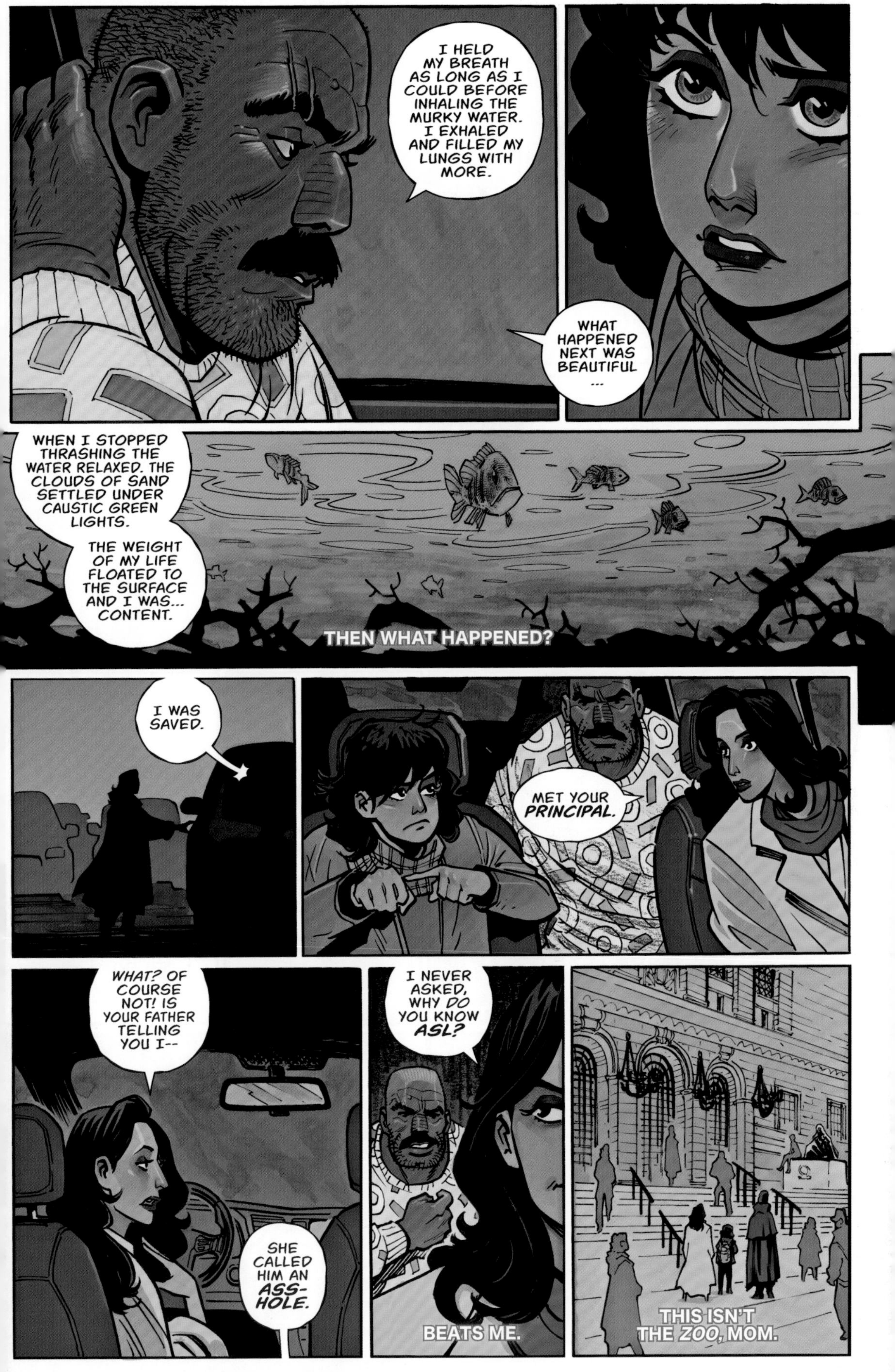
I HELD MY BREATH AS LONG AS I COULD BEFORE INHALING THE MURKY WATER. I EXHALED AND FILLED MY LUNGS WITH MORE.
WHAT HAPPENED NEXT WAS BEAUTIFUL...
WHEN I STOPPED THRASHING THE WATER RELAXED. THE CLOUDS OF SAND SETTLED UNDER CAUSTIC GREEN LIGHTS.
THE WEIGHT OF MY LIFE FLOATED TO THE SURFACE AND I WAS... CONTENT.
THEN WHAT HAPPENED?
I WAS SAVED.
MET YOUR PRINCIPAL.
WHAT? OF COURSE NOT! IS YOUR FATHER TELLING YOU I--
SHE CALLED HIM AN ASS-HOLE.
I NEVER ASKED, WHY DO YOU KNOW ASL?
BEATS ME.
THIS ISN'T THE ZOO, MOM.

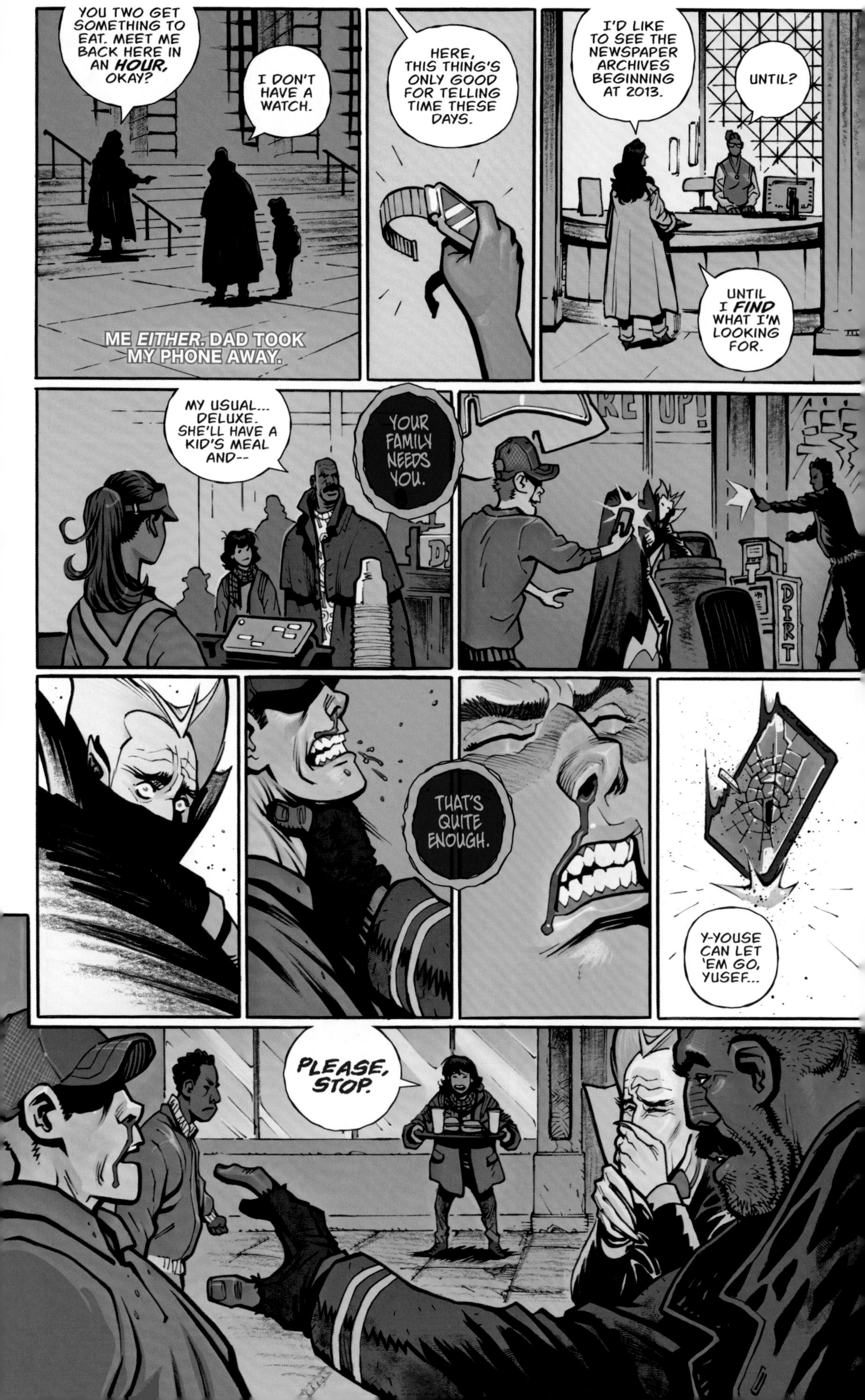
YOU TWO GET SOMETHING TO EAT. MEET ME BACK HERE IN AN HOUR, OKAY?
I DON'T HAVE A WATCH.
ME EITHER. DAD TOOK MY PHONE AWAY.
HERE, THIS THING'S ONLY GOOD FOR TELLING TIME THESE DAYS.
I'D LIKE TO SEE THE NEWSPAPER ARCHIVES BEGINNING AT 2013.
UNTIL?
UNTIL I FIND WHAT I'M LOOKING FOR.
MY USUAL... DELUXE. SHE'LL HAVE A KID'S MEAL AND--
YOUR FAMILY NEEDS YOU.
DIRT
THAT'S QUITE ENOUGH.
Y-YOUSE CAN LET 'EM GO, YUSEF...
PLEASE, STOP.

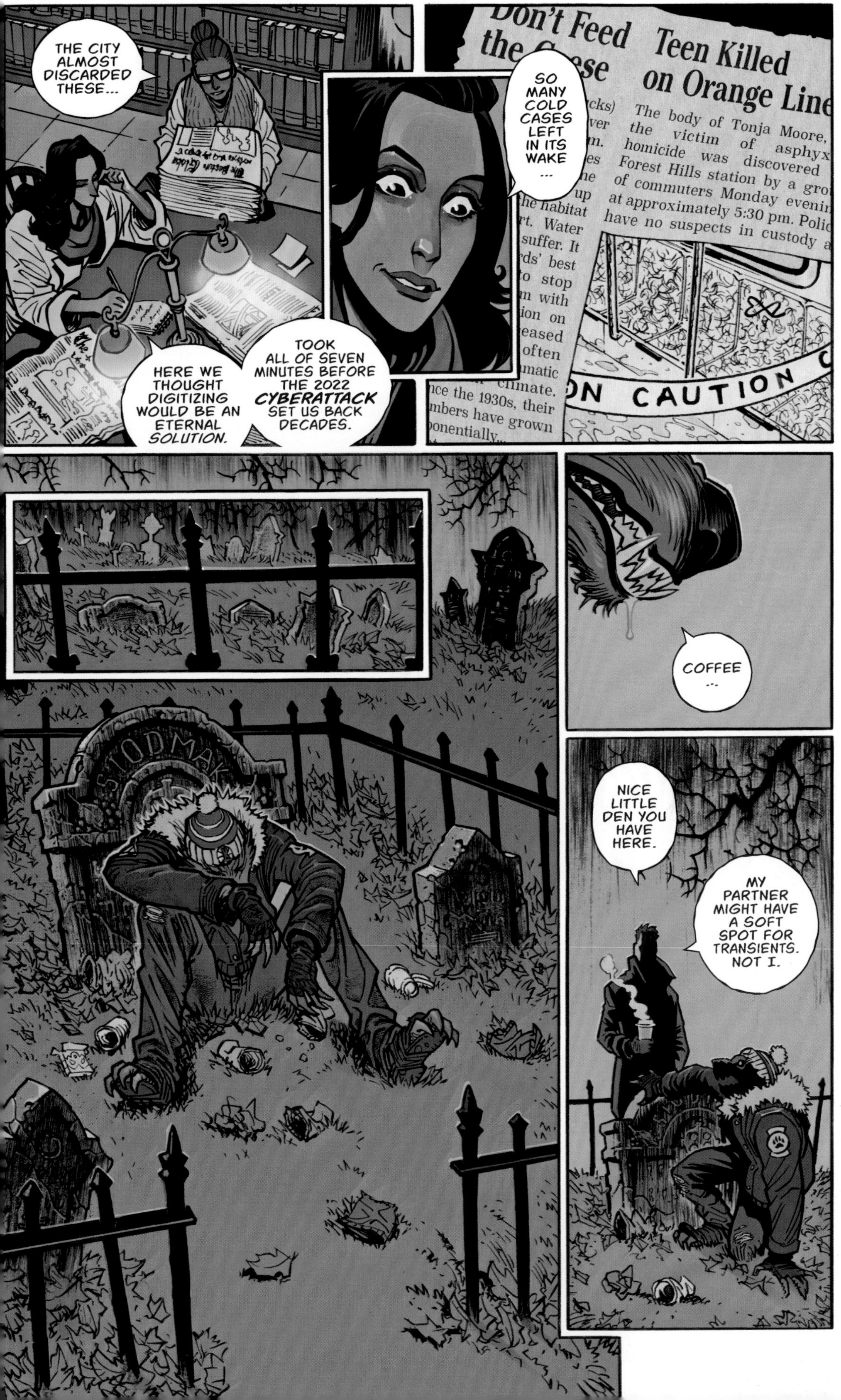

THE CITY ALMOST DISCARDED THESE...
HERE WE THOUGHT DIGITIZING WOULD BE AN ETERNAL SOLUTION.
TOOK ALL OF SEVEN MINUTES BEFORE THE 2022 CYBERATTACK SET US BACK DECADES.
SO MANY COLD CASES LEFT IN ITS WAKE ...
Don't Feed
Teen Killed on Orange Line
The body of Tonja Moore,
the victim of
homicide was discovered
Forest Hills station by a
of commuters Monday
at approximately 5:30 pm.
have no suspects in custody
the habitat
suffer. It
climate.
the 1930s, their
have grown
CAUTION
COFFEE ...
NICE LITTLE DEN YOU HAVE HERE.
MY PARTNER MIGHT HAVE A SOFT SPOT FOR TRANSIENTS. NOT I.

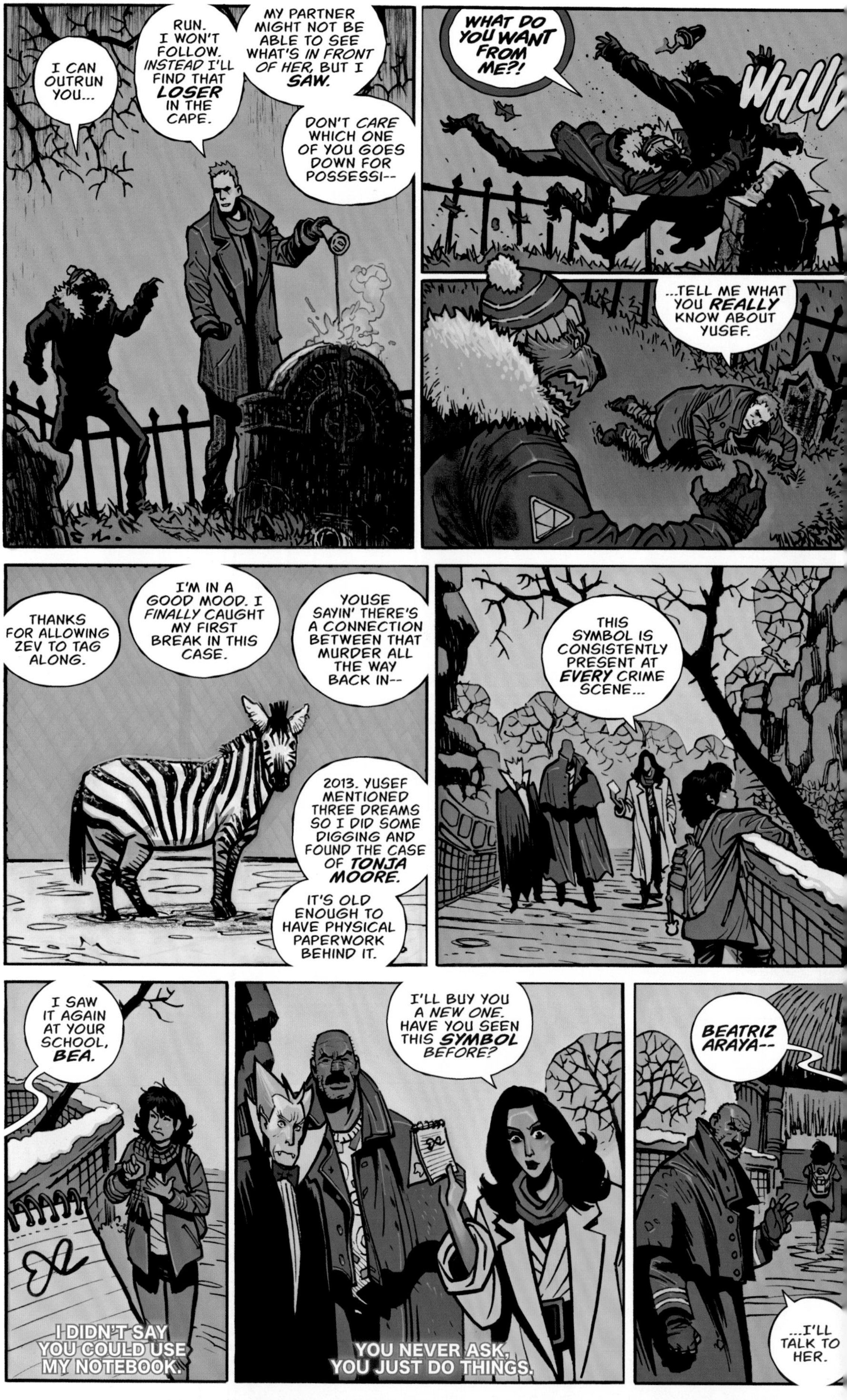
I CAN OUTRUN YOU...
RUN. I WON'T FOLLOW. INSTEAD I'LL FIND THAT LOSER IN THE CAPE.
MY PARTNER MIGHT NOT BE ABLE TO SEE WHAT'S IN FRONT OF HER, BUT I SAW.
DON'T CARE WHICH ONE OF YOU GOES DOWN FOR POSSESSI--
WHAT DO YOU WANT FROM ME?!
WHUV
...TELL ME WHAT YOU REALLY KNOW ABOUT YUSEF.
THANKS FOR ALLOWING ZEV TO TAG ALONG.
I'M IN A GOOD MOOD. I FINALLY CAUGHT MY FIRST BREAK IN THIS CASE.
YOUSE SAYIN' THERE'S A CONNECTION BETWEEN THAT MURDER ALL THE WAY BACK IN--
2013. YUSEF MENTIONED THREE DREAMS SO I DID SOME DIGGING AND FOUND THE CASE OF TONJA MOORE.
IT'S OLD ENOUGH TO HAVE PHYSICAL PAPERWORK BEHIND IT.
THIS SYMBOL IS CONSISTENTLY PRESENT AT EVERY CRIME SCENE...
I SAW IT AGAIN AT YOUR SCHOOL, BEA.
I DIDN'T SAY YOU COULD USE MY NOTEBOOK.
I'LL BUY YOU A NEW ONE. HAVE YOU SEEN THIS SYMBOL BEFORE?
YOU NEVER ASK, YOU JUST DO THINGS.
BEATRIZ ARAYA--
...I'LL TALK TO HER.

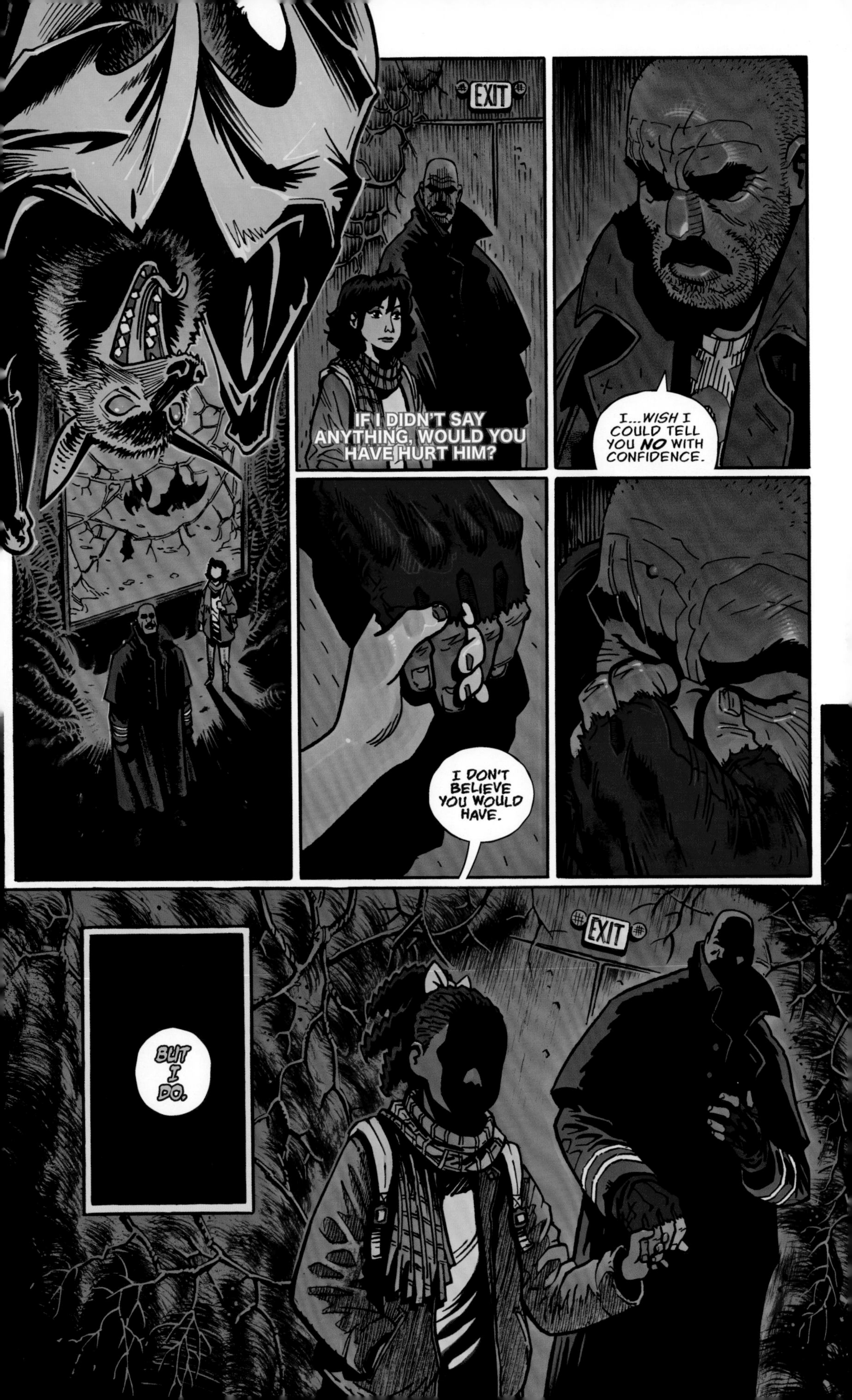
EXIT
IF I DIDN'T SAY ANYTHING, WOULD YOU HAVE HURT HIM?
I...WISH I COULD TELL YOU NO WITH CONFIDENCE.
I DON'T BELIEVE YOU WOULD HAVE.
EXIT
BUT I DO.

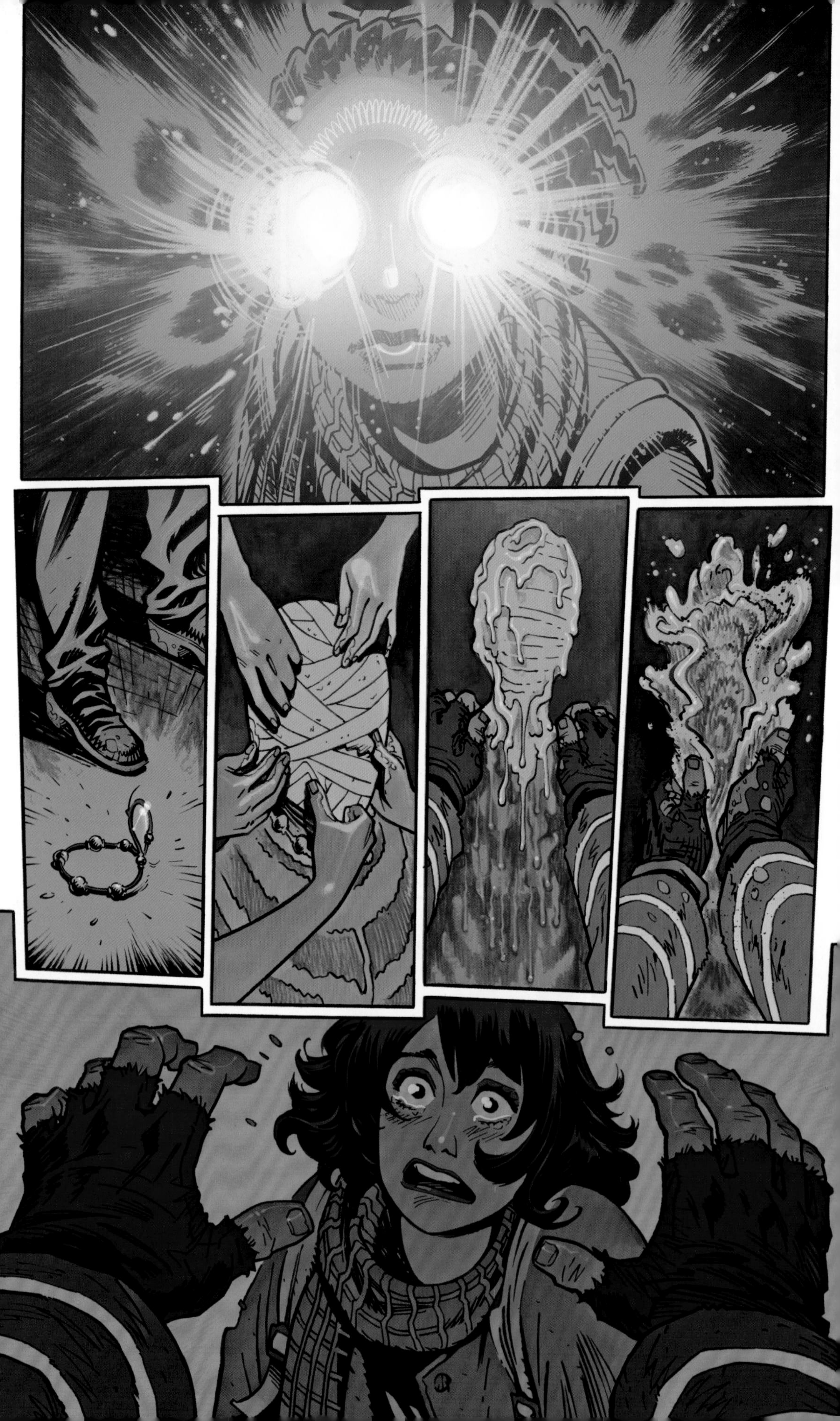

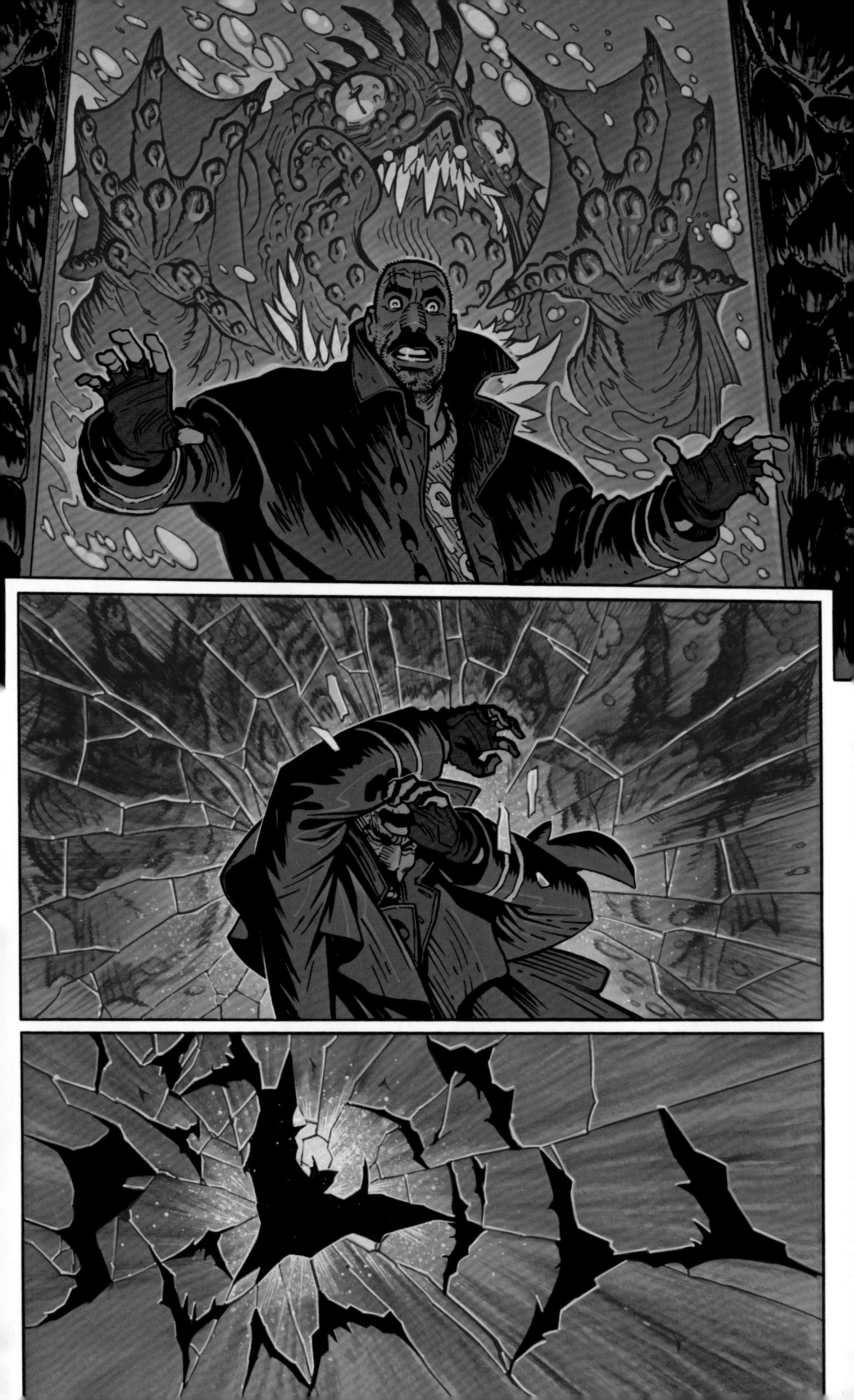

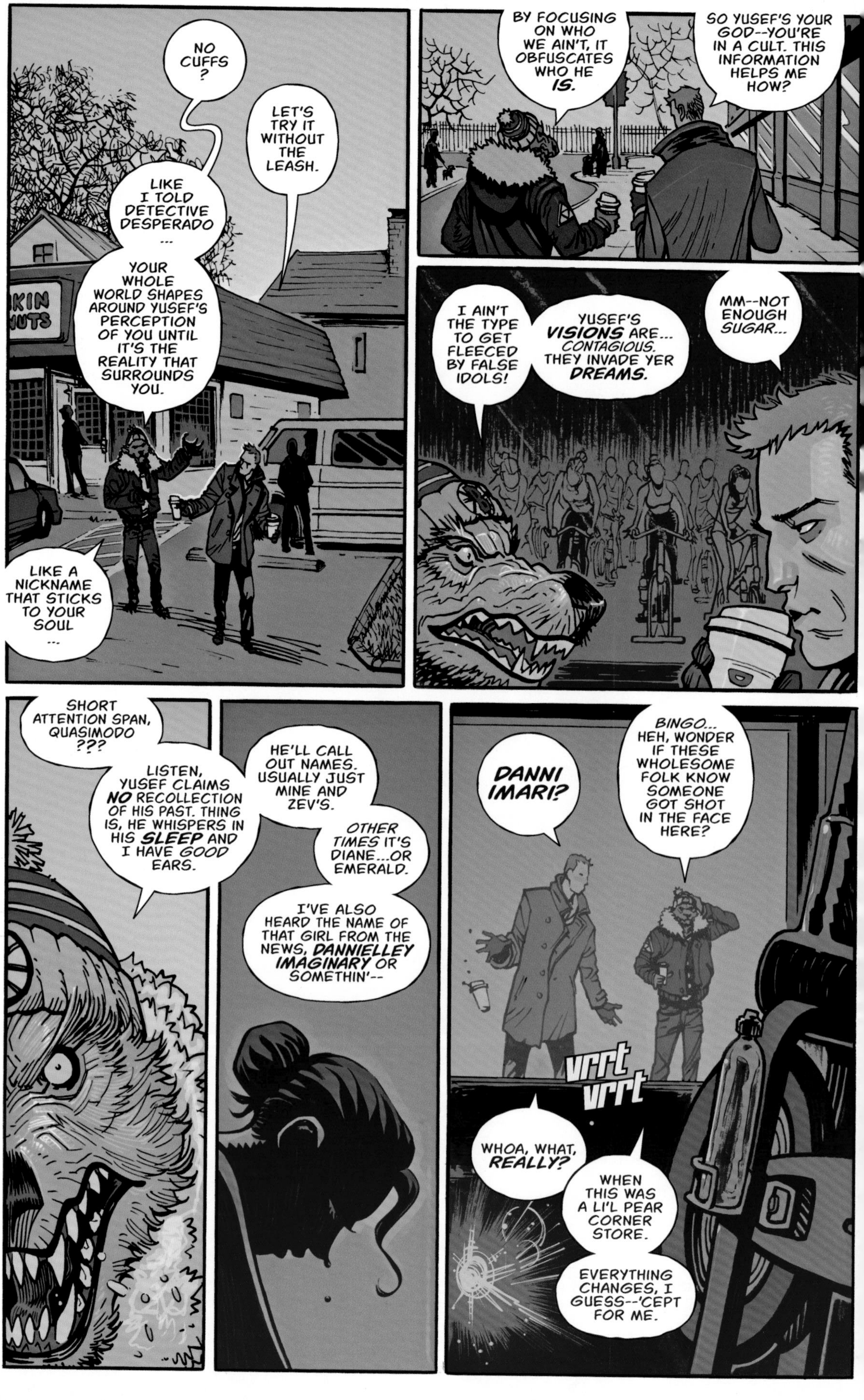
NO CUFFS ?
LET'S TRY IT WITHOUT THE LEASH.
LIKE I TOLD DETECTIVE DESPERADO ...
YOUR WHOLE WORLD SHAPES AROUND YUSEF'S PERCEPTION OF YOU UNTIL IT'S THE REALITY THAT SURROUNDS YOU.
LIKE A NICKNAME THAT STICKS TO YOUR SOUL ...
BY FOCUSING ON WHO WE AIN'T, IT OBFUSCATES WHO HE IS.
SO YUSEF'S YOUR GOD--YOU'RE IN A CULT. THIS INFORMATION HELPS ME HOW?
I AIN'T THE TYPE TO GET FLEECED BY FALSE IDOLS!
YUSEF'S VISIONS ARE... CONTAGIOUS. THEY INVADE YER DREAMS.
MM--NOT ENOUGH SUGAR...
SHORT ATTENTION SPAN, QUASIMODO ???
LISTEN, YUSEF CLAIMS NO RECOLLECTION OF HIS PAST. THING IS, HE WHISPERS IN HIS SLEEP AND I HAVE GOOD EARS.
HE'LL CALL OUT NAMES. USUALLY JUST MINE AND ZEV'S.
OTHER TIMES IT'S DIANE...OR EMERALD.
I'VE ALSO HEARD THE NAME OF THAT GIRL FROM THE NEWS, DANNIELLEY IMAGINARY OR SOMETHIN'--
DANNI IMARI?
BINGO... HEH, WONDER IF THESE WHOLESOME FOLK KNOW SOMEONE GOT SHOT IN THE FACE HERE?
VRRT VRRT
WHOA, WHAT, REALLY?
WHEN THIS WAS A LI'L PEAR CORNER STORE.
EVERYTHING CHANGES, I GUESS--'CEPT FOR ME.

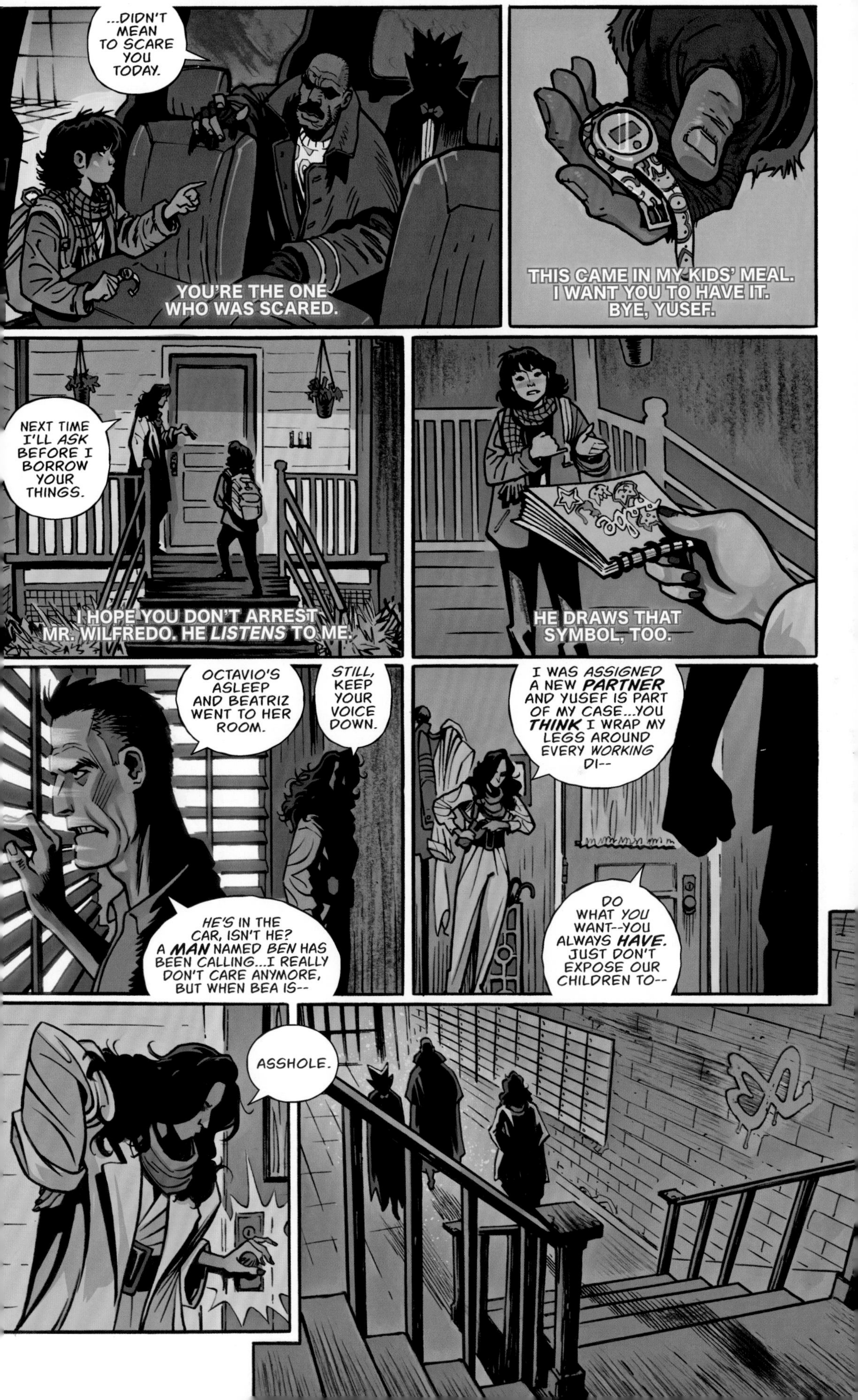

...DIDN'T MEAN TO SCARE YOU TODAY.
YOU'RE THE ONE WHO WAS SCARED.
THIS CAME IN MY KIDS' MEAL. I WANT YOU TO HAVE IT. BYE, YUSEF.
NEXT TIME I'LL *ASK* BEFORE I BORROW YOUR THINGS.
I HOPE YOU DON'T ARREST MR. WILFREDO. HE *LISTENS* TO ME.
HE DRAWS THAT SYMBOL, TOO.
OCTAVIO'S ASLEEP AND BEATRIZ WENT TO HER ROOM.
STILL, KEEP YOUR VOICE DOWN.
HE'S IN THE CAR, ISN'T HE? A ***MAN*** NAMED *BEN* HAS BEEN CALLING...I REALLY DON'T CARE ANYMORE, BUT WHEN BEA IS--
I WAS *ASSIGNED* A NEW ***PARTNER*** AND YUSEF IS PART OF MY CASE...YOU ***THINK*** I WRAP MY LEGS AROUND EVERY *WORKING* DI--
DO WHAT *YOU* WANT--YOU ALWAYS ***HAVE.*** JUST DON'T EXPOSE OUR CHILDREN TO--
ASSHOLE.

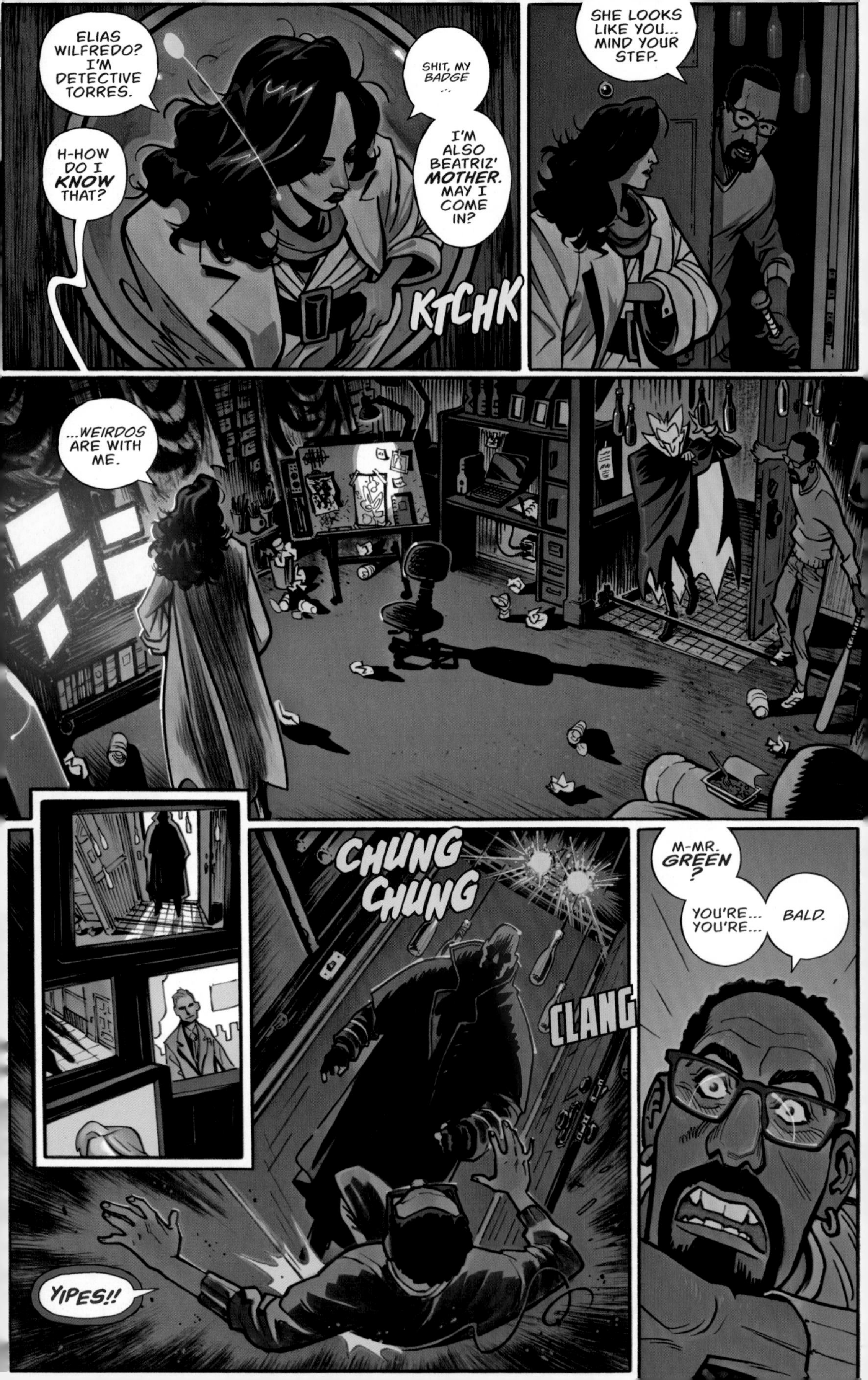
ELIAS WILFREDO? I'M DETECTIVE TORRES.
H-HOW DO I KNOW THAT?
SHIT, MY BADGE ...
I'M ALSO BEATRIZ' MOTHER. MAY I COME IN?
KTCHK
SHE LOOKS LIKE YOU... MIND YOUR STEP.
...WEIRDOS ARE WITH ME.
CHUNG CHUNG
CLANG
YIPES!!
M-MR. GREEN?
YOU'RE... YOU'RE...
BALD.

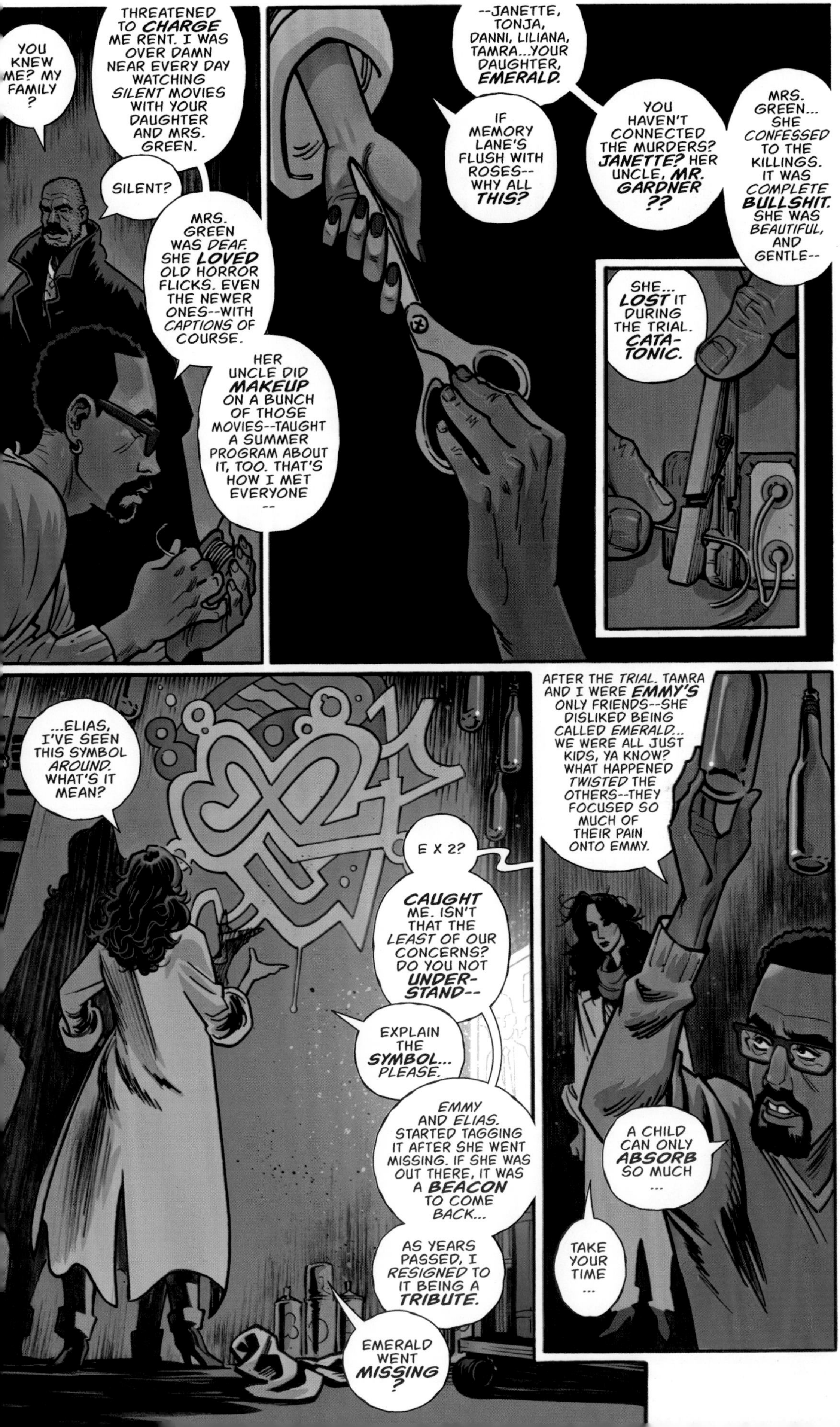
YOU KNEW ME? MY FAMILY?
THREATENED TO CHARGE ME RENT. I WAS OVER DAMN NEAR EVERY DAY WATCHING SILENT MOVIES WITH YOUR DAUGHTER AND MRS. GREEN.
SILENT?
MRS. GREEN WAS DEAF. SHE LOVED OLD HORROR FLICKS. EVEN THE NEWER ONES--WITH CAPTIONS OF COURSE.
HER UNCLE DID MAKEUP ON A BUNCH OF THOSE MOVIES--TAUGHT A SUMMER PROGRAM ABOUT IT, TOO. THAT'S HOW I MET EVERYONE--
--JANETTE, TONJA, DANNI, LILIANA, TAMRA...YOUR DAUGHTER, EMERALD.
IF MEMORY LANE'S FLUSH WITH ROSES--WHY ALL THIS?
YOU HAVEN'T CONNECTED THE MURDERS? JANETTE? HER UNCLE, MR. GARDNER??
MRS. GREEN... SHE CONFESSED TO THE KILLINGS. IT WAS COMPLETE BULLSHIT. SHE WAS BEAUTIFUL, AND GENTLE--
SHE... LOST IT DURING THE TRIAL. CATATONIC.
...ELIAS, I'VE SEEN THIS SYMBOL AROUND. WHAT'S IT MEAN?
E X 2?
CAUGHT ME. ISN'T THAT THE LEAST OF OUR CONCERNS? DO YOU NOT UNDERSTAND--
EXPLAIN THE SYMBOL... PLEASE.
EMMY AND ELIAS. STARTED TAGGING IT AFTER SHE WENT MISSING. IF SHE WAS OUT THERE, IT WAS A BEACON TO COME BACK...
AS YEARS PASSED, I RESIGNED TO IT BEING A TRIBUTE.
EMERALD WENT MISSING?
AFTER THE TRIAL, TAMRA AND I WERE EMMY'S ONLY FRIENDS--SHE DISLIKED BEING CALLED EMERALD... WE WERE ALL JUST KIDS, YA KNOW? WHAT HAPPENED TWISTED THE OTHERS--THEY FOCUSED SO MUCH OF THEIR PAIN ONTO EMMY.
A CHILD CAN ONLY ABSORB SO MUCH...
TAKE YOUR TIME...

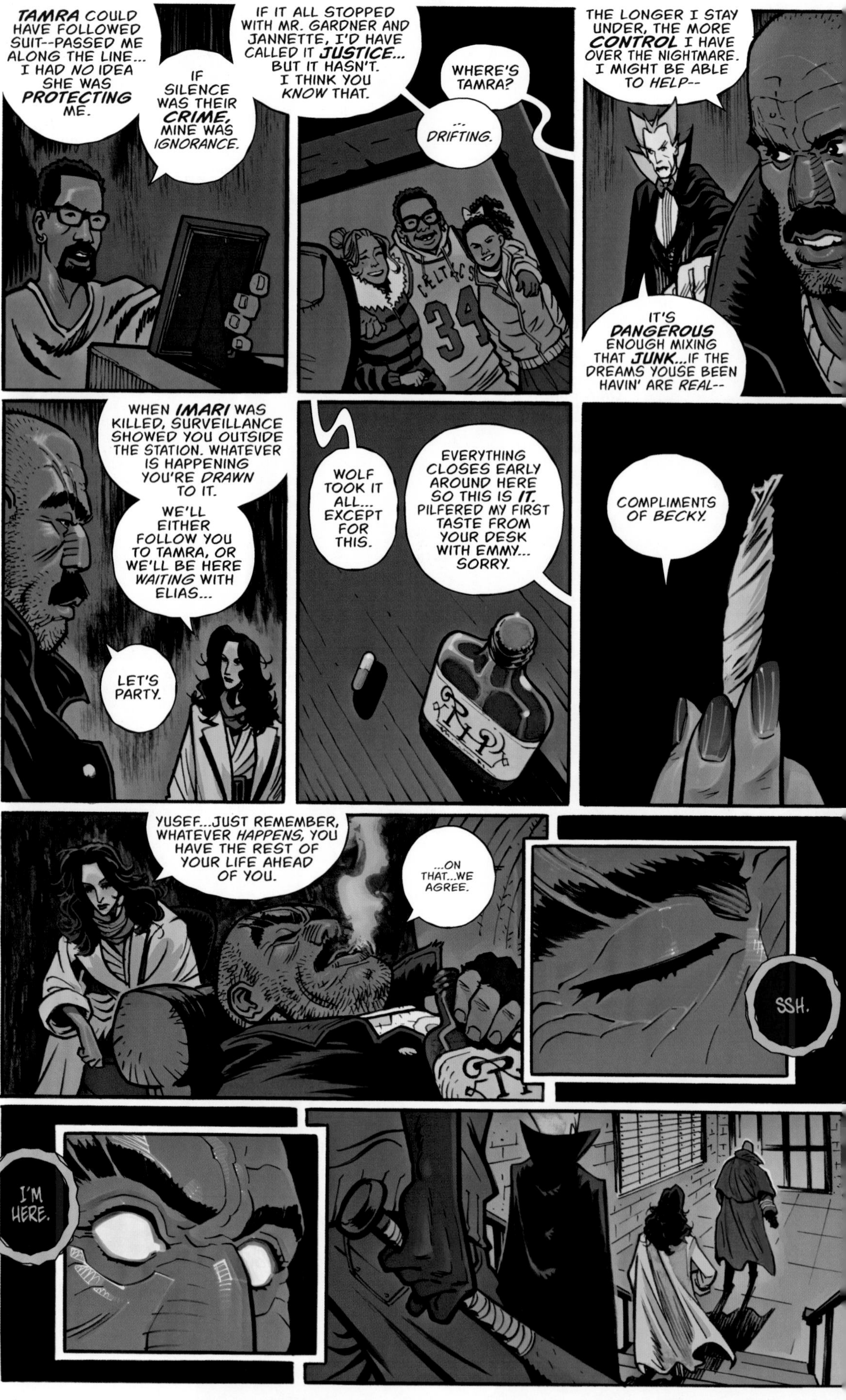

TAMRA COULD HAVE FOLLOWED SUIT--PASSED ME ALONG THE LINE... I HAD NO IDEA SHE WAS PROTECTING ME.
IF SILENCE WAS THEIR CRIME, MINE WAS IGNORANCE.
IF IT ALL STOPPED WITH MR. GARDNER AND JANNETTE, I'D HAVE CALLED IT JUSTICE... BUT IT HASN'T. I THINK YOU KNOW THAT.
WHERE'S TAMRA?
... DRIFTING.
THE LONGER I STAY UNDER, THE MORE CONTROL I HAVE OVER THE NIGHTMARE. I MIGHT BE ABLE TO HELP--
IT'S DANGEROUS ENOUGH MIXING THAT JUNK...IF THE DREAMS YOUSE BEEN HAVIN' ARE REAL--
WHEN IMARI WAS KILLED, SURVEILLANCE SHOWED YOU OUTSIDE THE STATION. WHATEVER IS HAPPENING YOU'RE DRAWN TO IT.
WE'LL EITHER FOLLOW YOU TO TAMRA, OR WE'LL BE HERE WAITING WITH ELIAS...
LET'S PARTY.
WOLF TOOK IT ALL... EXCEPT FOR THIS.
EVERYTHING CLOSES EARLY AROUND HERE SO THIS IS IT. PILFERED MY FIRST TASTE FROM YOUR DESK WITH EMMY... SORRY.
COMPLIMENTS OF BECKY.
YUSEF...JUST REMEMBER, WHATEVER HAPPENS, YOU HAVE THE REST OF YOUR LIFE AHEAD OF YOU.
...ON THAT...WE AGREE.
SSH.
I'M HERE.

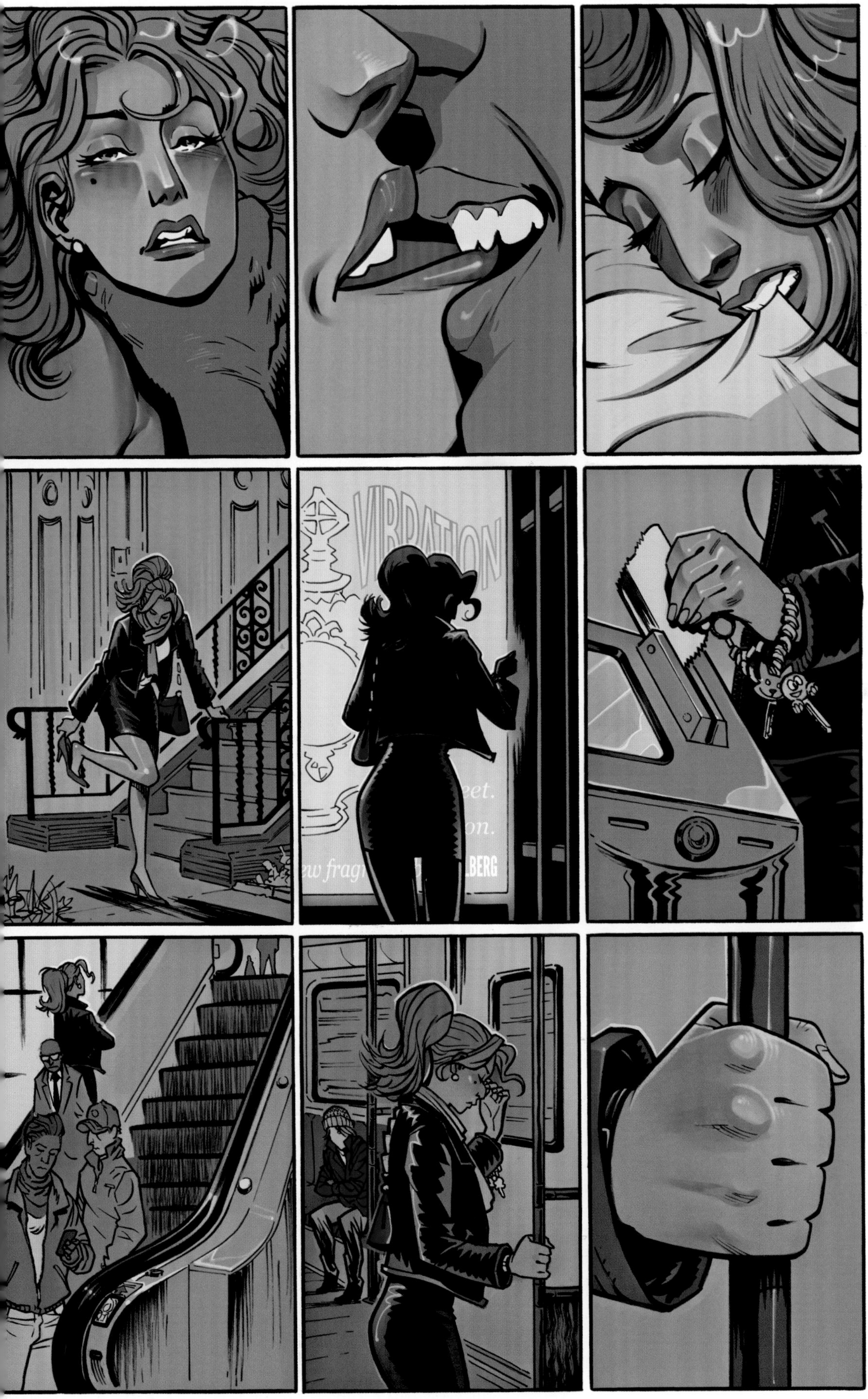
VIBRATION

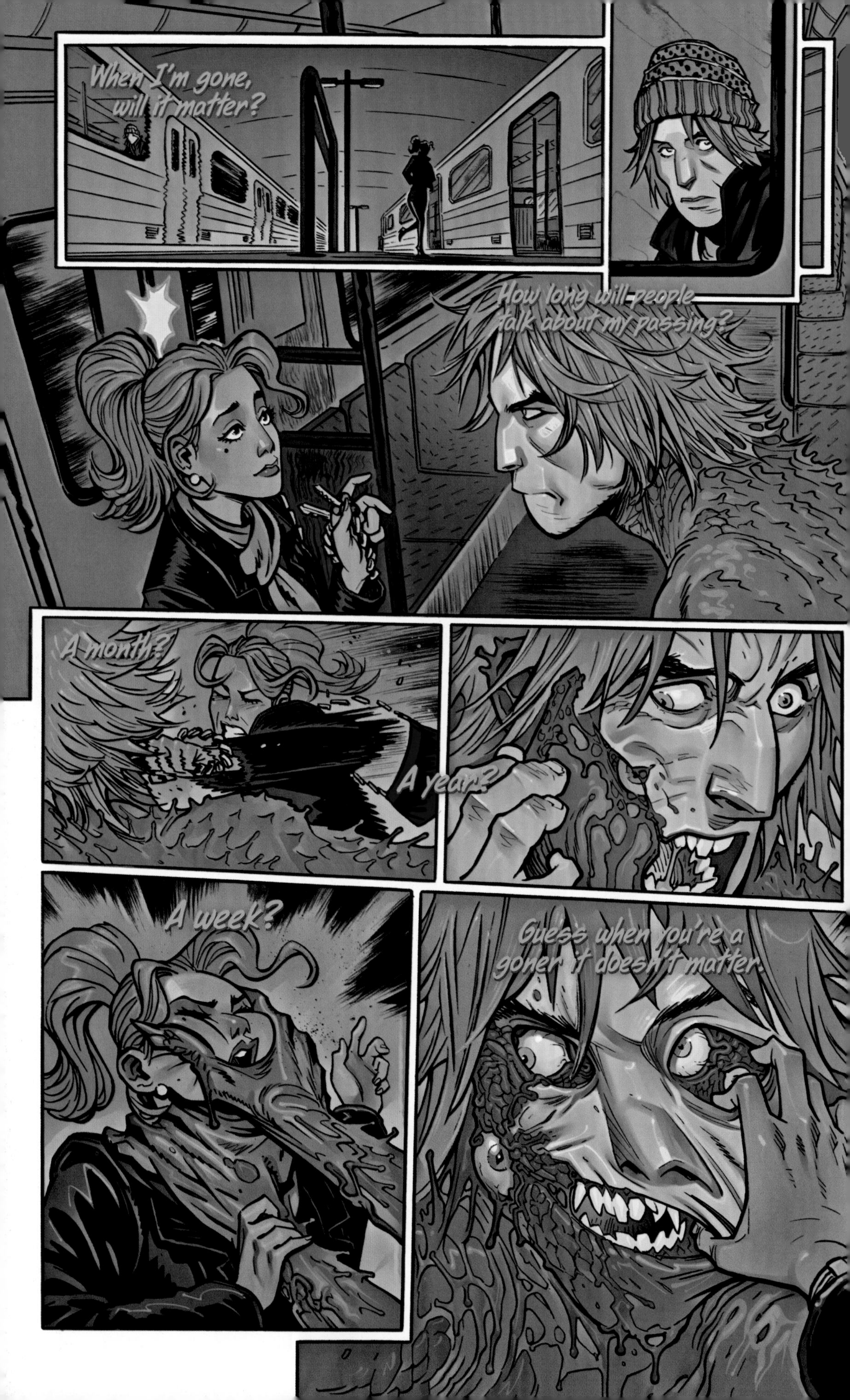
When I'm gone, will it matter?
How long will people talk about my passing?
A month?
A year?
A week?
Guess when you're a goner it doesn't matter.

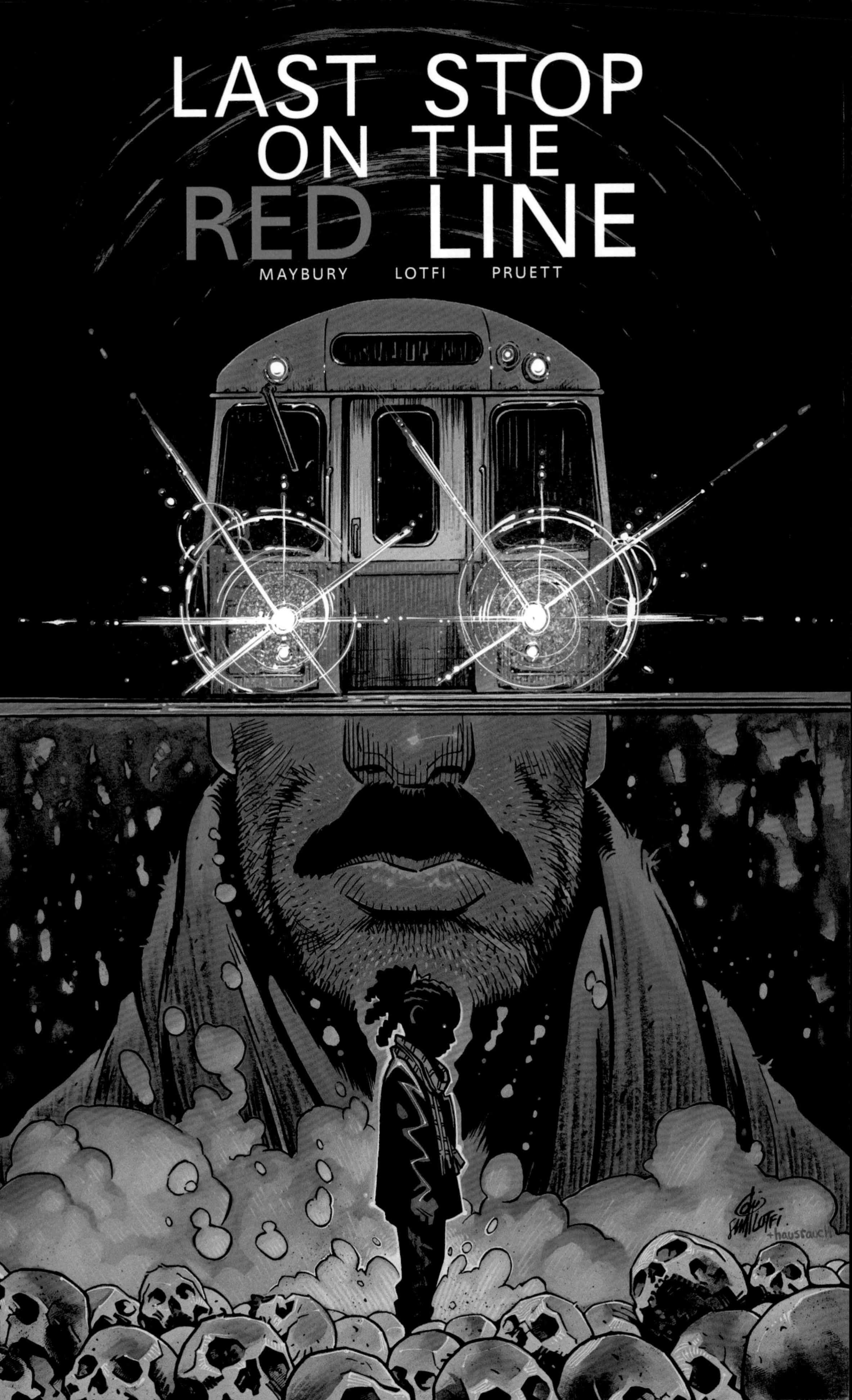
LAST STOP
ON THE
RED LINE
MAYBURY
LOTFI
PRUETT

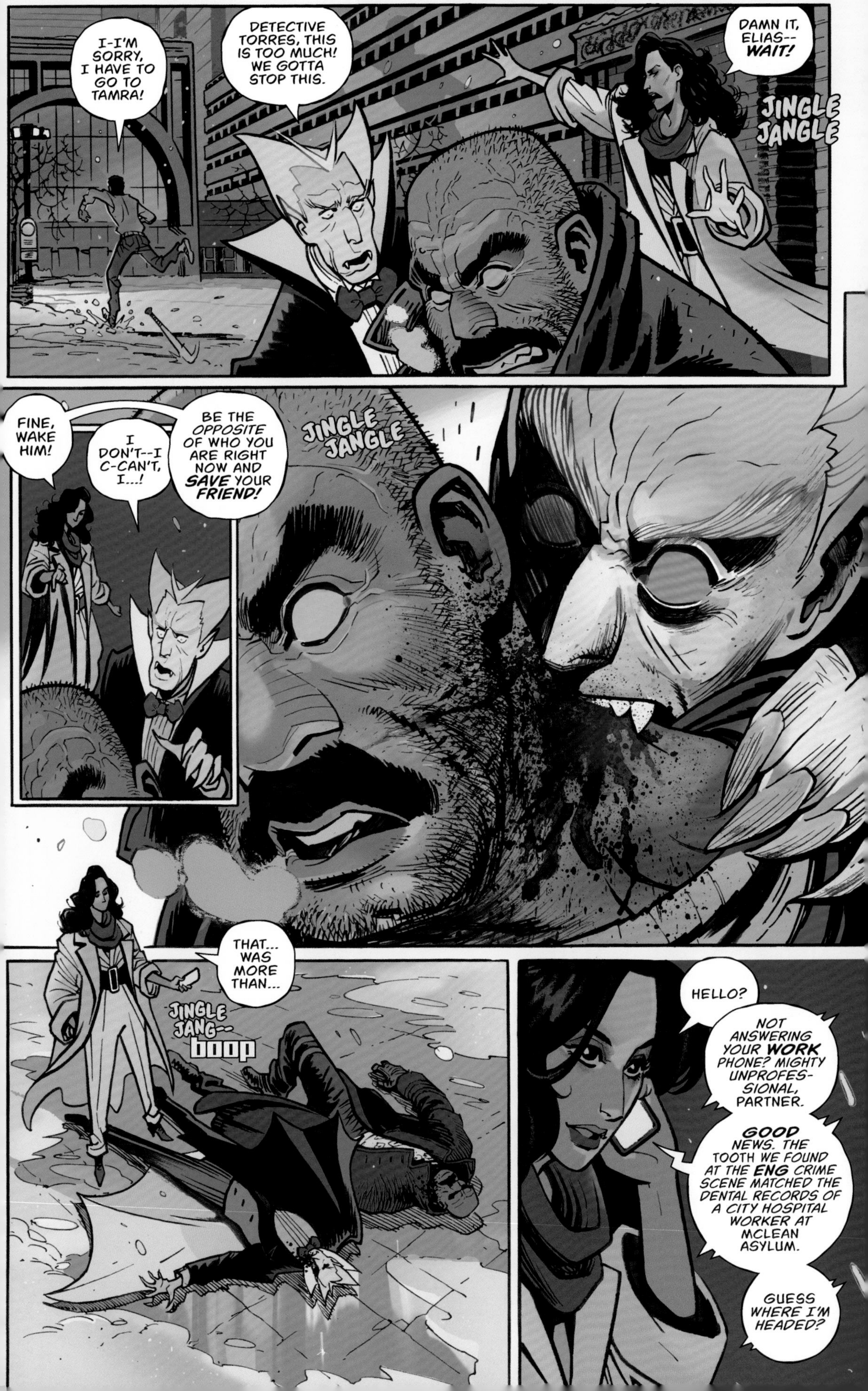
I-I'M SORRY, I HAVE TO GO TO TAMRA!
DETECTIVE TORRES, THIS IS TOO MUCH! WE GOTTA STOP THIS.
DAMN IT, ELIAS-- WAIT!
JINGLE JANGLE
FINE, WAKE HIM!
I DON'T--I C-CAN'T, I...!
BE THE OPPOSITE OF WHO YOU ARE RIGHT NOW AND SAVE YOUR FRIEND!
JINGLE JANGLE
THAT... WAS MORE THAN...
JINGLE JANG--
boop
HELLO?
NOT ANSWERING YOUR WORK PHONE? MIGHTY UNPROFES- SIONAL, PARTNER.
GOOD NEWS. THE TOOTH WE FOUND AT THE ENG CRIME SCENE MATCHED THE DENTAL RECORDS OF A CITY HOSPITAL WORKER AT MCLEAN ASYLUM.
GUESS WHERE I'M HEADED?

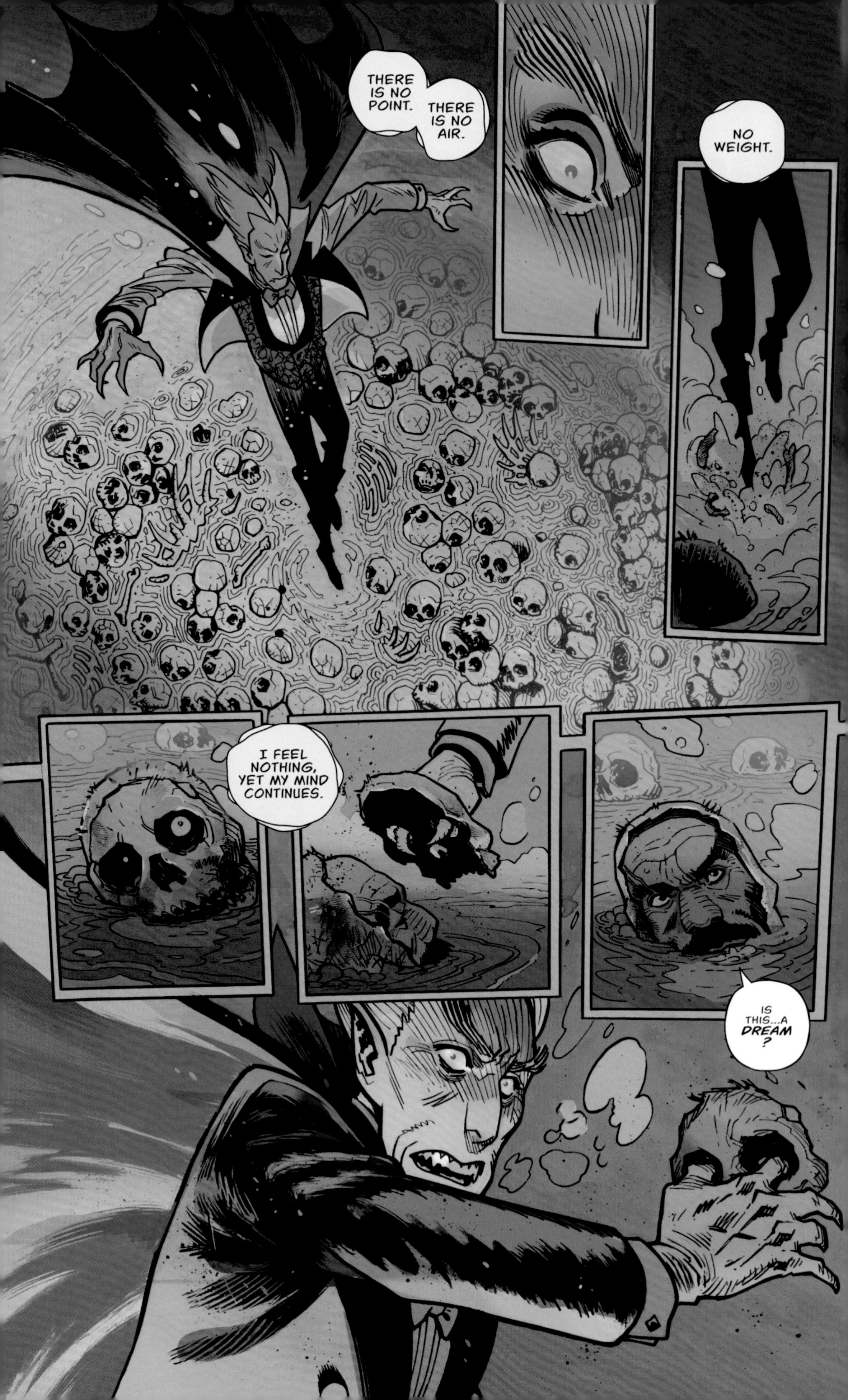
THERE IS NO POINT.
THERE IS NO AIR.
NO WEIGHT.
I FEEL NOTHING, YET MY MIND CONTINUES.
IS THIS...A DREAM?

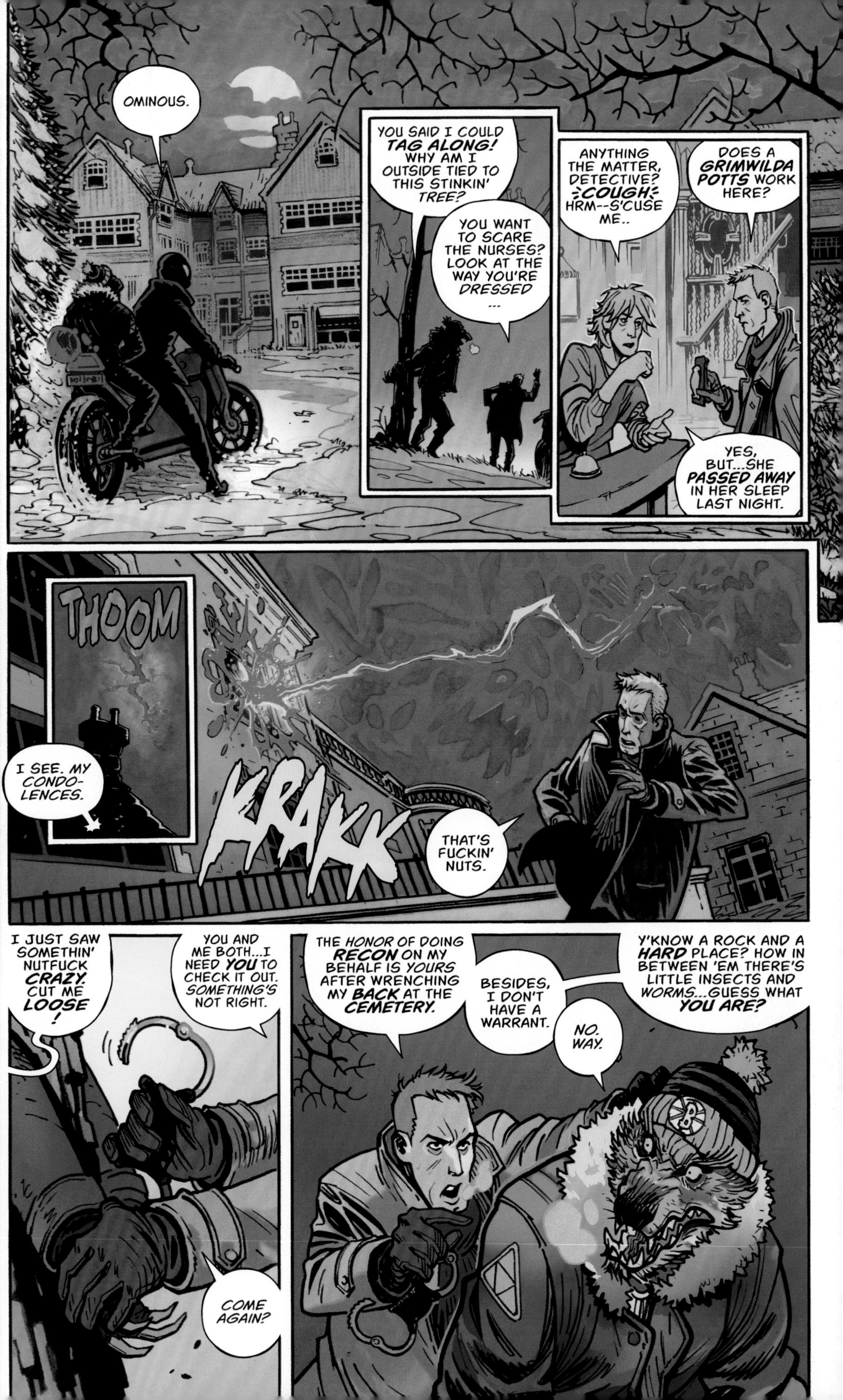
OMINOUS.
YOU SAID I COULD TAG ALONG! WHY AM I OUTSIDE TIED TO THIS STINKIN' TREE?
YOU WANT TO SCARE THE NURSES? LOOK AT THE WAY YOU'RE DRESSED ...
ANYTHING THE MATTER, DETECTIVE? COUGH! HRM--S'CUSE ME..
DOES A GRIMWILDA POTTS WORK HERE?
YES, BUT...SHE PASSED AWAY IN HER SLEEP LAST NIGHT.
THOOM
I SEE. MY CONDO-LENCES.
KRAKK
THAT'S FUCKIN' NUTS.
I JUST SAW SOMETHIN' NUTFUCK CRAZY. CUT ME LOOSE!
YOU AND ME BOTH...I NEED YOU TO CHECK IT OUT. SOMETHING'S NOT RIGHT.
COME AGAIN?
THE HONOR OF DOING RECON ON MY BEHALF IS YOURS AFTER WRENCHING MY BACK AT THE CEMETERY.
BESIDES, I DON'T HAVE A WARRANT.
NO. WAY.
Y'KNOW A ROCK AND A HARD PLACE? HOW IN BETWEEN 'EM THERE'S LITTLE INSECTS AND WORMS...GUESS WHAT YOU ARE?

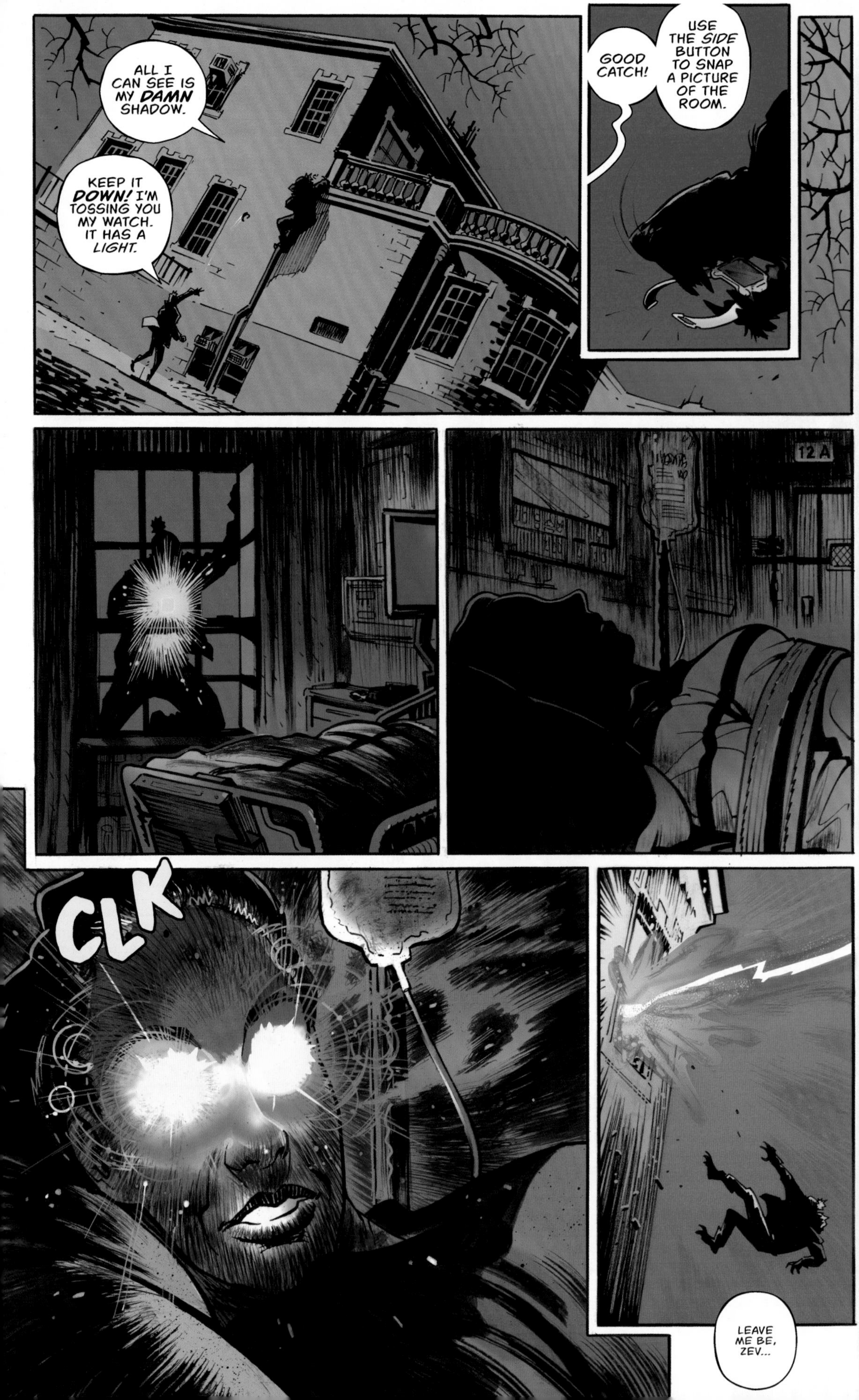
ALL I CAN SEE IS MY *DAMN* SHADOW.
KEEP IT *DOWN!* I'M TOSSING YOU MY WATCH. IT HAS A *LIGHT.*
GOOD CATCH!
USE THE *SIDE* BUTTON TO SNAP A PICTURE OF THE ROOM.
12 A
CLK
LEAVE ME BE, ZEV...

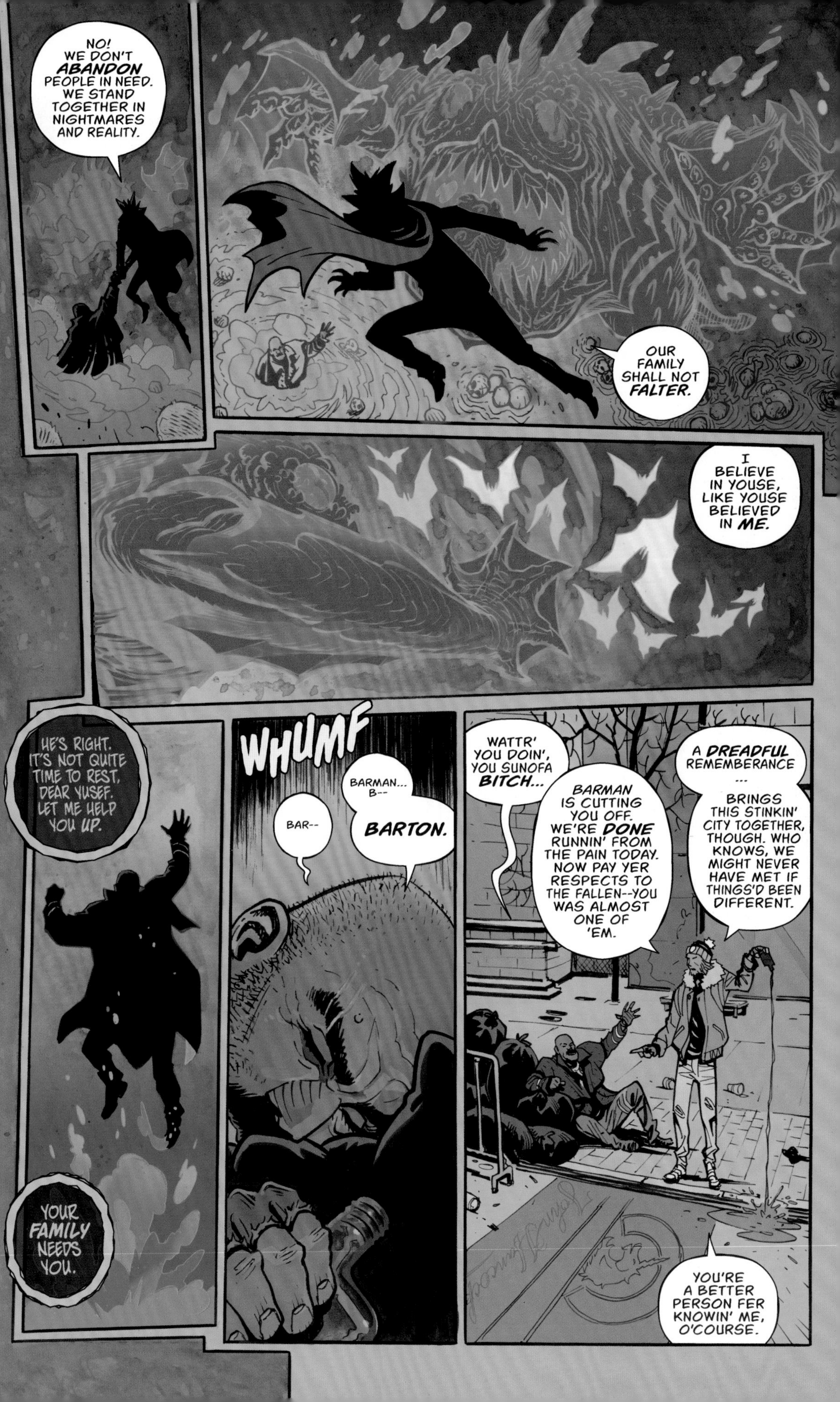

NO! WE DON'T ABANDON PEOPLE IN NEED. WE STAND TOGETHER IN NIGHTMARES AND REALITY.
OUR FAMILY SHALL NOT FALTER.
I BELIEVE IN YOUSE, LIKE YOUSE BELIEVED IN ME.
HE'S RIGHT. IT'S NOT QUITE TIME TO REST, DEAR YUSEF. LET ME HELP YOU UP.
YOUR FAMILY NEEDS YOU.
WHUMF
BAR--
BARMAN... B--
BARTON.
WATTR' YOU DOIN', YOU SUNOFA BITCH...
BARMAN IS CUTTING YOU OFF. WE'RE DONE RUNNIN' FROM THE PAIN TODAY. NOW PAY YER RESPECTS TO THE FALLEN--YOU WAS ALMOST ONE OF 'EM.
A DREADFUL REMEMBERANCE ...
BRINGS THIS STINKIN' CITY TOGETHER, THOUGH. WHO KNOWS, WE MIGHT NEVER HAVE MET IF THINGS'D BEEN DIFFERENT.
YOU'RE A BETTER PERSON FER KNOWIN' ME, O'COURSE.

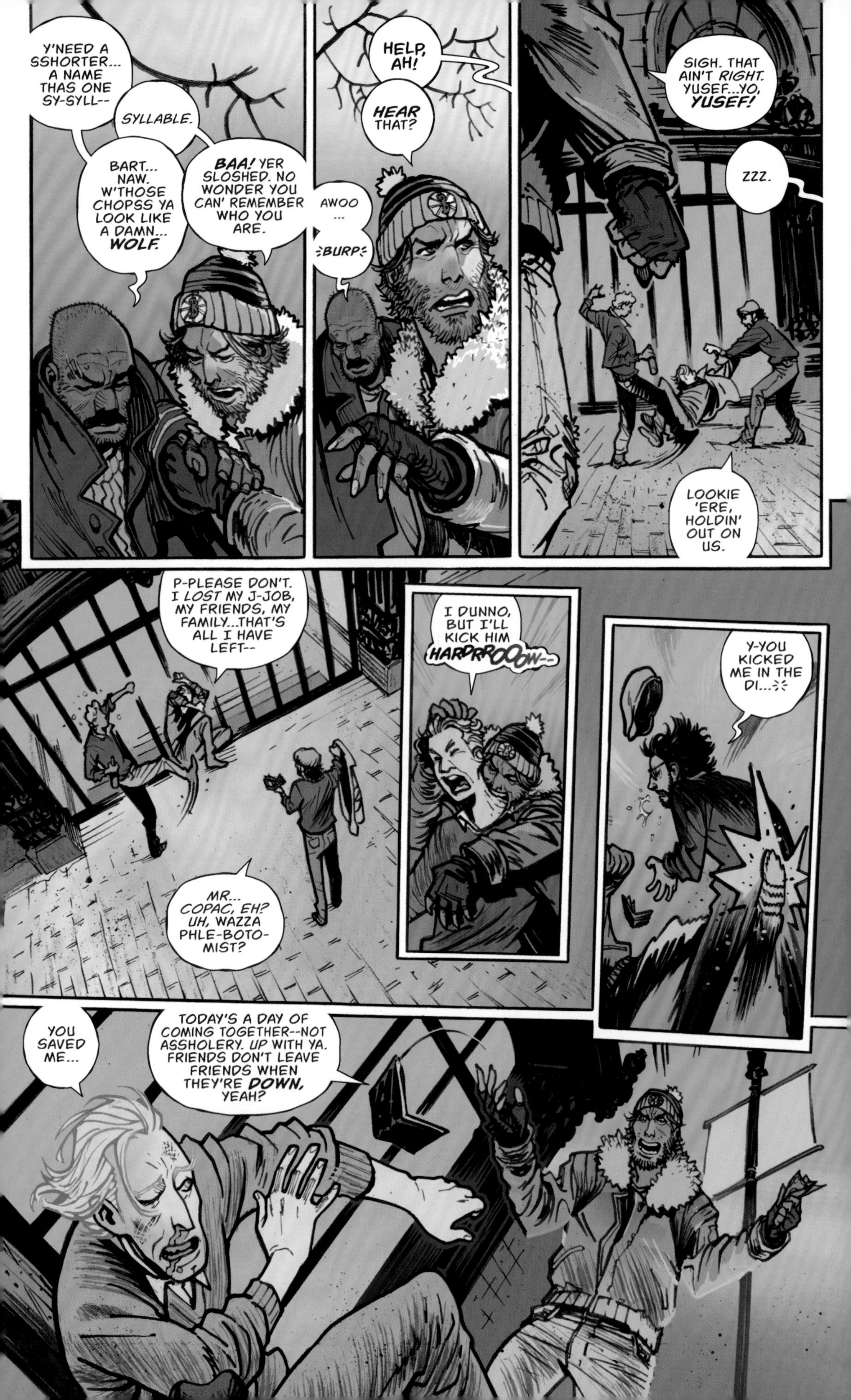
Y'NEED A SSHORTER... A NAME THAS ONE SY-SYLL--
SYLLABLE.
BART... NAW. W'THOSE CHOPSS YA LOOK LIKE A DAMN... WOLF.
BAA! YER SLOSHED. NO WONDER YOU CAN' REMEMBER WHO YOU ARE.
AWOO ...
BURP
HELP, AH!
HEAR THAT?
SIGH. THAT AIN'T RIGHT. YUSEF...YO, YUSEF!
ZZZ.
LOOKIE 'ERE, HOLDIN' OUT ON US.
P-PLEASE DON'T. I LOST MY J-JOB, MY FRIENDS, MY FAMILY...THAT'S ALL I HAVE LEFT--
MR... COPAC, EH? UH, WAZZA PHLE-BOTO-MIST?
I DUNNO, BUT I'LL KICK HIM HARDRROOOW--
Y-YOU KICKED ME IN THE DI...
YOU SAVED ME...
TODAY'S A DAY OF COMING TOGETHER--NOT ASSHOLERY. UP WITH YA. FRIENDS DON'T LEAVE FRIENDS WHEN THEY'RE DOWN, YEAH?

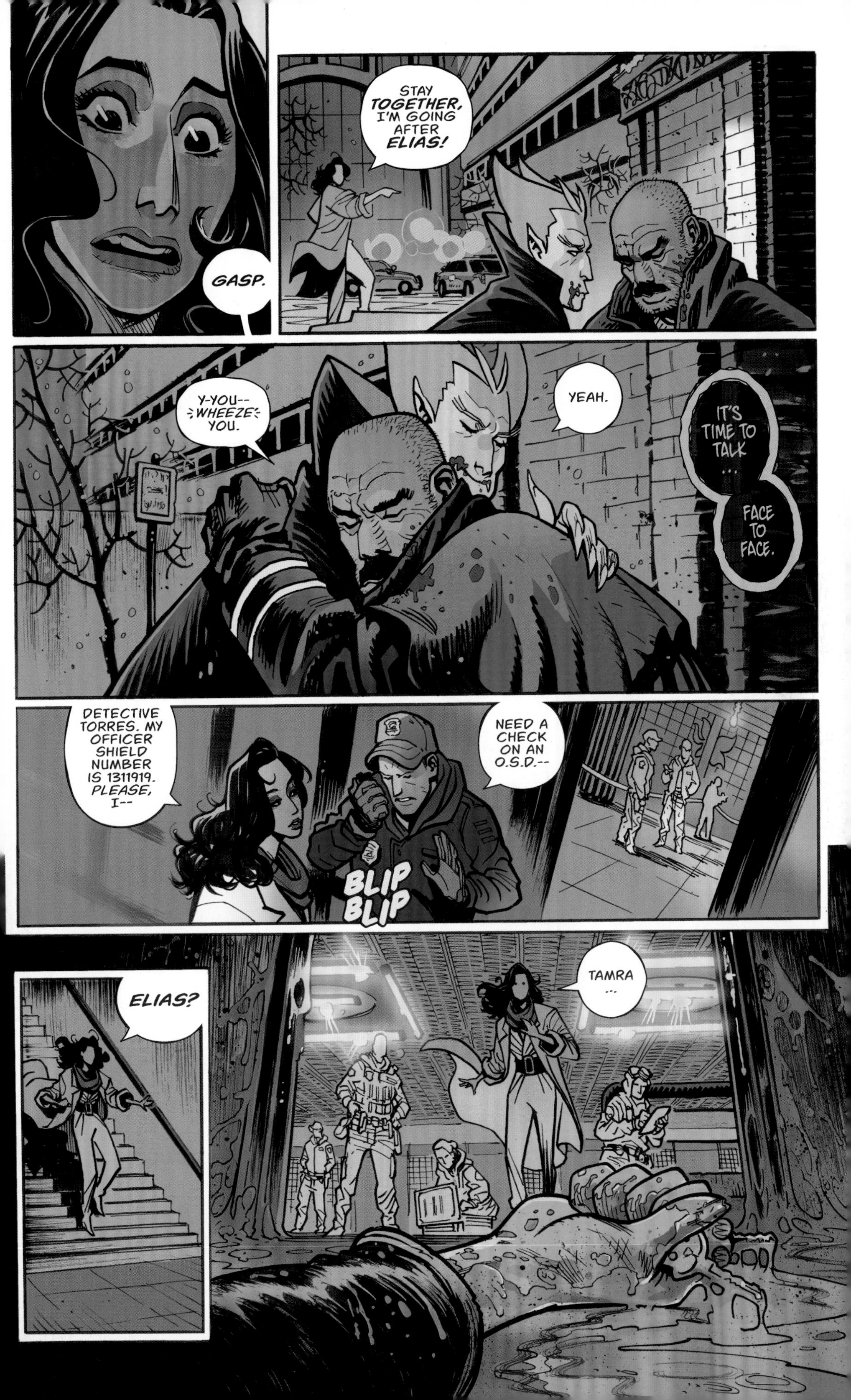
GASP.
STAY TOGETHER, I'M GOING AFTER ELIAS!
Y-YOU-- WHEEZE YOU.
YEAH.
IT'S TIME TO TALK...
FACE TO FACE.
DETECTIVE TORRES. MY OFFICER SHIELD NUMBER IS 1311919. PLEASE, I--
NEED A CHECK ON AN O.S.D.--
BLIP BLIP
ELIAS?
TAMRA...

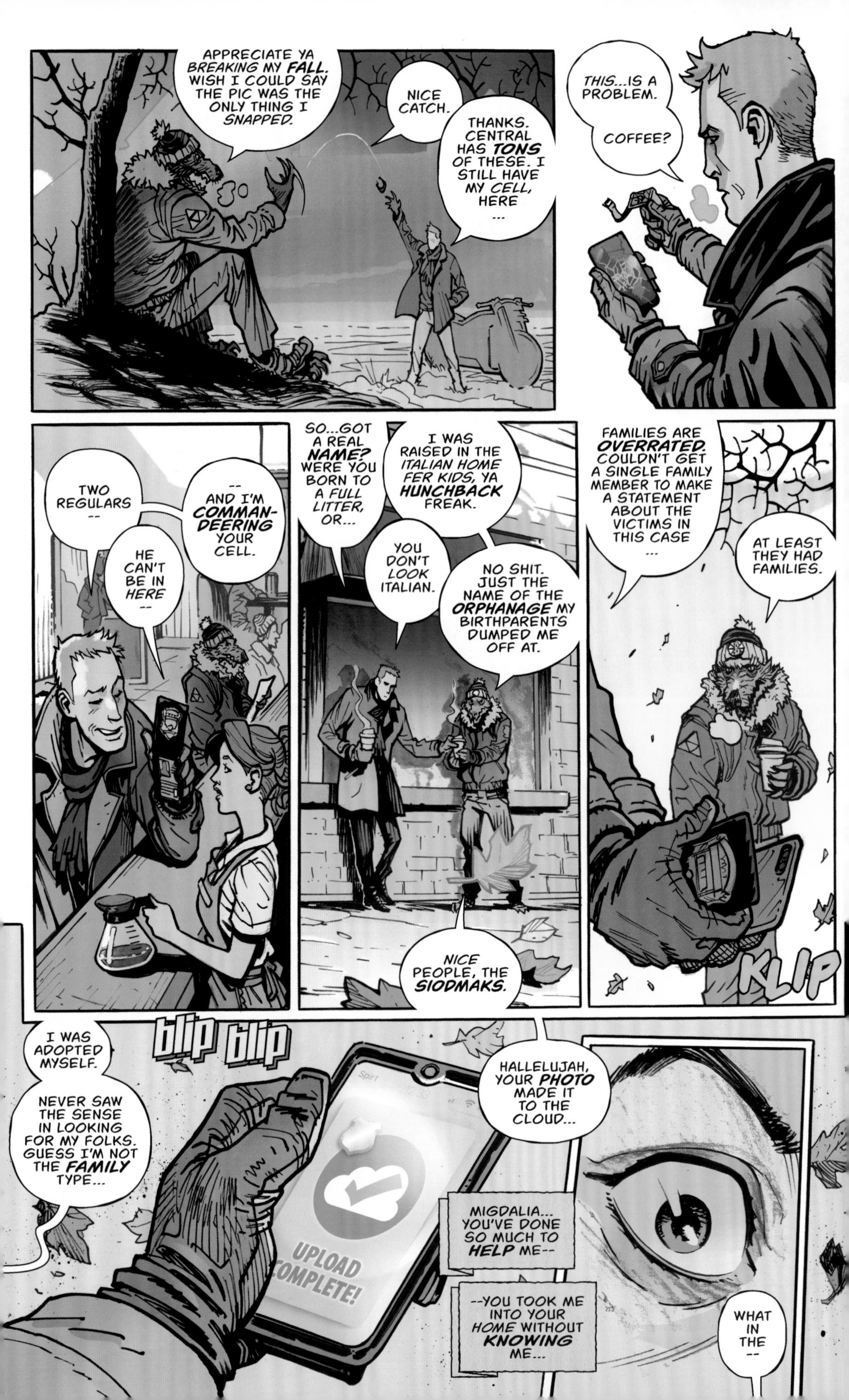
APPRECIATE YA BREAKING MY FALL. WISH I COULD SAY THE PIC WAS THE ONLY THING I SNAPPED.
NICE CATCH.
THANKS. CENTRAL HAS TONS OF THESE. I STILL HAVE MY CELL, HERE ...
THIS...IS A PROBLEM.
COFFEE?
TWO REGULARS --
-- AND I'M COMMANDEERING YOUR CELL.
HE CAN'T BE IN HERE --
SO...GOT A REAL NAME? WERE YOU BORN TO A FULL LITTER, OR...
I WAS RAISED IN THE ITALIAN HOME FER KIDS, YA HUNCHBACK FREAK.
YOU DON'T LOOK ITALIAN.
NO SHIT. JUST THE NAME OF THE ORPHANAGE MY BIRTHPARENTS DUMPED ME OFF AT.
FAMILIES ARE OVERRATED. COULDN'T GET A SINGLE FAMILY MEMBER TO MAKE A STATEMENT ABOUT THE VICTIMS IN THIS CASE ...
AT LEAST THEY HAD FAMILIES.
NICE PEOPLE, THE SIODMAKS.
KLIP
blip blip
I WAS ADOPTED MYSELF.
NEVER SAW THE SENSE IN LOOKING FOR MY FOLKS. GUESS I'M NOT THE FAMILY TYPE...
HALLELUJAH, YOUR PHOTO MADE IT TO THE CLOUD...
UPLOAD COMPLETE!
MIGDALIA... YOU'VE DONE SO MUCH TO HELP ME--
--YOU TOOK ME INTO YOUR HOME WITHOUT KNOWING ME...
WHAT IN THE --

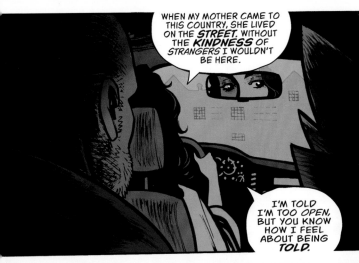

WHEN MY MOTHER CAME TO THIS COUNTRY, SHE LIVED ON THE *STREET.* WITHOUT THE *KINDNESS* OF STRANGERS I WOULDN'T BE HERE.

I'M TOLD I'M TOO OPEN, BUT YOU KNOW HOW I FEEL ABOUT BEING *TOLD.*

JINGLE JA-- *boop*

IT'S *ME.* I, UH, NEED... ⸰COUGH⸰ BACKUP ⸰COUGH⸰

DAMON? SPEAK UP.

I NEED BACKUP. WEIRD SHIT IS GOING ON. GREEN LIGHTS 'N' SPOOKY CLOUDS--

I'M ALREADY *HERE.*

YOU'RE *WHAT?* THEY'RE HIDING A MONSTER ON THE UPPER FLOOR. WAIT FOR ME, I'LL BE RIGHT-- *boop*

LISTEN, ONCE WE'RE INSIDE THERE'S SOMETHING I NEED TO DO. *ALONE.* I'M ASKING FOR MORE OF YOUR *TRUST...*

HOW'S YOUR ACTING?

EXIT

MY *COUSIN* EUGENE, HE'S *SICK* IN THE *HEAD.* TAKE THIS BURDEN OFF MY HANDS, MISTAH!

EXCUSE ME. WE HAVE A PROCESS FOR *ADMITTANCE,* YOU CAN'T SIMPLY BRING --

PLEASE ⸰COUGH⸰ LEAVE. I-I'M CALLING THE *POLICE!*

--LEFT AT THE STAIRS.

D- *DETECTIVE!* PLEASE-- ⸰COUGH⸰-- REMOVE THEM.

SHE'S POLICE.

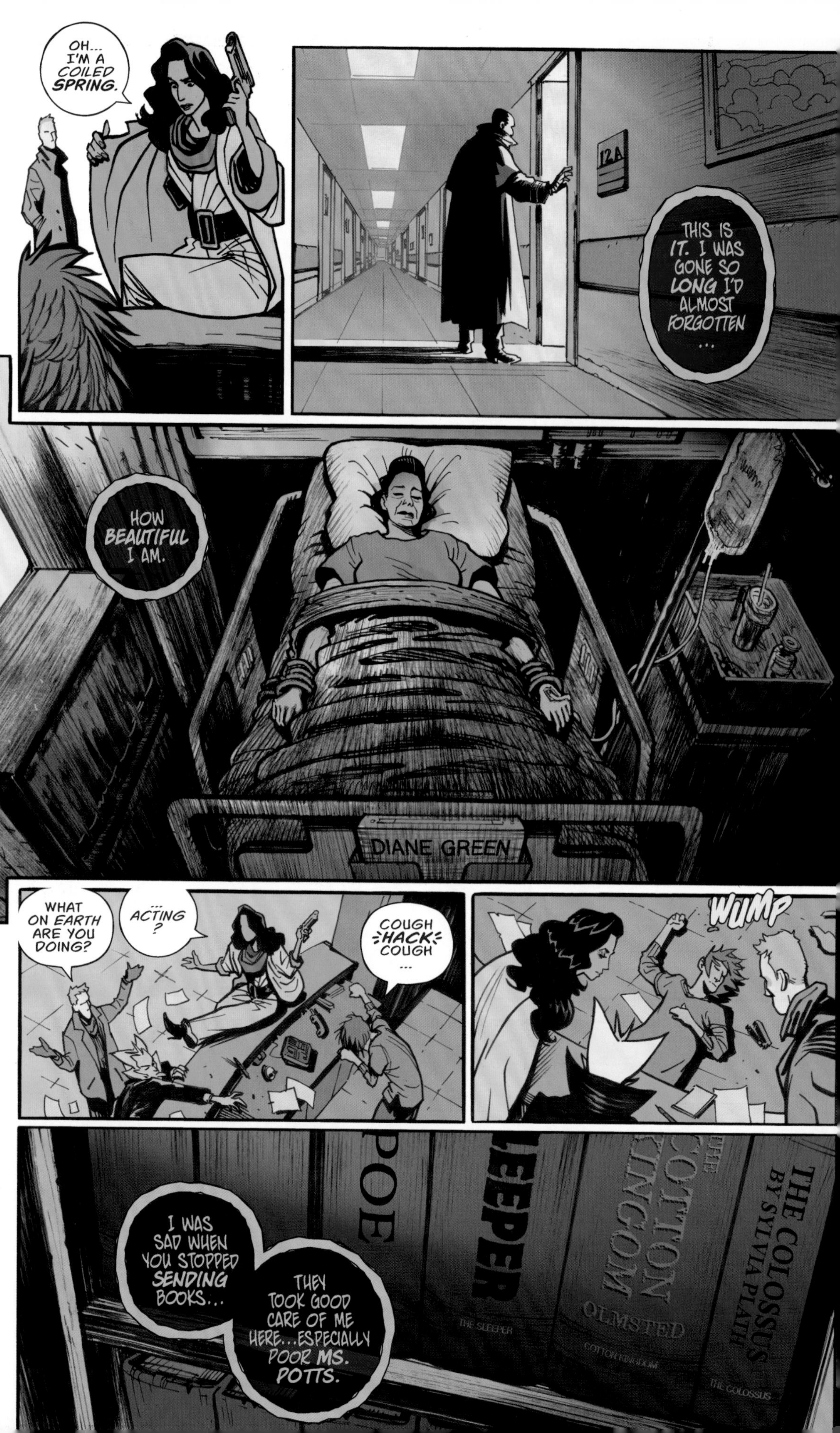

OH... I'M A COILED SPRING.
12A
THIS IS IT. I WAS GONE SO LONG I'D ALMOST FORGOTTEN ...
HOW BEAUTIFUL I AM.
DIANE GREEN
WHAT ON EARTH ARE YOU DOING?
... ACTING?
COUGH HACK COUGH ...
WUMP
POE
LEEPER
THE SLEEPER
THE COTTON KINGDOM
OLMSTED
COTTON KINGDOM
THE COLOSSUS BY SYLVIA PLATH
THE COLOSSUS
I WAS SAD WHEN YOU STOPPED SENDING BOOKS...
THEY TOOK GOOD CARE OF ME HERE...ESPECIALLY POOR MS. POTTS.

IT'S TIME TO STOP RUNNING, DEAREST HUSBAND...OUR DAUGHTER IS *LOST*, AND YOU ARE *COMPLICIT*.

REST, EMERALD. ELIAS HAS BECOME A GOOD MAN. INNOCENT PEOPLE ARE BEING HURT. KEEP YOUR *PROMISE* TO ME AND END THIS.

I'VE BROUGHT YOU YOUR FATHER.

EMMY... EMERALD IS HERE?

SHE LIES BEFORE YOU, IN MY *BODY.* TAKE OUR HAND IN YOURS...

WHEN DO I GET TO DO THIS-- *YOWCH!*

SAME AS BEFORE, CHILDREN ...

GAUZE.

COTTON.

LATEX.

SPIRIT GUM.

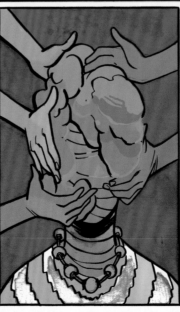

WELL DONE, CHILDREN. GO *OUTSIDE* AND PLAY HARD. IT'LL BE A GOOD COUPLE OF *HOURS...*

REMEMBER TO *LOCK* THE *DOOR* BEHIND YOU, JANETTE-- QUIETLY.

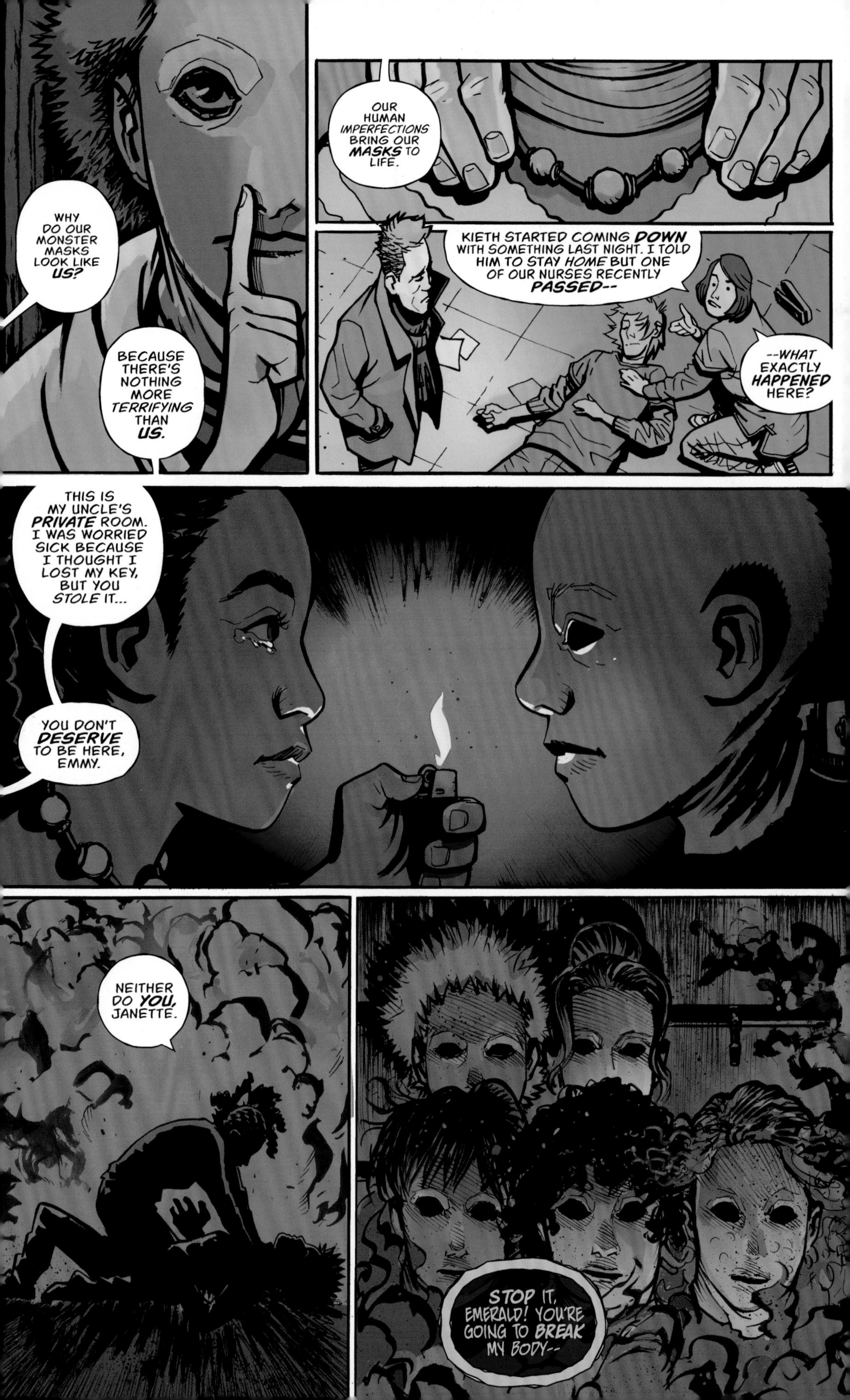
WHY DO OUR MONSTER MASKS LOOK LIKE US?
BECAUSE THERE'S NOTHING MORE TERRIFYING THAN US.
OUR HUMAN IMPERFECTIONS BRING OUR MASKS TO LIFE.
KIETH STARTED COMING DOWN WITH SOMETHING LAST NIGHT. I TOLD HIM TO STAY HOME BUT ONE OF OUR NURSES RECENTLY PASSED--
--WHAT EXACTLY HAPPENED HERE?
THIS IS MY UNCLE'S PRIVATE ROOM. I WAS WORRIED SICK BECAUSE I THOUGHT I LOST MY KEY, BUT YOU STOLE IT...
YOU DON'T DESERVE TO BE HERE, EMMY.
NEITHER DO YOU, JANETTE.
STOP IT, EMERALD! YOU'RE GOING TO BREAK MY BODY--

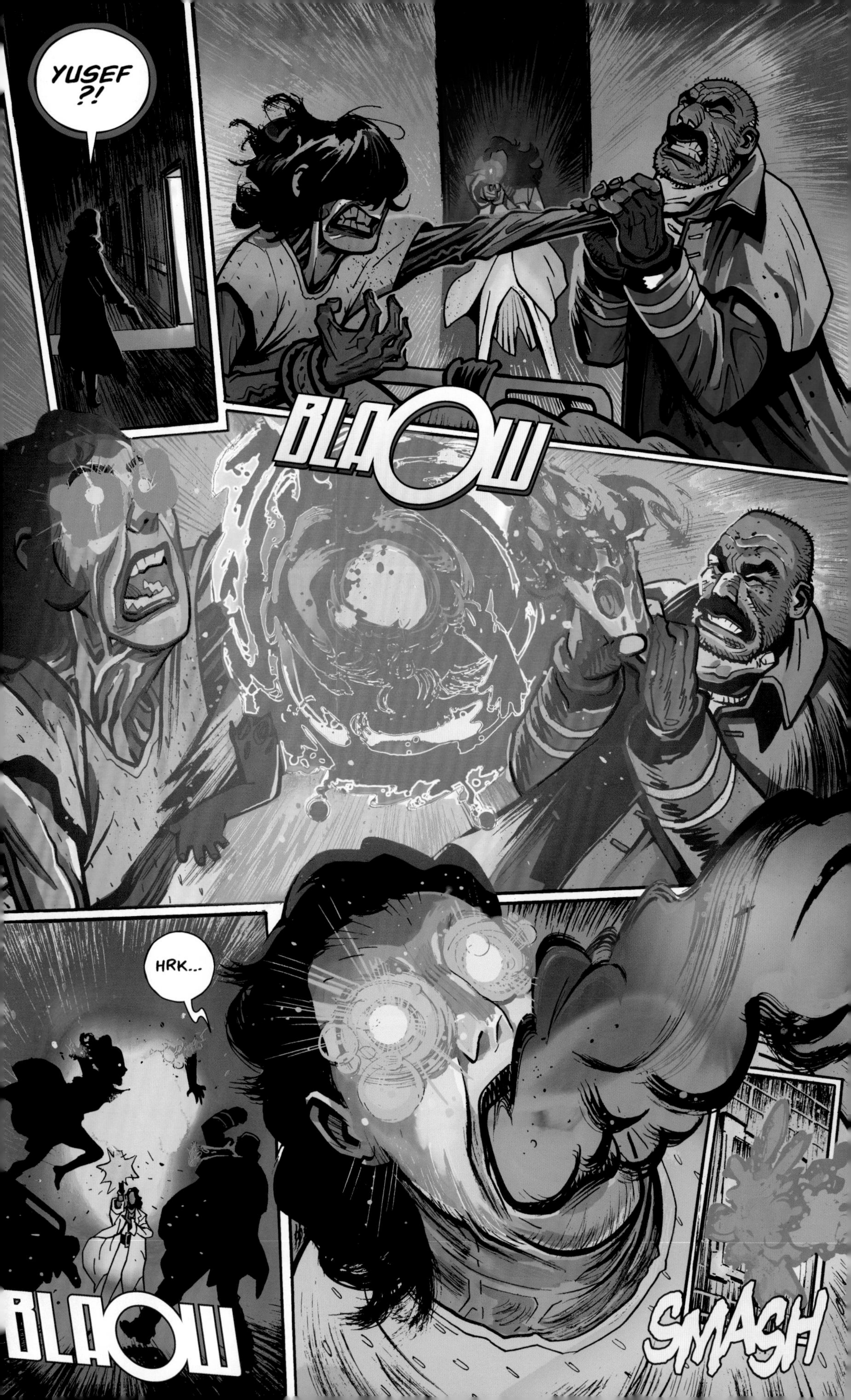
YUSEF ?!
BLAOW
HRK...
BLAOW
SMASH

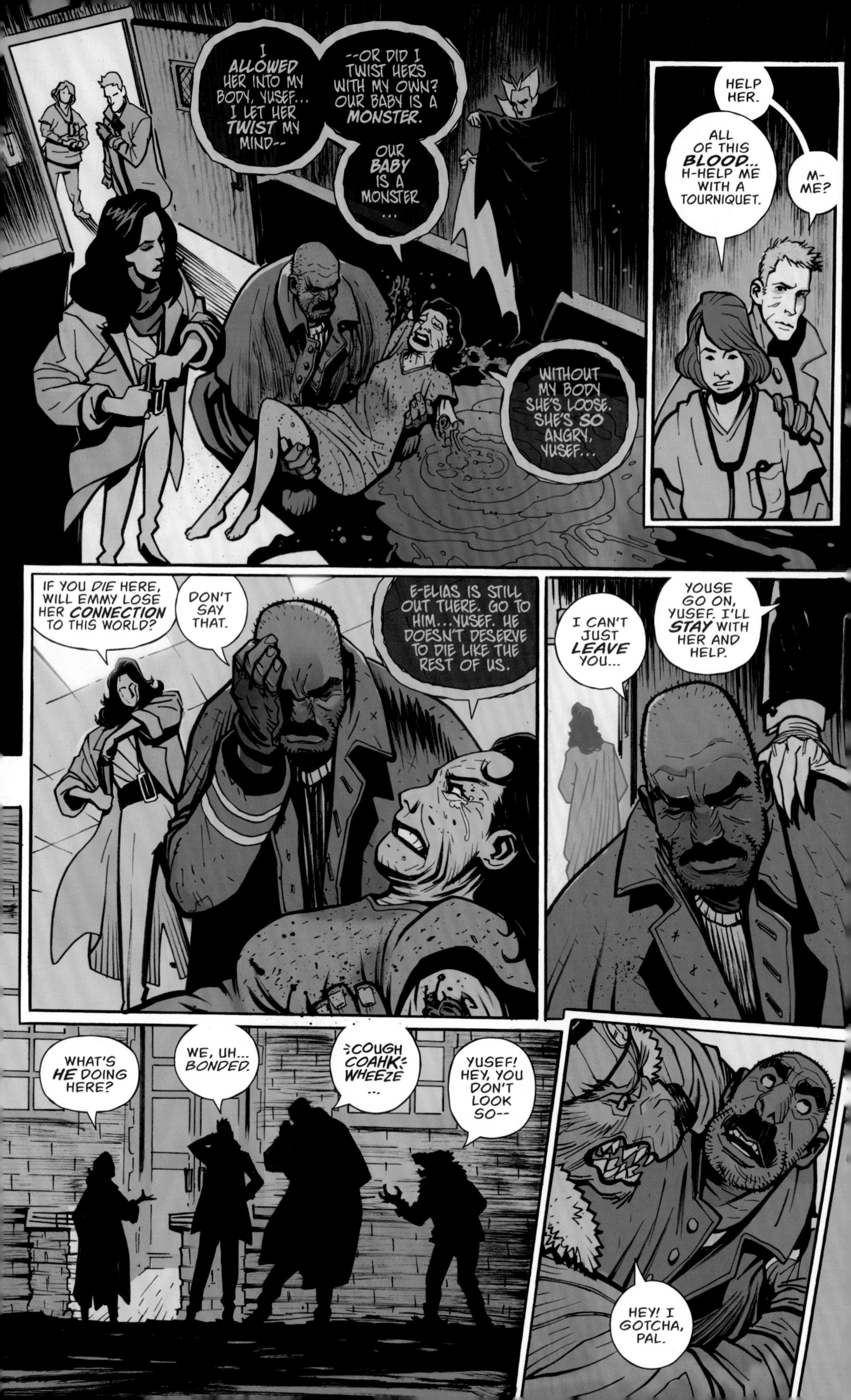
I ALLOWED HER INTO MY BODY, YUSEF... I LET HER TWIST MY MIND--
--OR DID I TWIST HERS WITH MY OWN? OUR BABY IS A MONSTER.
OUR BABY IS A MONSTER ...
WITHOUT MY BODY SHE'S LOOSE. SHE'S SO ANGRY, YUSEF...
HELP HER.
ALL OF THIS BLOOD... H-HELP ME WITH A TOURNIQUET.
M-ME?
IF YOU DIE HERE, WILL EMMY LOSE HER CONNECTION TO THIS WORLD?
DON'T SAY THAT.
E-ELIAS IS STILL OUT THERE. GO TO HIM...YUSEF. HE DOESN'T DESERVE TO DIE LIKE THE REST OF US.
I CAN'T JUST LEAVE YOU...
YOUSE GO ON, YUSEF. I'LL STAY WITH HER AND HELP.
WHAT'S HE DOING HERE?
WE, UH... BONDED.
COUGH COAHK WHEEZE ...
YUSEF! HEY, YOU DON'T LOOK SO--
HEY! I GOTCHA, PAL.

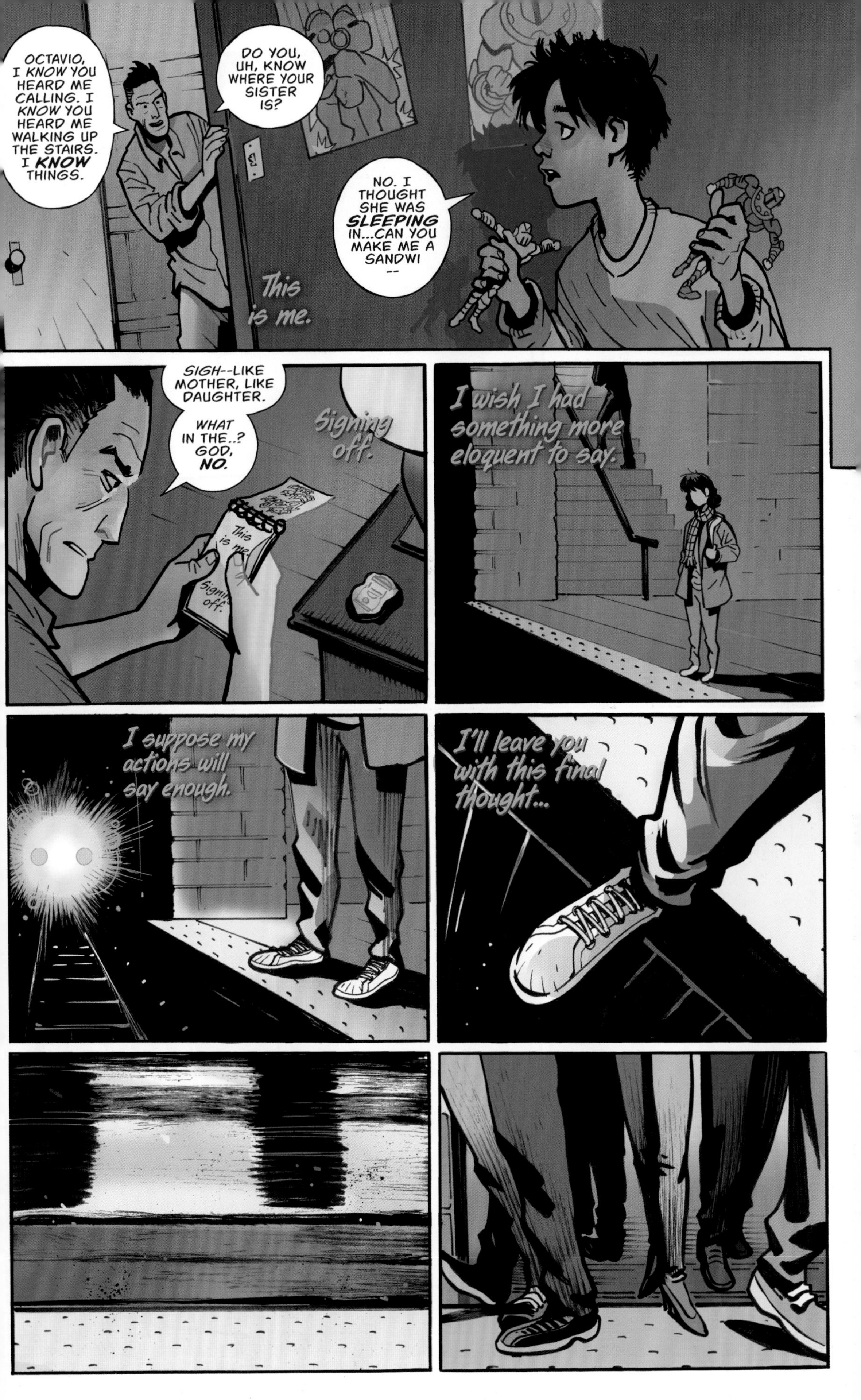
OCTAVIO, I KNOW YOU HEARD ME CALLING. I KNOW YOU HEARD ME WALKING UP THE STAIRS. I KNOW THINGS.
DO YOU, UH, KNOW WHERE YOUR SISTER IS?
NO. I THOUGHT SHE WAS SLEEPING IN...CAN YOU MAKE ME A SANDWI --
This is me.
SIGH--LIKE MOTHER, LIKE DAUGHTER.
WHAT IN THE..? GOD, NO.
Signing off.
This is me.
I wish I had something more eloquent to say.
I suppose my actions will say enough.
I'll leave you with this final thought...

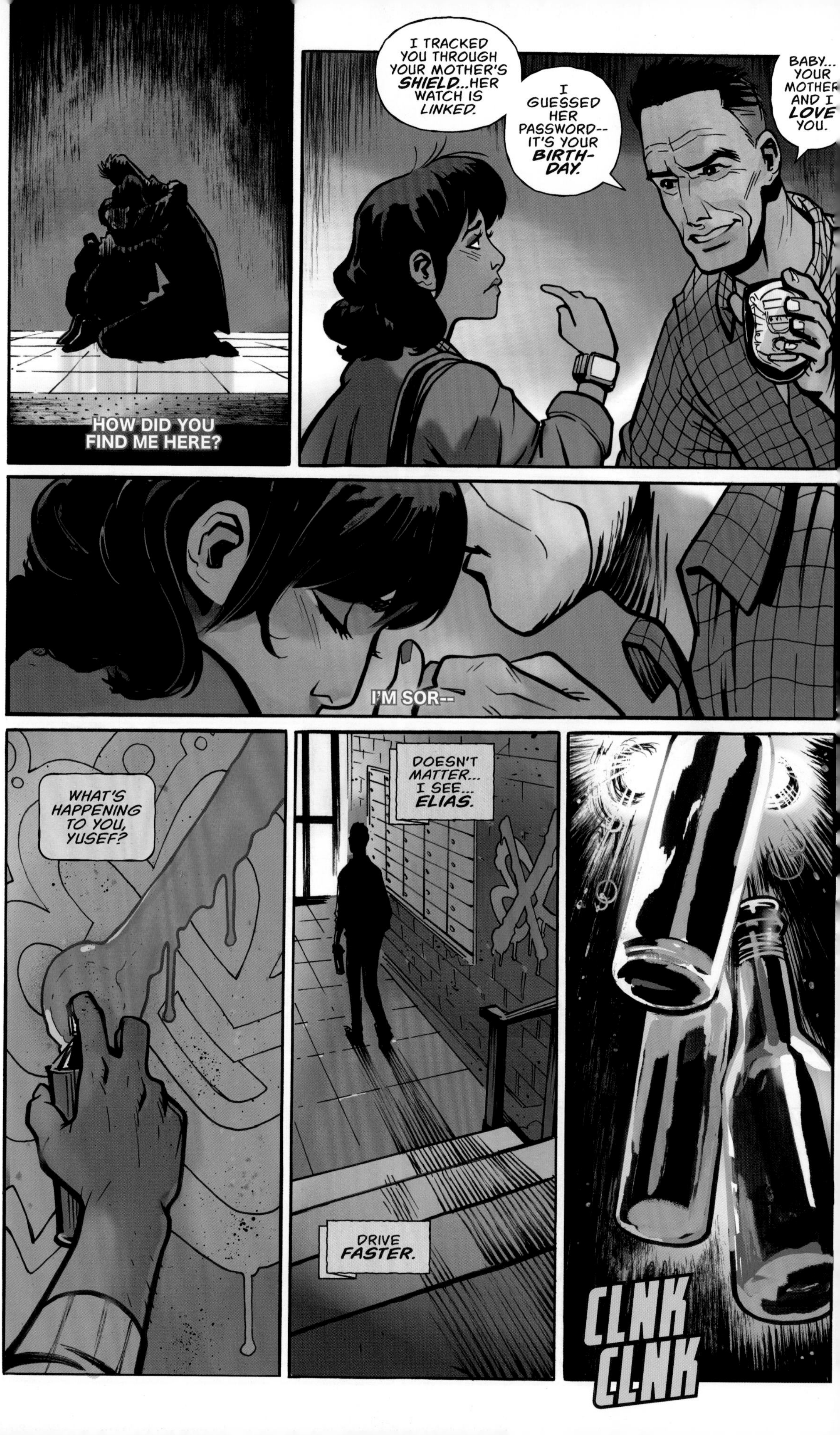
HOW DID YOU FIND ME HERE?
I TRACKED YOUR THROUGH YOUR MOTHER'S SHIELD...HER WATCH IS LINKED.
I GUESSED HER PASSWORD-- IT'S YOUR BIRTH-DAY.
BABY... YOUR MOTHER AND I LOVE YOU.
I'M SOR--
WHAT'S HAPPENING TO YOU, YUSEF?
DOESN'T MATTER... I SEE... ELIAS.
DRIVE FASTER.
CLNK CLNK

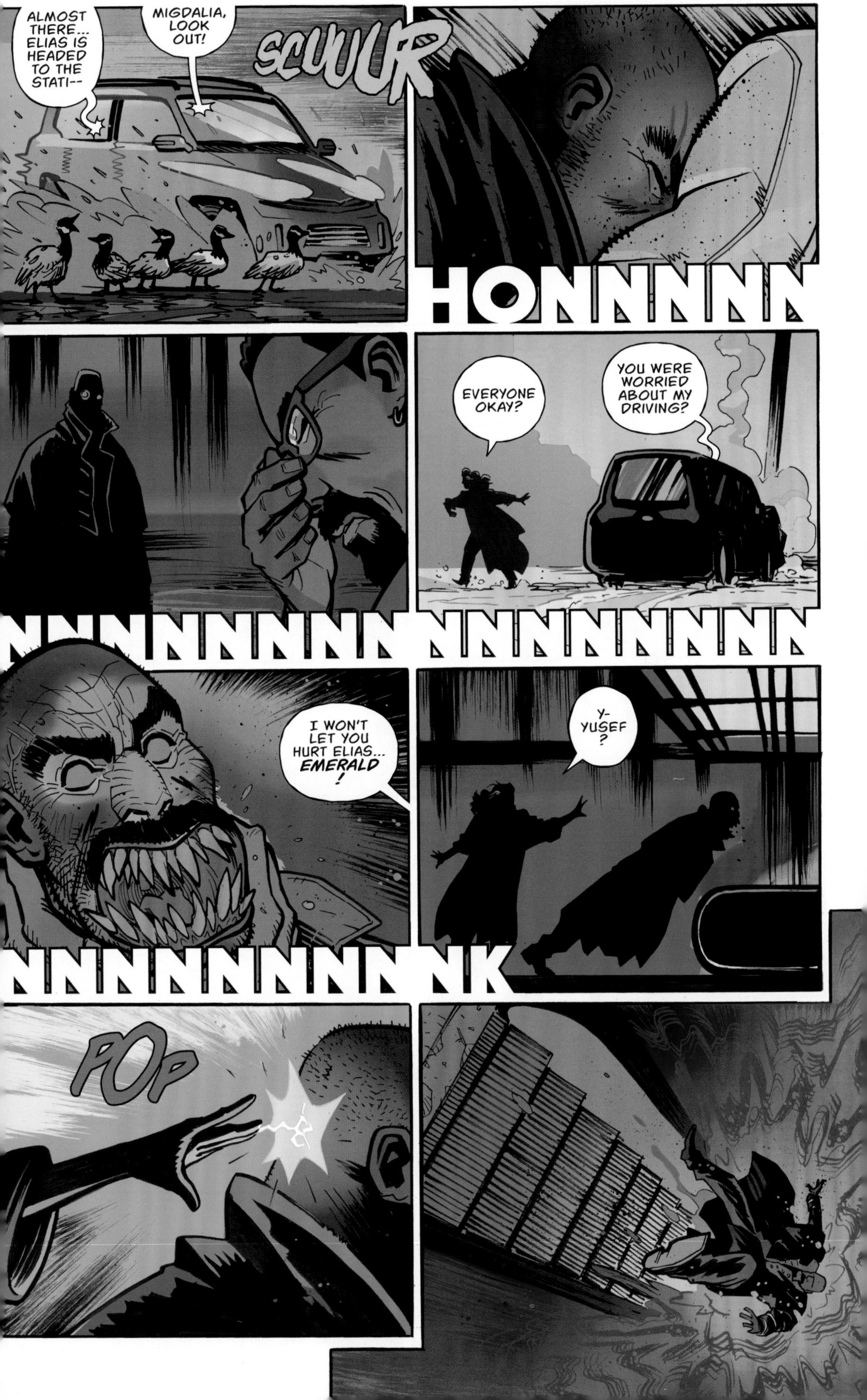
ALMOST THERE... ELIAS IS HEADED TO THE STATI--
MIGDALIA, LOOK OUT!
SCUUUR
HONNNNNNNNNNNNNNNNNNNNNNNNNNNNNNNNNNK
EVERYONE OKAY?
YOU WERE WORRIED ABOUT MY DRIVING?
I WON'T LET YOU HURT ELIAS... EMERALD!
Y-YUSEF?
POP

YUSEF, ARE YOU ALL RIGHT? HANG ON, I'M COMING!

NO.

I SAW...I REMEMBER **EVERYTHING**. THE THINGS THAT WERE **DONE** TO ME. THE THINGS I **DID** TO OTHERS...

--NEXT AND LAST STOP, ASHMONT.

I HAD FORGOTTEN MYSELF...

BUT MY PAST **REMEMBERED** ME.

AS THE LIGHTS TURNED FROM DIANE'S TRIAL TO THE NEXT SPECTACLE --

--WE BECAME INVISIBLE TO THE WORLD ONCE MORE.

LEAVING US TO OUR DARKNESS.

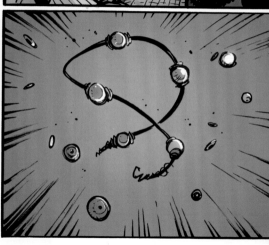

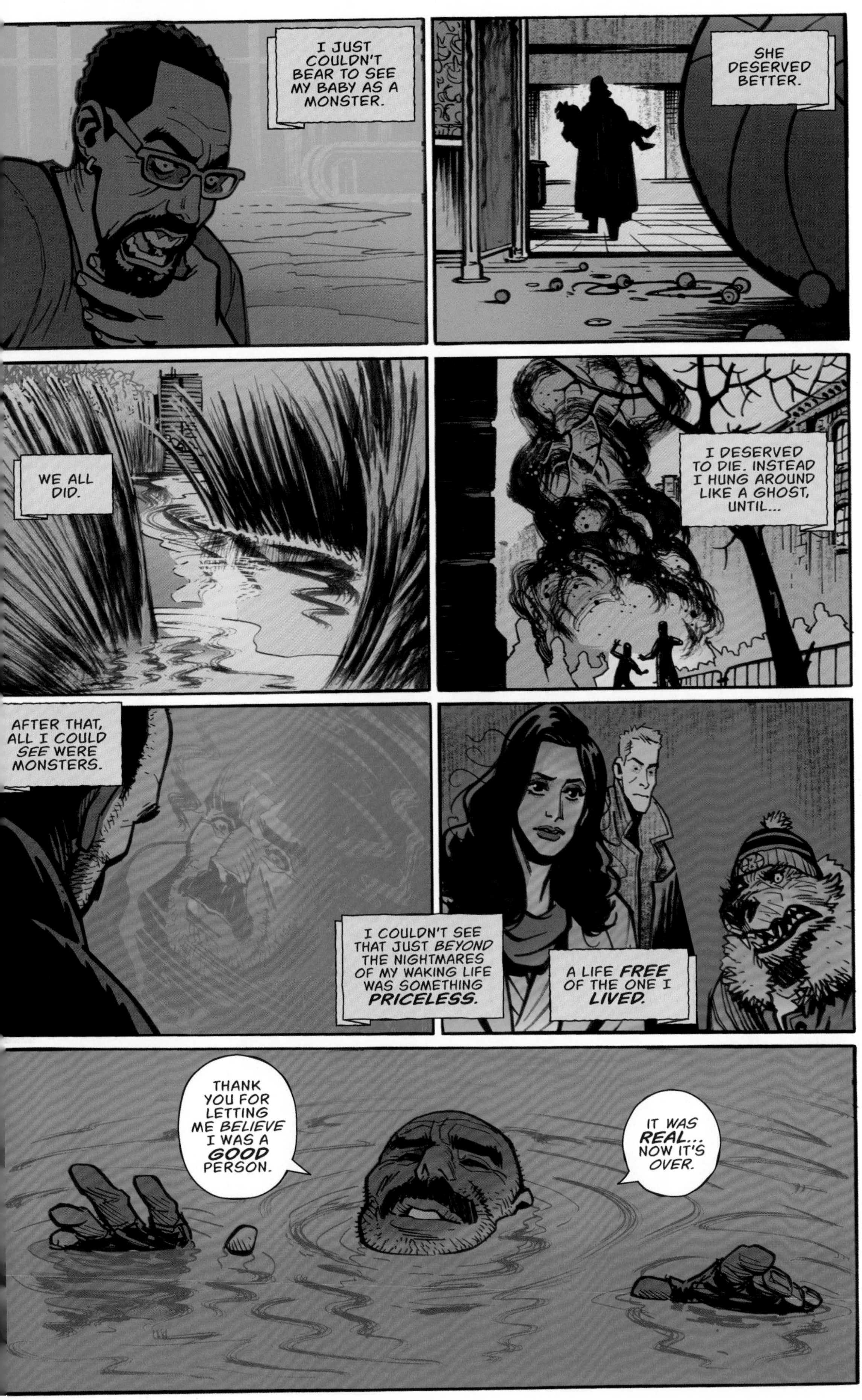
I JUST COULDN'T BEAR TO SEE MY BABY AS A MONSTER.
SHE DESERVED BETTER.
WE ALL DID.
I DESERVED TO DIE. INSTEAD I HUNG AROUND LIKE A GHOST, UNTIL...
AFTER THAT, ALL I COULD *SEE* WERE MONSTERS.
I COULDN'T SEE THAT JUST *BEYOND* THE NIGHTMARES OF MY WAKING LIFE WAS SOMETHING ***PRICELESS.***
A LIFE ***FREE*** OF THE ONE I ***LIVED.***
THANK YOU FOR LETTING ME *BELIEVE* I WAS A ***GOOD*** PERSON.
IT WAS ***REAL...*** NOW IT'S OVER.

There is good and evil in every person's soul.

But what that made me realize is...

-We're all monsters.

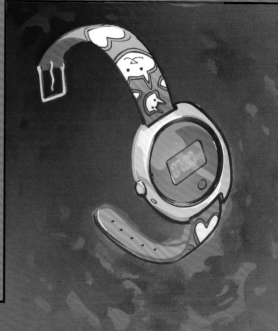

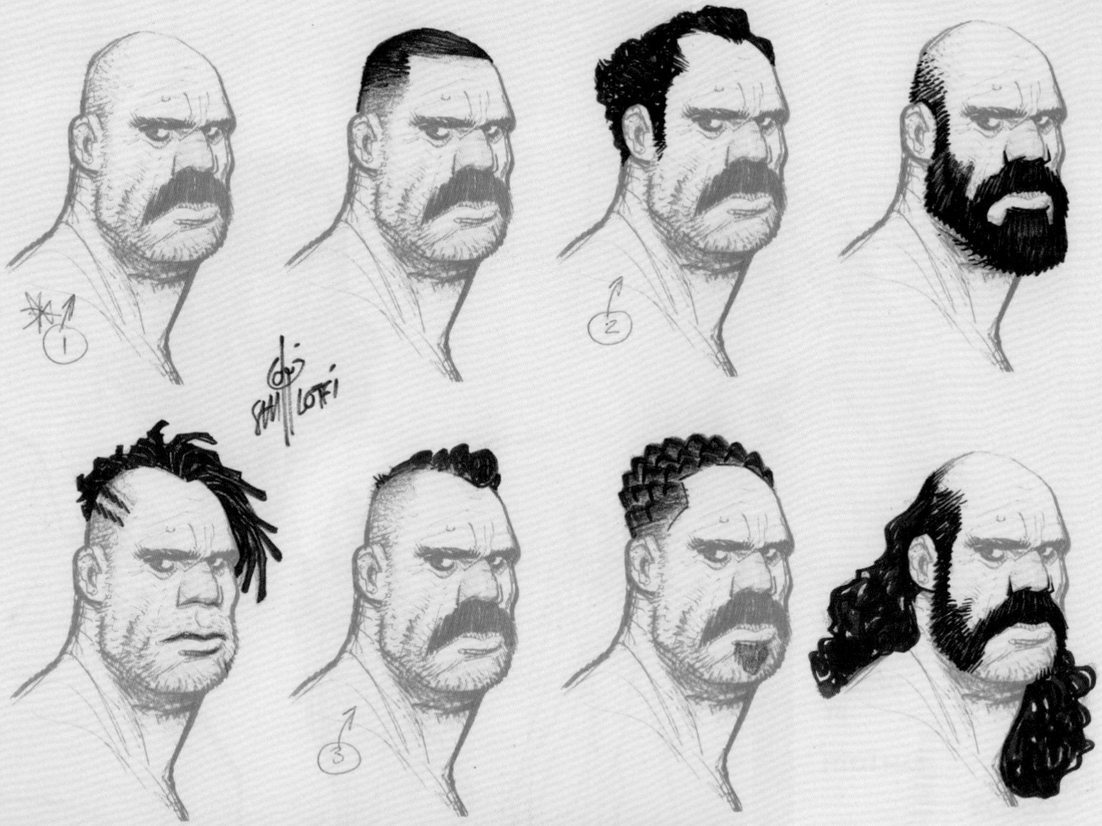
1
SAM LOTFI
2
3

SAM PROVIDED QUITE A FEW OPTIONS FOR HAIRSTYLES. ULTIMATELY, WE WENT WITH A BALD LOOK TO OBSCURE HIS ETHNICITY AND AGE.

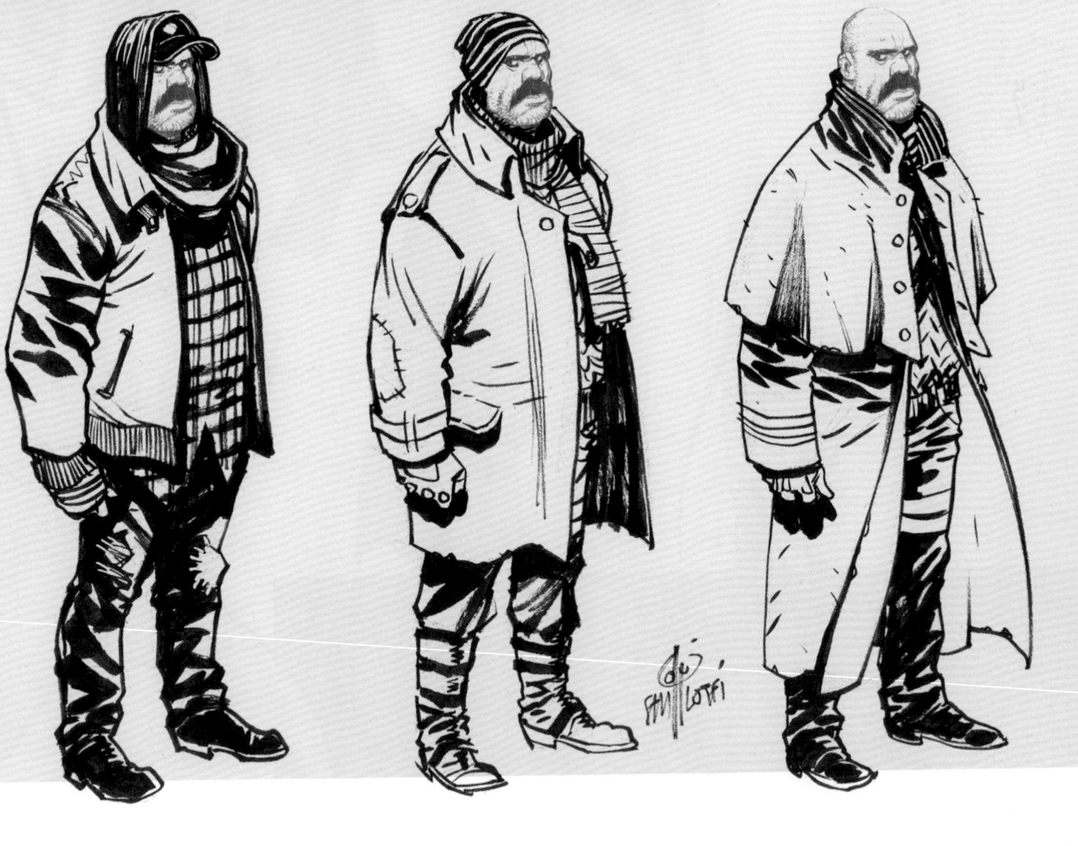
SAM LOTFI

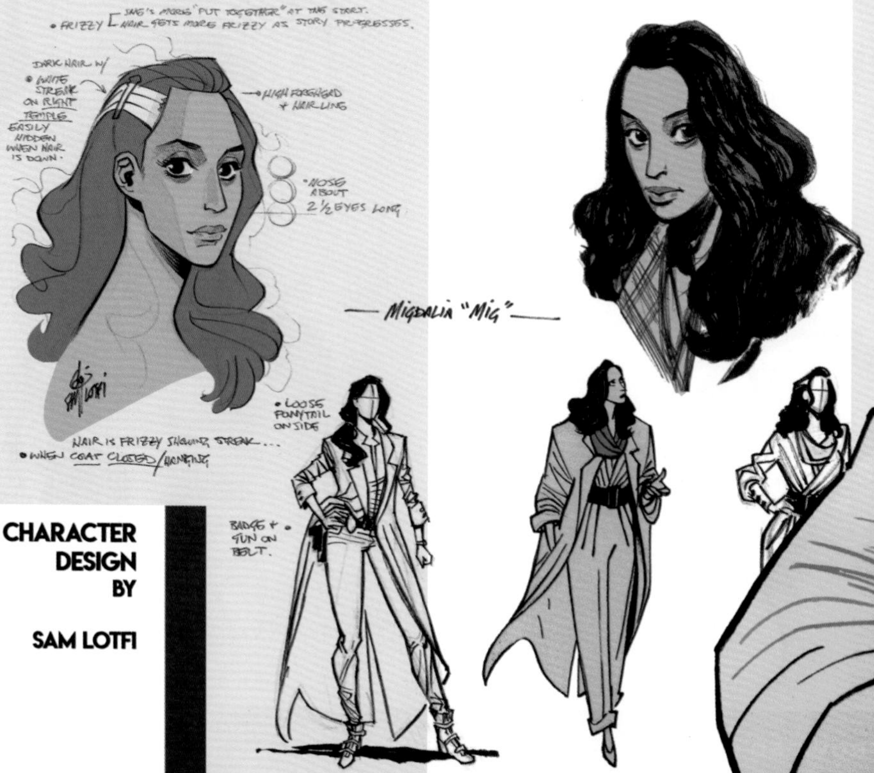
• FRIZZY
SHE'S MORE "PUT TOGETHER" AT THE START.
HAIR GETS MORE FRIZZY AS STORY PROGRESSES.
DARK HAIR W/
• WHITE STREAK ON RIGHT TEMPLE
EASILY HIDDEN WHEN HAIR IS DOWN.
HIGH FOREHEAD + HAIRLINE
• NOSE ABOUT 2 1/2 EYES LONG
HAIR IS FRIZZY SHOWING STREAK...
• WHEN COAT CLOSED/HANGING
MIGDALIA "MIG"
• LOOSE PONYTAIL ON SIDE
BADGE + GUN ON BELT.

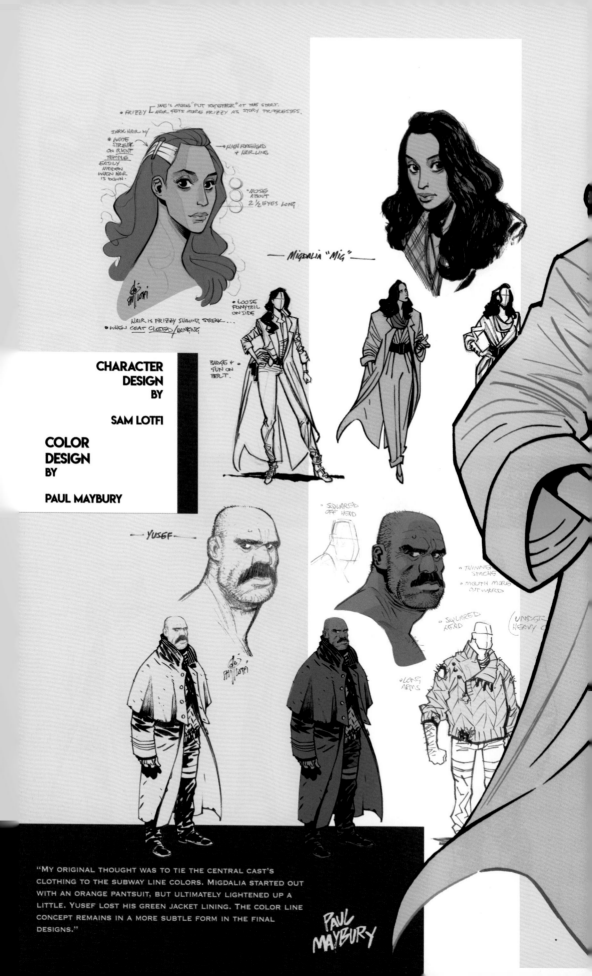

CHARACTER DESIGN BY

SAM LOTFI

COLOR DESIGN BY

PAUL MAYBURY

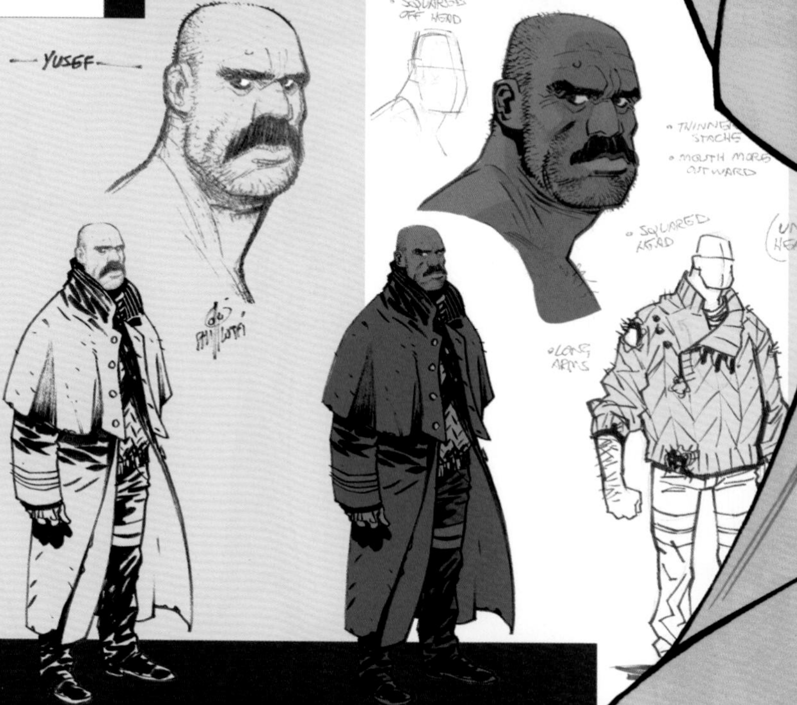
YUSEF
• SQUARED OFF HEAD
• MOUTH MORE OUTWARD
• SQUARED HEAD
• LONG ARMS

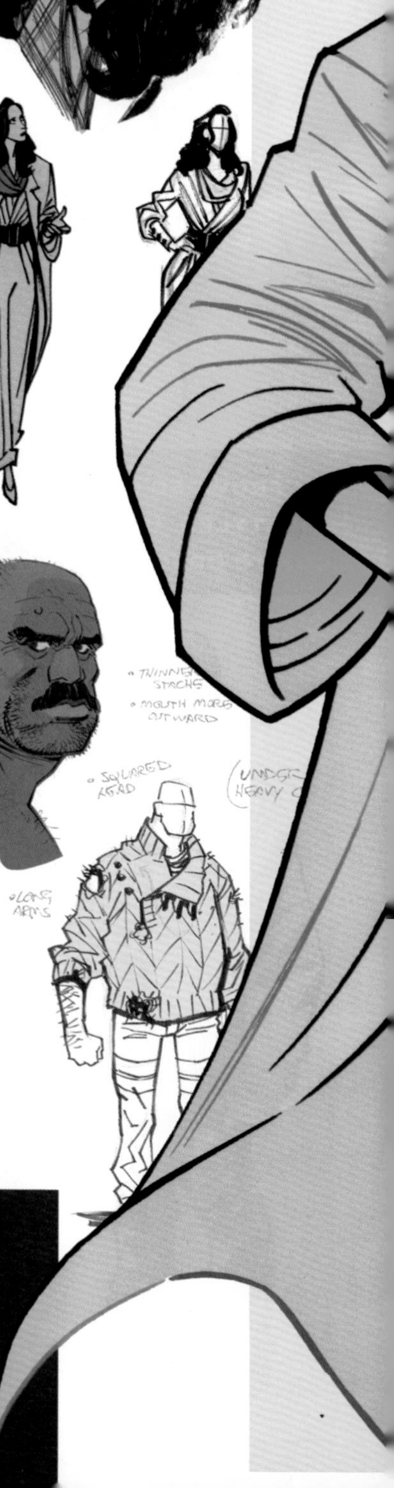

"MY ORIGINAL THOUGHT WAS TO TIE THE CENTRAL CAST'S CLOTHING TO THE SUBWAY LINE COLORS. MIGDALIA STARTED OUT WITH AN ORANGE PANTSUIT, BUT ULTIMATELY LIGHTENED UP A LITTLE. YUSEF LOST HIS GREEN JACKET LINING. THE COLOR LINE CONCEPT REMAINS IN A MORE SUBTLE FORM IN THE FINAL DESIGNS."

PAUL MAYBURY

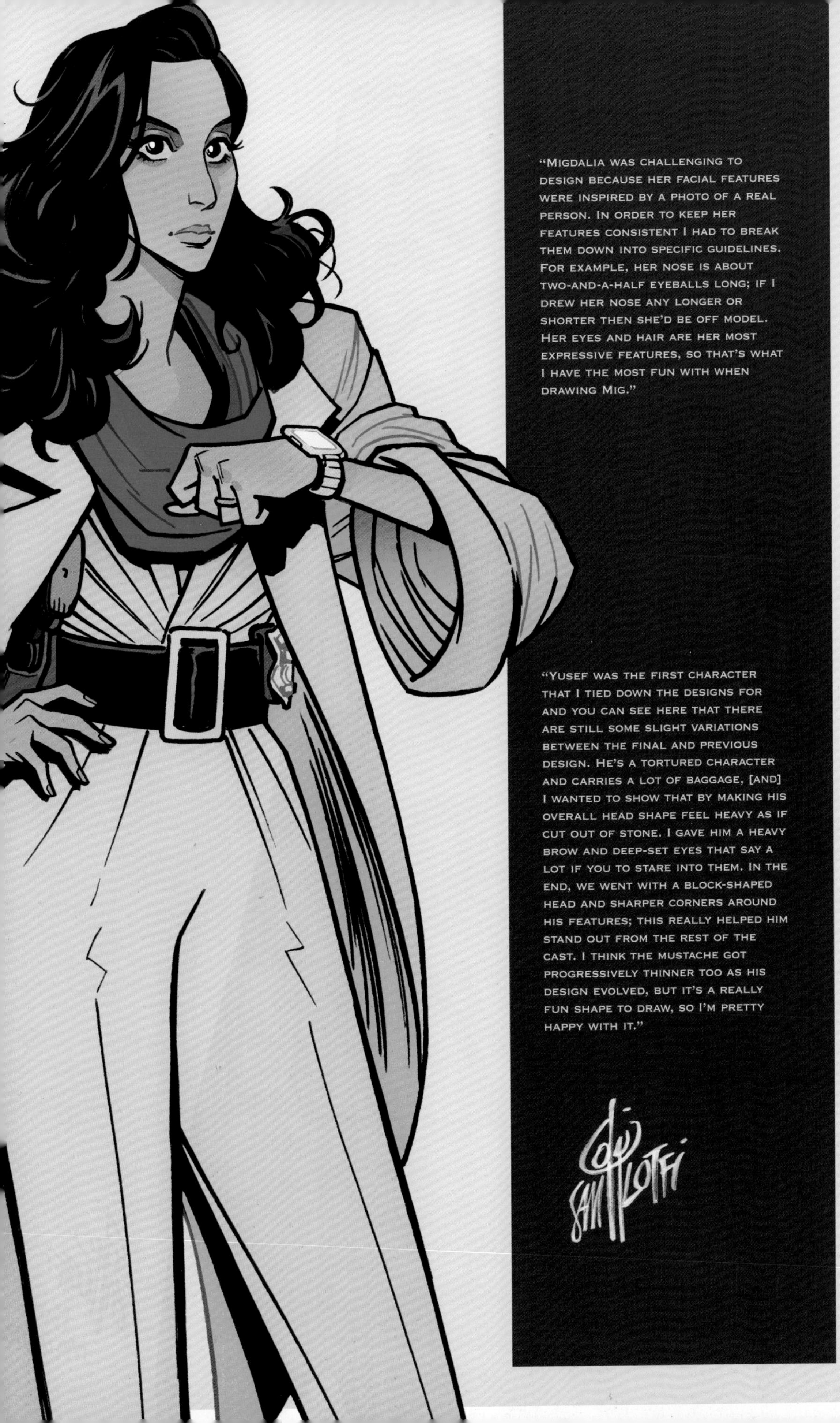

"Migdalia was challenging to design because her facial features were inspired by a photo of a real person. In order to keep her features consistent I had to break them down into specific guidelines. For example, her nose is about two-and-a-half eyeballs long; if I drew her nose any longer or shorter then she'd be off model. Her eyes and hair are her most expressive features, so that's what I have the most fun with when drawing Mig."

"Yusef was the first character that I tied down the designs for and you can see here that there are still some slight variations between the final and previous design. He's a tortured character and carries a lot of baggage, [and] I wanted to show that by making his overall head shape feel heavy as if cut out of stone. I gave him a heavy brow and deep-set eyes that say a lot if you to stare into them. In the end, we went with a block-shaped head and sharper corners around his features; this really helped him stand out from the rest of the cast. I think the mustache got progressively thinner too as his design evolved, but it's a really fun shape to draw, so I'm pretty happy with it."

Sam Lotfi

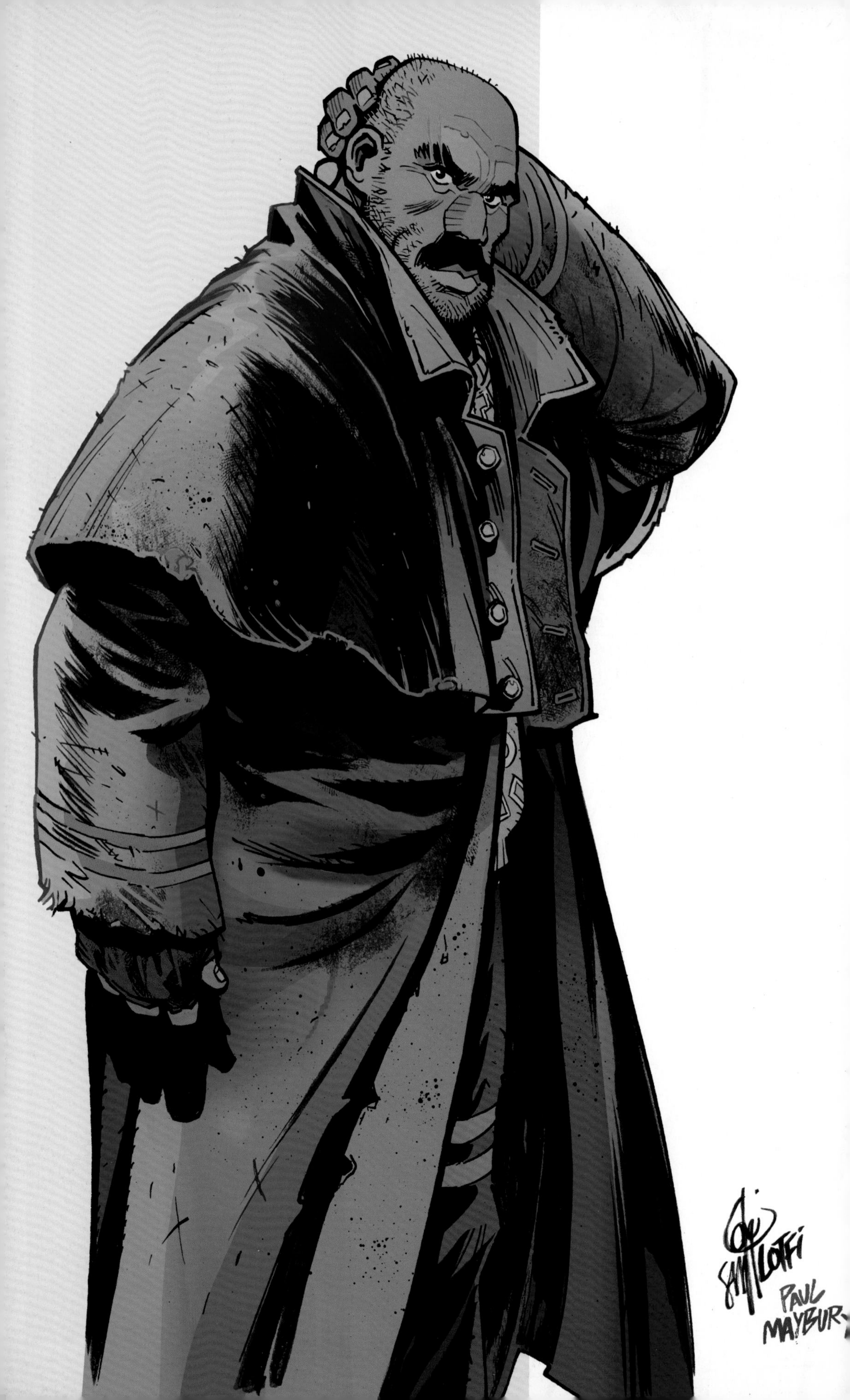
SAM LOTFI
PAUL MAYBUR